THE GREAT WAR

CALNE
DISTRICT
SOLDIERS

WAR--1914.

ROLL OF HONOUR.

NAMES OF MEN

FROM

HILMARTON AND HIGHWAY

SERVING WITH

His Majesty's Naval & Military Forces

IN

THE GREAT EUROPEAN WAR, 1914.

Atlay, Alec C., Hilmarton, Corpl. Kitchener's Army.
Atlay, J. Keith, Hilmarton, L.-Corpl.
Berry, William James, Hilmarton, Trooper, Royal Wilts Yeomanry.
Bicknell, Frederick, Cowage, 7th London Regt.
Bodman, Howard, Highway, Kitchener's Army.
Bridges, Donald, Goatacre, 7th London Regt.
Church, William, Corton, Army Reserve, Wilts Regt.
Creese, Harry, Hilmarton, Army Reserve, Gunner, Royal Field Artillery.
Dash, John, Kitchener's Army.
Dircox, Frank, Coombe Lane, H.M.S. Invincible.
Gage, Walter, Spilmans, Chief Stoker, H.M.S. Audacious.
Gage, Reginald, Spilmans, A.B. Gunner, H.M.S. Albemarle.
Gingell, George, Highway, H.M.S. Vernon.
Gingell, William, Goatacre, Kitchener's Army.
Gingell, William, Highway,
Halliday, Frank, Littlecott, Wilts Regt.
Hillier, Walter, Clevancy, Army Reserve, Wilts Regt.
Hobbs, George Nelson, Hilmarton, S.S.-Major, Royal Wilts Yeomanry.
Horton, James, Hilmarton, National Reserve, Kitchener's Army.
Horton, Reginald, Hilmarton, Kitchener's Army.
Horton, Augustus, Hilmarton, B Company, 8th Battalion.
Hunt, William, New Zealand,
Keevil, William, Rodwell,
Lewis, Frederick, Hilmarton,

Moore, James, Goatacre, National Reserve, Kitchener's Army.
Moore, Tom, Highway, Kitchener's Army.
Ponting, Charles, Cowage,
Reade, George, Goatacre, National Reserve, Kitchener's Army.
Reeves, Edward, Hilmarton,
Reeves, Walter, New Zealand, Kitchener's Army.
Reeves, Francis, Hilmarton,
Rivers, Walter, Hilmarton.
Rumming, William, Highway, L.-Corpl., Coldstream Guards.
Rumming, Thomas, Corpl., Wilts Regt.
Rumming, Frederick, Corton, Army Reserve, Wilts Regt.
Rumming, Charles, Rodwell, Kitchener's Army.
Slade, Edward, Cowage,
Slade, John, Cowage,
Slade, Herbert, Cowage,
Syms, Henry, Cowage,
Taylor, Robert, Hilmarton, 4th Wilts Regt.
Taylor, John, Goatacre, Kitchener's Army.
Taylor, Thomas, Goatacre
Townsend, Albert, Hopping Stones, Army Veterinary Corps.
Tuck, Alfred, New Zealand, 1st Class Stoker, Naval Reserve, H.M.S. Good Hope.
Tucker, Frederick, Goatacre, Kitchener's Army.
Whale, William, Highway,
Whale, Jessie, Goatacre,
Wilkins, Frank, Hilmarton,
Wilkins, Arthur, Hilmarton,
Wilkins, Thomas, Goatacre, 6th Leinster Regt.

GOD SAVE THE KING.

Printed at the "Wiltshire Gazette" Office, Devizes.

THE GREAT WAR

CALNE DISTRICT SOLDIERS

RICHARD BROADHEAD

Entrance to No. 2 camp at Yatesbury, Wiltshire 1918

Front piece:

Hilmarton & Goatacre Roll of Honour, given to all the families of men serving in 1914, it was paid for by Lord Islington, (Jon Poynder Dickenson Poynder).

First published 2009

O&B Services
The Annexe
Poynder Place
Hilmarton, SN11 8SQ

British Library Cataloguing in Publication Data.
A catalogue record for this book is available from the British Library.

ISBN 978 0 9563825 04

Printed by Cromwell Press Group, Trowbridge, Wiltshire

CONTENTS

FOREWORD

When thinking of the men and women who gave their lives in the major world conflicts I am often struck by the fact that many of them are known simply by their initials and surname as seen on War Memorials throughout the length and breadth of Britain and, for the non returning soldiers, the acres of War Graves throughout Europe and further afield.

Where no grave is to be found row after row of names on memorials such as The Menin Gate are all that outwardly exists to remind us of the death of our own countrymen. Here at The Menin Gate the fallen are remembered in a sombre memorial service that takes place every day. We find more information on those lost men and women whose bodies were found and a war grave provided, but this gives little more than their age, rank and regiment.

It is a sad fact that many of the young men killed were Uncles. So many had not had time to fall in love, get married and have families, so with the exception of the older conscripts and volunteers and members of the regular services, they had no wives, children or grandchildren to remember them.

In this book Richard Broadhead has gone behind the simple stone monuments and discovered real people, their names, how and where they lived, details about their families and finally how they met their fate. Some of this information is disturbing. Richard has discovered many cases of young men suffering from the mental torment and anguish from the constant sound of battle, stench of death, the loss of their friends and the gut wrenching fear of going 'over the top'. They were often treated as cowards and in some cases executed rather than shown the care and compassion, as they would be afforded today.

The amount of exhaustive research carried out by Richard has uncovered information that has not seen the light of day since The Great War 1914-18 and created poignant stories of a time which is almost outside living memory. In some cases he has even discovered photographs of the people that died and contemporary documents to support the research.

By combining his own research with existing records he has created one of the most comprehensive databases for Wiltshire soldiers, from that dreadful conflict, that has ever existed.

This is not only a fascinating read for anyone interested in those tumultuous times but an invaluable research tool for people discovering their family history.

Geoff Procter was Honorary Poppy Appeal Organiser for
The Royal British Legion Calne and District, Wiltshire
2003 to 2008

INTRODUCTION

A few years ago I attended a Remembrance Service during which a spokesman read out a list of names that were engraved on the war memorial. Whilst the initials and surnames of the fallen were being read out, I thought to myself 'how can we remember these men, when we know so little of them?'

Who was A. C. Smith? Where did he live? How old was he? What happened to him? These were some of the questions I would have liked to have known the answers to and, as the years progress, all we are left with is a list of the names of men who fell in the First World War. Lists are not always accurate, and are only as good as the people who compiled them.

I have tried to give the reader an indication of who these men were; where they lived; who their wives and parents were and where they lie today. Even for those with no known grave, I have tried to give an indication of where they fell and where it is likely their remains lie today. For each man I have identified in this book I have tried to cross reference with other sources to ensure that the information is accurate, but I apologise now for any mistakes made through information I have researched. For each man in the book I have tried to not only identify them, but also to find a connection with Calne and/or the surrounding area.

There are some names on local memorials for whom I have not been able to obtain any Military records but I have made a list of these on the next page. Some have notes identifying where they live and I believe some were older men who may have been associated with the Royal Defence Corps or some local volunteer force who acted like the home guard in the second world war. I have been unable to find these men on the Commonwealth War Grave Commission. Ernest Bennett who is included in the book, is not listed by the Commonwealth War Grave Commission but at the time of going to print I have written to them asking for him to be added to the list of remembrance.

I would like to thank those who gave me assistance while writing this book, including The Royal Gloucestershire, Berkshire & Wiltshire Regiment Museum, Salisbury. Brendan Dempsey and Olivia Water of Trinity College, Dublin and the many people from Calne and District, too many to mention individually.

Most of all I would like to thank my long-suffering wife, Anita, who has supported me beyond the call of duty during the writing of this book and of course to my two lovely boys, Jack-Harry and Tom-Tom who were kind enough to give me leave from playing games with them, and whom I sincerely hope never have to serve their country in such a way as those listed herein.

This book is not about the battles of the First World War or the men who directed the battles, it is a book about the great men who left their towns, whether as a volunteer or a conscript, to fight for our future. If we forget their sacrifice we open the door for future conflicts, which will mean that their deaths were to have been in vain.

Lest we forget.

Men on local memorials who I have yet to find military details.

Name	Memorial	Notes
H Andrews	Calne	
A B Burden	Calne	
Robert Clifford	Calstone Blacklands	Son of Aaron & Elizabeth Clifford of Calstone, Born 1894
A P Cooper	Calne	
E R Cooper	Calne	
L Gough	Calne	Louis Gough, born 1862
R H G James	Calne	
Thomas Edwin Orton	Calne	Born 1865 Husband of Elizabeth Orton (nee Angel) Son of Priscilla Orton of Sutton Poyntz Dorset
R E Parsons	Calne	
Andrew Rutherford	Calne	Son of Thomas & Elizabeth Rutherford died in Bristol in 1915 age 27
William Short	Derry Hill	Carpenter worked on Bowood Estate
A H Smith	Calne	Arthur Henry Born 1891
F Strange	Calne	
Hubert Victor Sumbler	Calne	Son of Thomas & Martha Sumbler Royal Garrison Artil lery Brother of A J Sumbler.
Frank Taylor	Bremhill	Born 1874
W Toogood	Calne	
W Wild	Calne	

My son Jack-Harry proudly finding Arthur Broadhead our relative and a member of a lost generation. He is buried in Lijssenthoek Military Cemetery, Belgium, with over 10,000 casualties of the Great War.

1
THE WAR OF HATE, 1914

In August 1914 the fuse was lit that would ignite a conflict that would change the world; it was to be given many names: the Great European War; The Great War for Civilisation and the First World War being but a few. There were many reasons for the commencement of hostilities, but once mobilisation of men had started, it triggered a domino effect throughout Europe and then on across the world.

Patriotism spread through countries like a plague, and, like a plague, it almost immediately claimed its victims. Men volunteered to fight for good and God against evil, in a war where keen, willing participants would be home for Christmas. The British Army was small but well trained, and had been developed to protect and control the British Empire, while relying on the powerful British Navy to protect the world trade routes.

In the August of 1914, Soldiers of the British Expeditionary Force marched across Belgium, a country that Great Britain had the treaty to protect, across fields where one hundred years earlier, the Duke of Wellington had defeated Napoleon Bonaparte. They marched to the town of Mons. The Great War had begun.

The Hate - La Haine - Der Hass

Walter Samuel Weston of Calne who fought in, and survived, the war wrote the following;

"The Germans were always talking of "Der-Tag", the day when they would start the war they were looking for an excuse. As history shows this came about in 1914. Let me say at this point, the young men, the young men of Britain were just as anxious as the Germans to have a war. All youth is restless, and this was an outlet, the realisation came later after much suffering. War had been glorified in all European countries; they thought in terms of the Franco Prussian 1870 and the Boer War 1900 type wars, they were to find this vastly different.

Young men flocked to the colours to get at the Germans; there was plenty of propaganda, like "Remember Belgium", and the sinking of the Lusitania, to attract men to the colours, But it wasn't really necessary. In fact I doubt many remembered these slogans or even had any hate for the Germans by the time they had been through the hoop in such places as Salisbury Plain and the long valley at Aldershot. However, these young men trained, became disciplined, proud of their regiment. I can see them now in my minds eye, bronzed and alert. I can also see them later, lying in rows dead, sightless eyes seemingly staring skywards, still, it was an adventure they wanted the reality came later.

The war dragged on, it seemed it would never end, my own 2nd/7th Battalion the Royal Warwickshire Regiment, like many more, would have to advance, lose men, rest, reinforce, then more attacks, until the 11th hour of the 11th day of the 11th month 1918."

Hasslied

French and Russian, they matter not,
A blow for a blow, a shot for a shot,
We fight the battle with bronze and steel,
And the time that is coming Peace will seal.
You will hate with a lasting hate,
We will never forego our hate,
Hate by water and hate by land,
Hate of the head and hate of the hand,
Hate of the hammer and hate of the crown,
Hate of seventy millions choking down.
We love as one, we hate as one,
We have one foe and one alone

ENGLAND!

by Ernst Lissauer

23rd AUGUST 1914 – THE BATTLE OF MONS, BELGIUM
26th AUGUST 1914 – THE BATTLE OF LE CATEAU, FRANCE

Calne's First Casualty

Corporal Walter Brindle		*1st Bn Royal Berkshire Regiment*	
Service No.	9772	Age:	21
Place of Birth:	Castle Eaton, Wiltshire	Home Country:	England
Date of Death:	26/08/1914	Cause of death:	Killed in action
Memorial:	Calne & Avebury		
War cemetery:	Maroilles Communal Cemetery		
Theatre of war:	France		
Next of Kin:	Joseph & Mary Brindle		
Address:	West Kennet, Wiltshire		

Walter came from a military family; his father Joseph was an old soldier who had served in the Zulu War and been awarded a medal; six of his seven brothers served during the Great War and Frank, Walter's youngest brother, had joined the Royal Army Medical Corps before he was 16. After the death of his father, Walter's mother remarried becoming Mrs Hicks and lived at 3 Patford Street, Calne.

Walter arrived in France on Thursday 13th August 1914, one of the first troops to do so. He was in the retreat from Mons, when some of his men fell into a canal and being a good swimmer, he plunged in and rescued his comrades. While climbing out onto the embankment a German shell exploded killing him instantly.

The war diary for his regiment states that on Wednesday 26th August they were located at Maroilles, France and at 1.30 am ordered to make a night attack and take the bridge over the River Sarne, suffering 61 killed, wounded and missing. It is likely that this is where Walter saved his comrades and was killed.

TO THE GLORY OF GOD
AND IN MOST LOVING MEMORY OF
HARRY STANLEY,
LEGION D'HONNEUR.
CAPT. NORTHUMBERLAND FUSILIERS,
KILLED IN ACTION ON THE AISNE SEPT. 14TH 1914.
SIDNEY MILES. M.C.,
MAJOR ROYAL ARTILLERY,
KILLED NEAR YPRES SEPT. 27TH 1917.
THE TWO DEAR ONLY SONS OF
MAJ·GENERAL & MRS TOPPIN,
OF BLACKLANDS HOUSE.

Above: Memorial to Harry Toppin and his brother Sidney, in the Church of St. Peter, Blacklands, Calne.

Left: Harry Toppin.

6th SEPTEMBER 1914 – THE BATTLE OF MARNE, FRANCE
9th SEPTEMBER 1914 – THE BATTLE OF FERE CHAMPENOISE, FRANCE
14th SEPTEMBER 1914 – FIRST BATTLE OF THE AISNE, FRANCE

Captain Harry Stanley Toppin   *1st Bn Northumberland Fusiliers*
Service No.   N/A   Age: 40
Place of Birth: Elham, Kent   Home Country: England
Date of Death: 14/09/1914   Cause of death: Killed in action
Memorial: Private Memorial Blacklands Church & Branksome Dorset.
War cemetery: La Ferte Sous Jouarre Memorial
Theatre of war: France
Next of Kin: Maj. Gen. Toppin & Mrs Jane Toppin
Address: Blacklands Park, Calne

Harry had inherited Blacklands Park on the death of Mr Brown. He was one of many experienced officers called to the front having gained fame and distinction in the field of exploration. He was gazetted to the Northumberland Fusiliers in 1895 when, in his twenty first year, he served with the Nile expedition of 1898, and in the South African war. Subsequently he was employed for four years, 1904 to 1908, on survey work in the Uganda Protectorate, after he acted as Peruvian Commissioner for the Bolivian frontier of Peru. Notes on Peru were submitted to the Royal Geographical Society and it was hoped he would read a paper before the society on the results of his labors. Unfortunately the out break of war curtailed his interests and he returned to his regiment.

Harry had been mentioned in dispatches and was awarded the Chevalier of the Legion of Honor (France). He was killed in action on Monday 14th September 1914 during the battle of the Aisne and is remembered on the La Ferte Sous Jouarre Memorial with nearly 4,000 other soldiers who died in the area during the early part of the war and have no known grave.

Above: Belgium Refugees flee from the German advance.

Left: Charles Hillier is remembered on his wife's grave at All Saints Churchyard, Yatesbury. Ada was to die almost exactly one year later in September 1915.

Lance Corporal Charles William Hillier		*1st Bn Royal Berkshire Regiment*	
Service No.	7604	Age:	32
Place of Birth:	Calne, Wiltshire	Home Country:	England
Date of Death:	19/09/1914	Cause of death:	Killed in action
Memorial:	Yatesbury & Devizes Odd Fellows		
War cemetery:	La Ferte Sous Jouarre Memorial		
Theatre of war:	France		
Next of Kin:	Ada Phoebe Hillier (wife); Henry and Sarah Hillier (parents)		
Address:	Yatesbury, Wiltshire		

Charles arrived in France on Thursday 13th August 1914 with the British Expeditionary Force. He took part in the retreat from Mons in Belgium and would have marched continuously from 23rd of August. On Saturday 19th September he found himself on a ridge near La Mets Ferme, France, the weather was wet and misty. He was one of eight members of his regiment killed in action by shell fire. He has no known grave.

24th SEPTEMBER 1914 – THE BATTLE OF ALBERT, FRANCE

Lance Corporal Stewart Cecil Hawkins		*9th Lancers*	
Service No.	5573	Age:	24
Place of Birth:	Lyneham, Wiltshire	Home Country:	England
Date of Death:	18/10/1914	Cause of death:	Killed in action
Memorial:	Calne - Calstone & Blacklands		
War cemetery:	Sanctuary Wood Cemetery		
Theatre of war:	Belgium		
Address:	Quemerford, Calne, Wiltshire		

Cecil would have been based at Tidworth, Hampshire before the Great War; he arrived in France on Tuesday 15th September as part of the 1st Cavalry Division. He was killed in action on Sunday 18th October, a day before the start of the First battle of Ypres, Belgium. He is buried in Sanctuary Wood Cemetery; the wood took its name from acting as a screen from German artillery where troops could be in relative safety.

A Soldier
of the
KING.

AFTER the War every man who has served will command his Country's gratitude. He will be looked up to and *respected* because he answered his country's call.

The Regiments at the Front are covering themselves with Glory.

Field-Marshal Sir John French wrote in an Order of the day,

"It is an Honour to belong to such an Army."

Every fit man from 19 to 38 is eligible for this great honour. Friends can join in a body, and serve together in the same regiment.

Rapid Promotion.

There is rapid promotion for intelligence and zeal. Hundreds who enlisted as private soldiers have already become officers because of their merits and courage, and thousands have reached non-commissioned rank.

Enlist To-day.

At any Post Office you can obtain the address of the nearest Recruiting Office. **Enter your name to-day on the Nation's Roll of Honour and do your part.**

GOD SAVE THE KING.

Above: Members of the 1st Battalion Wiltshire Regiment, in trenches in Belgium 1914

Left: This recruiting advert appeared in 1914 at the start of the war. The age range for recruits, of 19 to 38 years, was varied throughout the war with the result that in 1918 eighteen year olds were legally sent into action. Rapid promotion was almost a guarantee with the losses during the war; if you survived there was a strong chance you would be promoted as an experienced soldier.

19th OCTOBER 1914 – THE FIRST BATTLE OF YPRES, BELGIUM

Corporal William John Bennett　　　　　　*1st Bn Wiltshire Regiment*

Service No.	8726	Age:	21
Place of Birth:	Calne, Wiltshire	Home Country:	England
Date of Death:	24/10/1914	Cause of death:	Killed in action
Memorial:	Calne		
War cemetery:	Le Touret Memorial		
Theatre of war:	France		
Next of Kin:	John & Elizabeth Bennett		
Address:	13 Patford Street, Calne, Wiltshire		

William was a regular soldier when the war started and was a champion runner for his battalion. He was highly respected in the Calne district and described as a promising young soldier. He arrived in France on Friday 14th August 1914 and took part in many of the early engagements of the war.

He was killed in action on Saturday 24th October 1914 at Neuve Chapelle, France. An extract from the war diary for the 1st Bn Wiltshire Regiment states;

"9.45a.m. shelling of village and trenches commenced. Ceased for a few hours and was again continued without a break from 2 till 7p.m. Companies in trenches suffered from shell fire, their trenches being blown in by these heavy shells. Village suffered a good deal. B Coy

in dug outs outside the village also suffered. Trenches report an attack about 5p.m. Sent up what could be collected of B Coy to reinforce trenches.
2nd Lieut Riddell slightly wounded. 8 men killed, 36 wounded and 23 men missing. It is feared that most of these 23 men were buried in the dug outs."

William is remembered on the Le Touret Memorial with over 13,000 soldiers who were killed in this area of France and have no known grave.

Private Alford Edward Heavens		*2nd Bn Wiltshire Regiment*	
Service No.	8807	Age:	22
Place of Birth:	Oaksey, Wiltshire	Home Country:	England
Date of Death:	24/10/1914	Cause of death:	Killed in action
Memorial:	Not known		
War cemetery:	Ypres Menin Gate		
Theatre of war:	Belgium		
Next of Kin:	Edward & Mary Anne Evans		
Address:	Spillmans, Hilmarton, Wiltshire		

On Saturday 24th October the 2nd Battalion Wiltshire Regiment were in the trenches at Beselare, Belgium. At 5.30am, just before daybreak, the Germans attacked with a very superior force but were driven back with heavy losses. The Germans then attacked again and fighting carried on continuously for two hours, the Germans had hundreds of casualties killed and wounded but eventually broke through. With the exception of about thirty non commissioned officers and men mostly from the trenches on the right, the remainder of the Battalion were killed and a large number captured.
A note was made in the Battalions war diary stating;

"Special mention should be made of the gallant worth of Capt Comyn, the medical officer and stretcher bearers who for the last three days and nights were continuously handling wounded or burying dead."

One of the dead was Alford Heavens. He is remembered on the Ypres Menin Gate with nearly 55,000 soldiers who died in Belgium and have no known grave.

Private William Golding		*1st Bn Wiltshire Regiment*	
Service No.	5616	Age:	32
Place of Birth:	Calne, Wiltshire	Home Country:	England
Date of Death:	25/10/1914	Cause of death:	Killed in action
Memorial:	Not known		
War cemetery:	Le Touret Memorial		
Theatre of war:	France		
Next of Kin:	William & Sarah Golding		

William arrived in France on Monday 21st September 1914; it is likely he was a reservist who had been called up as the 1st Battalion Wiltshire Regiment had been on the continent since August.
He was one of 37 men killed in action on Sunday 25th October at Neuve Chapelle, France. The trenches were shelled all day, the village had been reduced to ruins and the roads cut up by heavy shells. William is remembered on the Le Touret memorial and has no known grave.

Private William Henry Gee   *1st Bn Wiltshire Regiment*

Service No.   6868   Age: 32
Place of Birth: Ashton Keynes, Wiltshire   Home Country: England
Date of Death: 26/10/1914   Cause of death: Killed in action
Memorial: Not known
War cemetery: Le Touret Memorial
Theatre of war: France
Next of Kin: Annie Gertrude Gee (wife); William & Annie Gee (parents)
Address: 9 Omdurman Street, Gorse Hill, Swindon; Lower Penn, Hilmarton

William was an employee of the Great Western Railway Works in Swindon and worked in the Carriage & Wagon Paint Shop. At the start of 1912 he married Annie Gertrude Price. Another reservist, he arrived in France on Saturday 12th September 1914.

On Monday 26th October 1914 William was with the 1st Battalion Wiltshire regiment at Neuve Chapelle, France. At 4.30pm the Germans began to attack and, just as it was beginning to get dark they began entrenching 200 yards in front of the British positions. Three platoons of C Coy attacked the Germans with the bayonet and drove them back into the burning village behind, killing and wounding a certain number of them and taking about 6 prisoners.

At 6pm a plan was made to retake the village from the Germans, but after much delay and further attacks and counter attacks it was decided that a general advance could not take place without Artillery support. The fighting continued through the night, the casualties of the fighting were 20 men killed, 40 men wounded, and 10 reported missing.

One of the casualties was William. He is remembered on the Le Touret Memorial and has no known grave.

Private Ernest Arthur Elsip   *1st Bn Wiltshire Regiment*

Service No.   7665   Age: 26
Place of Birth: Calne, Wiltshire   Home Country: England
Date of Death: 27/10/1914   Cause of death: Killed in action
Memorial: Not known
War cemetery: Le Touret Memorial
Theatre of war: France
Next of Kin: Sarah Anne Adlam (Stepmother)
Address: Kington St Michael, Wiltshire

As dawn broke on Tuesday 27th October the 1st Battalion Wiltshire regiment found themselves almost completely surrounded by German snipers in trees, houses and ditches which made movement very difficult. Many message bears, known as runners, were shot while trying to deliver reports and communication was severely hampered.

At 3.30pm British troops were seen to be retiring with a party of 50 to 100 Germans in pursuit. The Germans were engaged and immediately retired toward the village. After being reinforced the Germans again attacked which the British then checked. The Germans were beginning to break the British line and at dusk the Wiltshire's retired. Just after dark the Germans set fire to haystacks which lit up the British positions making it difficult to move around and dig trenches. The Wiltshire's then retired again to a point 500 to 600 yards to the rear. Casualties for the day were officers killed 2, wounded 5, other ranks killed 45, wounded 153 and missing 150.

Ernest was one of the casualties, he had been in France two months, he is remembered on the Le Touret Memorial and has no known grave.

Private Daniel Hillier   *13th Hussars*

Service No.	4745	Age:	35
Place of Birth:	Heddington, Wiltshire	Home Country:	England
Date of Death:	30/10/1914	Cause of death:	Killed in action
Memorial:	Calne		
War cemetery:	Ypres Menin Gate		
Theatre of war:	Belgium		
Next of Kin:	Annie Hillier (wife); Mary A Sumbler (stepmother)		
Address:	13 Mill Street, Calne, Wiltshire.		

Daniel was a baker and married Annie Smart in Calne at the end of the year 1908. It is likely he was a reservist and was called up for service. He landed in France on 7th October 1914, 23 days before he was killed. He is remembered on the Ypres Menin Gate and has no known grave.

Major Charles George Francis Mercer Nairne   *1st Bn Royal Dragoons*

Service No.	N/A	Age:	40
Place of Birth:	Not known	Home Country:	England
Date of Death:	30/10/1914	Cause of death:	Killed in action
Memorial:	Calne & Derry Hill		
War cemetery:	Ypres Town Cemetery		
Theatre of war:	Belgium		
Next of Kin:	Henry Charles Keith, 5th Marquis of Lansdowne		
Address:	Bowood, Calne, Wiltshire		

Lord Charles Mercer Nairne was killed on Friday 30th October while serving with the 1st (Royal) Dragoons and information was at once sent not only to Lansdowne House but to Buckingham Palace and Sandringham where the King and Queen were in residence, his Lordship being an equerry to the King. He was born February 12th 1874 and was the second son of the Marquis and Marchioness of Lansdowne, his eldest brother was the Earl of Kerry, M.P. He was educated at Eton and at the age of 19 became a subaltern in the Old Edinburgh Light Infantry Militia. After two years service in this unit of the Royal Scots he joined the 1st

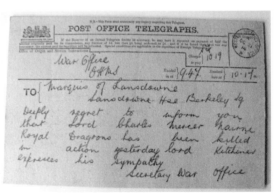

Above: the telegram to the Marquis of Lansdowne reporting his sons death.

Left: Lord Charles Mercer Nairne

Above: Map of the grave location given to the Marquis of Lansdowne.

Left: The original grave marker of Lord Charles Mercer-Nairne at Ypres Town Cemetery.

Dragoons, and just before the Boer War he was appointed aide de camp to Earl Roberts, who was commanding in Ireland. He preceded Lord Roberts to the Cape and served in the actions fought in Natal for the relief of Sir George White's force. He received the Queens Medal with four clasps; came home with Lord Roberts, getting his captaincy shortly afterwards. He was employed on Lord Roberts personal staff at the war office.

He became an Equerry to his Majesty when he was the Prince of Wales and continued to discharge the duties of that office until the outbreak of the Great War, when Lord Charles earnestly requested to be relieved of his attendance at court in order that he might go with his Regiment on active service. His Majesty gave his consent and Lord Charles went to the front.

Lord Charles Mercer-Nairne derived the surname, which he assumed in lieu of his patronymic of Fitzmaurice, from his paternal grandmother, Emily Jane Mercer Elphinstone de Flahault, who established her claim to the Scots Barony of Nairne (Cr. 1681) in 1874. Her mother, Baroness Nairne was the daughter of Lord Keith, the famous admiral of the Nelson period, by the eldest daughter and co-heir of Mercer of Aldie, whose estates, together with Meikleour and tully beagles in Perthshire, were transferred to Lord Charles as from January 1914. Thus the name and estates of Nairne and Aldie pass to a junior branch while the barony still vests with Lord Lansdowne, and after him will pass to the elder line.

The Memorial to Lord Charles Mercer Nairne in the mausoleum at Bowood, near Chippenham..

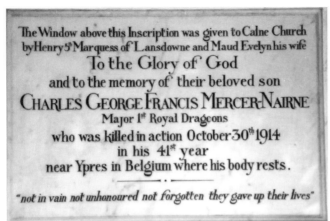

The Window above this Inscription was given to Calne Church by Henry 5th Marquess of Lansdowne and Maud Evelyn his wife

To the Glory of God

and to the memory of their beloved son

CHARLES GEORGE FRANCIS MERCER-NAIRNE

Major 1st Royal Dragoons

who was killed in action October 30th 1914

in his 41st year

near Ypres in Belgium where his body rests.

"not in vain not unhonoured not forgotten they gave up their lives"

Above: Part of the Memorial Window.

Left: Plaque in St. Mary's Church, Calne.

Lord Charles, who was himself the son of a former viceroy of India, married in January 1909 Lady Violet Elliot, daughter of Earl of Minto, who was at the time Viceroy of India. The wedding was celebrated at Calcutta with befitting ceremony and a few months later the bridegroom was appointed equerry to the Prince of Wales, who went on to be King George, who afterwards was a sponsor to Lord Charles's son in January 1913.

Memorial services were held at Derry Hill, Calne and St. Margaret's as well as at Westminster, London, which was attended by many dignitaries. In the summer of 1917 a memorial window was installed in St. Mary's Church in Calne. The design depicts three personages. In the center is St. Michael on whose right is St. George, and the left is St. Louis of France. In the background of St. George is an un-invaded England; behind St Louis is a desolated and burning Ypres. Underneath are the arms of Lord Nairne and the cross which marks his grave at Ypres with his name inscribed on it, over all is the sun of France.

The window was formally unveiled prior to the service on Sunday 5th August 1917.

Private Alfred John Cleverly		*1st Bn Wiltshire Regiment*	
Service No.	7058	Age:	27
Place of Birth:	Calne, Wiltshire	Home Country:	England
Date of Death:	31/10/1914	Cause of death:	Killed in action
Memorial:	Calne, Derry Hill		
War cemetery:	Le Touret Memorial		
Theatre of war:	France		
Next of Kin:	William & Sarah Cleverly		
Address:	New Road, Studley, Wiltshire		

Alfred was a groom prior to the Great War. He had enlisted in the Wiltshire Militia in August 1904 and it is likely he transferred to the Territorial Army in 1908. At the outbreak of war he volunteered for service to bring the regular regiment up to strength. In January 1915 news reached Derry hill that Alfred was missing and had not been since Saturday 31st October 1914. He was one of many names on a long casualty list of wounded, missing and killed.

Thirty seven members of the 1st Battalion Wiltshire regiment were killed on the same day. Alfred had arrived in France on Monday 31st August 1914. He is remembered on the Le Touret Memorial and has no known grave.

Private Albert Selby   *1st Bn Wiltshire Regiment*
Service No.   3/8974   Age: 28
Place of Birth: Hook, Wiltshire   Home Country: England
Date of Death: 31/10/1914   Cause of death: Killed in action
Memorial: Calne
War cemetery: Le Touret Memorial
Theatre of war: France
Next of Kin: Annie Maria Selby (wife); William & Elizabeth Selby (parents)
Address: Corton, Hilmarton, Wiltshire; Hook, Wiltshire

In the winter of 1911 Albert Selby married Annie Maria Cannons in Calne; three years later Albert was in France having arrived on Monday 21st September 1914. Annie, his wife, would learn in January 1915 that he had been missing since the end of October and later that he was assumed killed in action on Saturday 31st October 1914. It is likely he was killed near Richbourg St Vaast when the 1st Battalion Wiltshire regiment were shelled by the Germans while resting. He is remembered on Le Touret Memorial.

Private Frederick Knight   *1st Bn Wiltshire Regiment*
Service No.   8031   Age: 23
Place of Birth: Avebury, Wiltshire   Home Country: England
Date of Death: 31/10/1914   Cause of death: Killed in action
Memorial: Not known
War cemetery: Le Touret Memorial
Theatre of war: France
Next of Kin: James & Kate Knight
Address: Compton Bassett, Wiltshire

Frederick had arrived in France on Friday 14th of August 1914 and in early 1915 he was reported wounded, most likely near Richbourg St Vaast. In mid March 1915 news reached his parents that he was wounded and missing. He was never seen again and later it was assumed he had been killed in action on Saturday 31st October 1914, he is remembered on the Le Touret Memorial.

Private Frederick James Wheeler   *1st Bn Wiltshire Regiment*
Service No.   6274   Age: 32
Place of Birth: Hilmarton, Wiltshire   Home Country: England
Date of Death: 31/10/1914   Cause of death: Killed in action
Memorial: Calne, Wiltshire
War cemetery: Le Touret Memorial
Theatre of war: France
Next of Kin: William & Sarah Anne Wheeler
Address: Fishers Brook Cottages, Whitley, Calne, Wiltshire

Frederick was an army reservist at the start of the Great War and would have been one of many men called to the colours at the commencement of hostilities. It was reported that he had been wounded on a casualty list that appeared in December 1914. Later he was assumed to have been killed in action on Saturday 31st October 1914 near Richbourg St Vaast. He has no known grave and is remembered on the Le Touret Memorial.

H.M.S. Goodhope

Stoker 1st Class Alfred Tuck   *H.M.S. Goodhope Royal Navy*

Service No.   308496   Age: 28
Place of Birth: Bremhill, Wiltshire   Home Country: England
Date of Death: 01/11/1914   Cause of death: Killed in action
Memorial: Hilmarton & Calne
War cemetery: Portsmouth Navel Memorial
Theatre of war: At Sea
Next of Kin: Bertha Tuck (wife); Charles and Jane Tuck (parents)
Address: New Zealand, Wiltshire

Alfred was the local postman in Hilmarton and Goatacre and was described as highly respected for his genial, quiet and straight forward manner. He was also a Naval reservists and had been away on his annual training when War broke out and was not allowed to return home.

  He was killed on Sunday 1st November when his ship HMS Goodhope was sunk, along with HMS Monmouth, by the German armoured cruisers Scharnhorst and Gneisenau under Admiral Graf Maximilian von Spee with the loss of her entire complement of 900 hands in the Battle of Coronel, off the Chilean coast.

  He is remembered on the Portsmouth Naval Memorial which commemorates nearly 10,000 naval personnel who lost their lives at sea during the Great War.

Captain Arthur Edward Bruce O'Neill   *2nd Bn Life Guards*

Service No.   N/A   Age: 38
Place of Birth: London   Home Country: England
Date of Death: 06/11/1914   Cause of death: Killed in action
Memorial: Not known
War cemetery: Ypres Menin Gate
Theatre of war: Belgium
Next of Kin: Lady Annabel O'Neill
Address: Not known

Arthur O'Neill was the first Member of Parliament to be killed in the Great War and was the son of the 2nd Baron O'Neill and Lady O'Neill, of Shanes Castle, Antrim, Ireland. He was a principle land owner in the neighbourhood of Calne and the Marquis of Crewe. He was in the 2nd Life Guards and was a Unionist Member for Mid Antrim.

The senior remaining officer wrote the following letter to Lieutenant Petersons Parents (an officer who was killed in the same attack as Arthur) describing the events which led to Arthurs death;

"Yesterday afternoon, November 5, we were ordered to support and recapture a village out of which the French had been driven. The whole regiment dismounted and advanced under heavy rifle fire on the village, which was charged at the point of the bayonet by us. Your son - Lt. Peterson was shot through the heart during this charge. I am most profoundly grieved; he was such a splendid fellow and such a great friend.

We cleared the village at the point of the bayonet killing about 30 Germans and capturing about 20. I was the only officer left after this attack as our commanding officer, Major Dawney, a most gallant man was killed sitting next to me in the trench by a shrapnel shell. We also lost Captain O'Neill, killed, and Mr. Johnson and Mr. Hobson wounded, during this attack.

Our brigade, the regiment itself, were known to stay in the trenches longer than anyone else. Your brother died with two other officers of the regiment, Major Dawney, commanding and Captain Arthur O'Neill, in driving the Germans back; they accomplished this work and in so doing actually saved most likely a great defeat of our arms; the fact is recognised by the General. I heard, I do not vouch for the truth of it - your brother killed 16 Germans before he was killed. As the senior officer left with the regiment, and as I was also the squadron leader, I write to let you know that he died leading his troops most gallantly as we advanced under enemy fire."

Arthur was killed in action on Friday 6th November 1914 and is remembered on the Ypres Menin Gate. His two brothers in law were killed in action on Friday 30th October 1914 near Zantvoorde, Belgium. All three have no known grave.

Right: Captain Arthur Edward Bruce O'Neill

Below: Belgium cavalryman displaying his prizes, his German foes sword and horse

7th November 1914 – British Forces Land in the Persian Gulf to Protect British Oil Interests

Private Arthur Besant		*1st Bn Duke of Cornwall's Light Infantry*	
Service No.	8027	Age:	29
Place of Birth:	Bremhill, Wiltshire	Home Country:	England
Date of Death:	28/11/1914	Cause of death:	Killed in action
Memorial:	Not known		
War cemetery:	Rue Petillion Military Cemetery Fleurbaix		
Theatre of war:	France		
Next of Kin:	Emma Besant		
Address:	Charlcutt, Wiltshire.		

On the declaration of war the 1st Battalion Duke of Cornwall's Light Infantry who were based at Curragh, Ireland, were mobilized and arrived in France in mid August. Arthur was killed in action on Saturday 28th November 1914. The war diary for this time states the condition of some of the men had become terrible, that they were incapable of walking and some had to be carried out of the line.

Private Ernest John Angell		*2nd Bn Royal Berkshire Regiment*	
Service No.	8361	Age:	31
Place of Birth:	Calne, Wiltshire	Home Country:	England
Date of Death:	07/12/1914	Cause of death:	Died of wounds
Memorial:	Calne		
War cemetery:	Estaires Communal Cemetery		
Theatre of war:	France		
Next of Kin:	Winifred Angell (wife); John & Sarah Angell (parents)		
Address:	8 Alma Terrace, Calne; North Street, Calne, Wiltshire		

Ernest was married with two young children when he left for France, arriving on the continent on Friday 6th November 1914. He was wounded in the trenches at Fauquissart, France and died of his wounds on Monday 7th December 1914 at Estaires, France. He had been in France for just one month.

Private John Newman		*2nd Bn Wiltshire Regiment*	
Service No.	8208	Age:	22
Place of Birth:	Bremhill, Wiltshire	Home Country:	England
Date of Death:	07/12/1914	Cause of death:	Died of wounds
Memorial:	Not known		
War cemetery:	Merville Communal Cemetery		
Theatre of war:	France		
Next of Kin:	Frederick James and Emily Newman (stepmother)		
Address:	30, Christian Malford, Wiltshire		

John Volunteered for service. He had arrived in France on Sunday 4th October 1914. Early in 1915 news was received that he had died of wounds at a Casualty Clearing Station at Merville, France.

18th December 1914 – The Battle of Givenchy, France

British and German troops meet in no mans land to celebrate Christmas together.

25th DECEMBER 1914 – UNOFFICIAL CHRISTMAS TRUCE

"We had a surprise on Christmas morning. When the fog cleared we saw the Germans outside the trenches. We shouted to them and wished them merry Christmas and they waved back. Some of our chaps took courage and walked across. Then most of us went and had a chat some of them could speak good English. It seemed rather funny to see two foes talking together. We exchanged 'fags' and they had cigars, quite a treat to smoke one, but they were not up to much, they soon burnt out. Some of the men were quite young, but they were biggish chaps and looked well at all events they did not look as rough as we did. Anyway, their trenches are better than ours drier too I believe. " - Private Plank of Wiltshire Regiment

"We have had no firing the last few days as it was Christmas. We obliged the Germans by not firing and let them enjoy their Christmas as we did. The Germans sang us a song, and we sang them back a song. Then we cheered one another, and sang 'The King.'
They seemed to be short of food. We threw then some corned beef, and they walked half way between the trenches and fetched it. They shouted 'Don't fire, gentlemen' and after we had permission from our officers we said 'All right' They had no equipment on when they walked on top of the trenches. It was as a treat to see how friendly they were, but we didn't take too much notice of it." - Private J. Bullock of Wiltshire Regiment

"Christmas Day No Firing. An unofficial armistice took place and troops of both sides met and buried the dead. The Battalion fixed up a board with " a merry xmas" written on it in German midway between the trenches and was evidently much appreciated by the enemy."
- 2nd Battalion Wiltshire Regiment Diary

2
1915 - THE WAR THAT SHOULD HAVE BEEN OVER BY CHRISTMAS

Private Frederick Evans
Service No.   8913
Place of Birth: Calne, Wiltshire
Date of Death: 16/01/1915
Memorial: Derry Hill & Lacock
War cemetery: Wytschaete Military Cemetery
Theatre of war: Belgium
Next of Kin: Harry & Annie Evans
Address: Cantax Hill, Lacock, Wiltshire

1st Wiltshire Regiment
Age: 19
Home Country: England
Cause of death: Killed in action

Nineteen year old Frederick was killed in action on Saturday 16th January 1915 while in the trenches facing the Germans at Kemmel, Belgium. The war diary of the Wiltshires for the day states;

"Trenches. A quiet day, a farm just in rear of Battn. HQ took fire, and the enemy put some shrapnel over, presumably at the smoke. Relieved about 7p.m. by 5th Fusiliers. 2 men killed.1 man wounded."

Frederick was one of the two men killed, he is buried in Wytschaete Military Cemetery, Belgium with 329 casualties of the Great War.

Left: Members of the Wiltshire regiment in the trenches near Kemmel, Belgium.

Below: German soldier at the entrance to his dugout near the Yser, Belgium.

Private Walter Henry Rivers   *1st Bn Wiltshire Regiment*

Service No.	11049	Age:	21
Place of Birth:	Hilmarton, Wiltshire	Home Country:	England
Date of Death:	01/03/1915	Cause of death:	Killed in action
Memorial:	Hilmarton		
War cemetery:	Kemmel Chateau Military Cenetery		
Theatre of war:	Belgium		
Next of Kin:	Richmond & Jane Rivers		
Address:	Hilmarton, Wiltshire		

Walter had volunteered to join Kitcheners Army in September 1914 with many other young men from Hilmarton. He had arrived in France on Monday 4th of January 1915. The weather was cold and wet in the trenches, something for which this new army were ill prepared. In February Walter received a parcel for himself and his comrades from Hilmarton. It contained for each a pair of socks, a tin of cocoa, sweets and beef tea.

Edward Slade, who had volunteered with Walter, wrote to his parents on the 23rd February 1915 about one of their experiences;

"I and six more were in a trench on Monday night when a German came creeping up to us, and I was on lookout and saw him coming, and not knowing what he was up to I stopped him and we took him prisoner.
This is the first German I have been close to and he was all of a tremble, and begged me not to shoot him. He had a purse full of money and a good watch, and I expect he was around our trenches to see what was about."

Edward Slade was to die the following year at the Battle of the Somme.

In mid march 1915 Walter's parents received a letter from one of his comrades explaining that Walter had been shot in the hip going towards the British trenches, and crawling into the trench received a shot through the head, death being instantaneous. He was buried quite comfortably, and a service was held over him. The war diary for the Monday 1st March 1915 states;

"In trenches. Enemy dropped heavy shells at KEMMEL Cross roads and then traversed to the North. A good deal of rifle fire by night. One man killed."

Walter was 31 years old and had been in the firing line nearly two months. He was very popular being full of life and sport and to use a phrase of his comrades he made *"an excellent soldier ."*

Another comrade wrote, *"It was so sad about poor Walter, and if we are spared to return we shall miss him so much."*

Private Albert W Henly   *2nd Bn Wiltshire Regiment*

Service No.	18295	Age:	34
Place of Birth:	Calne, Wiltshire	Home Country:	England
Date of Death:	10/03/1915	Cause of death:	Killed in action
Memorial:	Calne		
War cemetery:	Le Touret Memorial		
Theatre of war:	France		

Next of Kin:	Not known
Address:	7 Cow Lane, Calne, Wiltshire

Albert worked in the collieries of South Wales and was employed as an underground hauler, he was a Kitchener volunteer and had arrived in France Wednesday 17th February 1915. Three weeks later on Wednesday 10th March Alfred was in the support trenches at Neuve Chapelle. This was to be the British armies first major offensive of 1915 but was destined to end in failure. The Germans heavily shelled the British positions constantly during the day and Alfred was one of six members of the 2nd Battalion Wiltshire Regiment killed.

He is remembered on the Le Touret Memorial.

Private James Henry Summers		*Royal Marine Light Infantry*	
Service No.	PO/16698	Age:	20
Place of Birth:	Derry Hill, Wiltshire	Home Country:	England
Date of Death:	11/03/1915	Cause of death:	Died
Memorial:	Derry Hill & Bremhill - Foxham - East Tytherton Morovian Church		
War cemetery:	Portsmouth Naval Memorial		
Theatre of war:	At Sea		
Next of Kin:	Joseph John & Elizabeth Anne Summers		
Address:	Pond Cottage, Charlcutt, Wiltshire		

James, a farm labourer, enlisted in the Royal Marine Light Infantry on 29th July 1913 and on 18th October 1914 he was posted to the Bayano.

The liner Bayano was taken over early in the First World War for service as an auxiliary cruiser. On Thursday 11th March she was on her way to Liverpool from the North Sea when the vessel was intercepted by the German Submarine U 27. At 5.15am off Corsewell point near Stranraer, Scotland, the U boat attacked. H.M.S. Bayano sank rapidly and only four officers and 22 ratings were saved. Fourteen officers, including, Commander Carr the ships Captain and 181 ratings were killed. The S.S. Castlereagh, went to the rescue of the sailors and it was reported there was a great deal of wreckage and many dead bodies in the water. The Castlereagh was prevented from making a search due to the presence of the U27.

The U 27 was herself to become a victim of what was described as a "war crime" when she was sank on 19th August 1915 by H.M.S. Baralong, a Q ship, which was a war ship disguised as a merchant ship. It was the intention to lure U boats close to the ship and then open fire with concealed guns. This led in turn to U Boats sinking ships without warning.

Twenty year old James was one of the 195 casualties of the Bayano and is remembered on the Portsmouth Naval Memorial.

H.M.S. Bayano before she was requisitioned by the Navy.

10ᵗʰ MARCH 1915 – THE BATTLE OF NEUVE CHAPELLE, FRANCE

Neuve Chapelle first came to prominence for the people of Calne in newspaper reports and letters concerning the British Expeditionary Forces' eastward advance to the north of Le Bassee in October 1914. The fighting toward the end of October 1914 had been described as murderous and had forced the British out of the village of Neuve Chapelle.

Neuve Chapelle was, like many other in this part of French Flanders, an unimportant collection of houses and small farms, scattered about a junction of country roads with a church at its centre. It was really quite a small place, but owing to the universal tendency of all these villages to straggle, each house being apparently built without any reference to neighbours, it covered considerable ground.

On the western side of the village there were some detached houses of a better class, surrounded by enclosures and orchards bounded by tall hedgerows. The ground all round is completely flat and, except in the open space which extends round the village and beyond the enclosures, view was restricted by the hedges and pollard trees.

After the fighting of 1914 and the advances and retreats, a static line of entrenched positions stretched from the North Sea to Switzerland. Sir John French the commander of the British Forces was under pressure to regain the confidence of his French allies and to break out of the trenches and return to a more mobile war. The battle began on Wednesday 10ᵗʰ March 1915.

By April 1915 after the battle from the west, all that could be seen of the place was a few ruined, crumbling red brick houses, nearly all roofless, and in their midst a tall white shapeless mass which represented the church. The ground between the Le Bassee road and the village was an expanse of pasture and arable land seamed with trenches. The original configuration of the German first line was in many places hard to trace, for the ground had been so furrowed and pitted by shells that there remained nothing but confused mounds, which represented the former parapets; and hollows representing the trenches and dugouts, in which could be seen calico sand bags, articles of equipment, the remains of food, ammunition, Pickelhauben helmets and Jagers' shakos. In many areas the original trenches had been reversed by the British attacking troops, who had prepared them against counter attack by the Germans.

In spots the ground appeared to be powdered with a bright yellow fungus growth, and the stagnant water in the older shell craters were covered in scum of the same hue. This was due to the lyddite from the British High explosive shells.

In the orchard close to the church near the centre of the village the fruit trees were nearly all torn about, while one large oak four feet in diameter was broken in half about a yard above the roots. The ground was strewn with branches and pitted with craters, the older ones being full of water, and the ditches which in the water-logged country, were dug all round the houses and enclosures had their banks blown in. One result was that the water had over-flowed into various hollows of the ground, forming large pools and patches of bog.

The appearance of the village itself looked as though an earth quake had wrought havoc, for the place resembled a huge rubbish heap; it was almost impossible to distinguish the streets amongst the rubble and bricks which had been hurled across and obliterated them. Here and there portions of houses were still standing, but these were few and far between, and were dangerous to enter for falling tiles and tottering walls.

In the churchyard the very dead had been uprooted, only to be buried again under masonry which had fallen from the church, and crosses from the heads of the tombs lay scattered in all directions. The sole thing in the cemetery that had escaped damage was a wooden crucifix standing erect amid the medley of overturned graves. There was another large crucifix still standing at the crossroads at the north end of the village where, at the time British soldiers entered, a dead German was lying at its foot.

Collected together at different points behind the British line were the graves of many of the British Soldiers. In some places the dead had been buried where they fell either singly or in little groups; in others there are regular cemeteries.

All the graves had been carefully made, a wooden cross having been erected over each, with the name and regiment of the dead marked on it, and many had been turfed and had flowers placed on them.

Private Montague Rowland Bridgeman		*1st Bn Wiltshire Regiment*	
Service No.	8003	Age:	27
Place of Birth:	Dauntsey, Wiltshire	Home Country:	England
Date of Death:	12/03/1915	Cause of death:	Killed in action
Memorial:	Calne & Christian Malford		
War cemetery:	Ypres Menin Gate		
Theatre of war:	Belgium		
Next of Kin:	Frederick Edward & Myrah Urania Bridgeman		
Address:	11 Dodford Cottages, Christian Malford, Wiltshire		

It is likely Montague was a reservist. He arrived in France on Wednesday 7th October 1914. On Friday 12th March 1915 the 1st Battalion Wiltshire Regiment were in the trenches near Kemmel in Belgium opposite a German position called the Spranbroek Molen, waiting to assault the Germans. The Wiltshires had arrived at 5.30 and the morning was dull and misty. The Artillery bombardment which was to precede the assault on Spranbroek Molen had to be delayed because of the weather. The mist began to clear and the war diary states;

"At 2.30pm the Artillery bombardment began and continued with a slight pause till 4.10p.m. It consisted of field guns firing shrapnel to cut the hostile wire, and large quantities of heavy HE (High Explosives) to beat down the German parapets and blow in his trenches, in this it appeared to be fairly successful, but, it was afterwards observed that the enemy's front line trenches were almost intact."

At 4.10pm the Wiltshires attacked and as soon as they passed the British wire the Germans opened fire with what was described as very heavy using both rifles and machine guns. Some small parties of men managed to get to the German wire which was a distance of 200 yards away but the majority of the Wiltshires were unable to get more than 50 yards from the British trenches, unable to move because of the heavy fire. At 5pm the British began to fall back to their trenches and suffered many casualties from the German fire and most of the Wiltshires withdrew at 7pm under the cover of darkness. The war diary goes on to tell us:

"It was observed that the enemy were holding this position very strongly and did not seem unduly shaken by our Artillery fire".

The Wiltshires casualties for the day were 33 killed, 48 wounded and 12 missing. Montague was first reported as missing, then reported wounded and then reported killed in action on that day. His is remembered on Ypres Menin gate and has no known grave. His brother, Walter, was to die of wounds just 7 days later while serving with the 2nd Battalion Wiltshires at Neuve Chapelle.

Lance Corporal Maynard Summers   *1st Bn Wiltshire Regiment*

Service No.	7775	Age:	27
Place of Birth:	Heddington, Wiltshire	Home Country:	England
Date of Death:	12/03/1915	Cause of death:	Killed in action
Memorial:	Heddington		
War cemetery:	Ypres Menin Gate		
Theatre of war:	Belgium		
Next of Kin:	Jacob & Emma Summers		
Address:	Stockley, Wiltshire		

Maynard Summers was a regular soldier and had been on the continent since Friday 14th August 1914 which was one week after the start of the Great War. He was killed in action on the same day as Montague Bridgeman and is remembered on the Ypres Menin Gate Memorial.

Corporal William Wiltshire   *2nd Bn Wiltshire Regiment*

Service No.	8309	Age:	25
Place of Birth:	Calne, Wiltshire	Home Country:	England
Date of Death:	12/03/1915	Cause of death:	Killed in action
Memorial:	Calne		
War cemetery:	Le Touret Memorial		
Theatre of war:	France		
Next of Kin:	William & Edith Wiltshire		
Address:	Quemerford Common, Calne, Wiltshire		

William was a regular soldier who had been in the service of his Country for six years; he had arrived in France on Wednesday 7th October 1914.

On Friday 12nd March the 2nd Battalion Wiltshire Regiment was at the heart of the battle of Neuve Chapelle in the forward trenches. Just as the rations arrived at 5.30am the Germans attacked with bombs (hand grenades) and confusion overtook the British trenches. Eventually the Germans were stopped and the Wiltshires counter attacked to try to retake the trenches that had been lost. Initially the attack made good progress but coming under heavy machine gun fire the British were driven back; these attacks prevented some of the Wiltshires getting water and their rations. Other Regiments attacked the Germans during the day but all ended in failure and by the end of the day the British front line was held by a jumbled mass of Wiltshires, Gordons, Warwicks and Scots Guards.

Then about 50 members of the 2nd Battalion Wiltshire Regiment were killed and one of these was William. Initially in March he was reported missing; in April it had been reported he was missing or a prisoner and in June the news arrived that he had been killed in action on Friday 12th March 1915. He is remembered on the Le Touret Memorial.

Private William John Keevil   *2nd Bn Wiltshire Regiment*

Service No.	12470	Age:	19
Place of Birth:	Hilmarton, Wiltshire	Home Country:	England
Date of Death:	12/03/1915	Cause of death:	Killed in action
Memorial:	Hilmarton		
War cemetery:	Le Touret Memorial		
Theatre of war:	France		
Next of Kin:	John Richard & Amy Keevil		
Address:	Rodwell Farm, Hilmarton, Wiltshire		

Nineteen year old William was another victim of the fighting that took place at Neuve Chapelle on Friday 12th March 1915. He was a Kitchener volunteer and had only arrived in France nine days earlier. First reports stated he was missing and then in April it was stated he was wounded and missing. His body was never found and he is remembered on the Le Touret Memorial.

Mr Moxey, the current owner of Rodwell Farm, informed me that William's brother had visited the Farm and told him that the weather vain still had the marks where he and William used to use it for target practice.

Lance Sergeant Alec Chapman Atlay		*2nd Bn Wiltshire Regiment*	
Service No.	11034	Age:	27
Place of Birth:	Lockington, Yorkshire	Home Country:	England
Date of Death:	13/03/1915	Cause of death:	Died of wounds
Memorial:	Hilmarton		
War cemetery:	Le Touret Memorial		
Theatre of war:	France		
Next of Kin:	Thomas Ware and Nancie Atlay		
Address:	Hilmarton, Wiltshire		

On the evening of Tuesday 1st September 1914 a public meeting was held at the School in Lyneham to support Lord Kitchener's call for additional recruits for the army. Herbert Gaisford, chairman of the parish council, explained the purpose of the gathering and W. Arnold Forster gave a stirring speech. He explained why the British were fighting and what was the duty of the Englishman on this supreme occasion. Many of his points were met with rousing cheers and he appealed to those present who fulfilled the necessary conditions of enlistment to come forward and give their names for national service. Thirteen volunteers came forward, the first turned to the audience and exclaimed,

"Gentlemen I have been shot at before in the Boer war, and I am willing to be shot at again."

Alec Atlay and his brother Keith both volunteered on that night, They were the sons of the Headmaster of Hilmarton School. On Wednesday 11th November just two months later Alec was in France as part of a draft for the 2nd Battalion Wiltshire Regiment. In March 1915 he was in the trenches at Neuve Chapelle. On Saturday 13th March the Wiltshire were being pulled out of the front line after the disaster that they had been part of the previous day. Between the 10th and the 13th March the 2nd Battalion Wiltshire regiment casualties were 64 killed, 173 wounded and 56 missing.

Initial reports on the 23rd of March stated Alec was wounded but shortly after news was received by his parents that he was wounded and missing. Nancie Atlay, Alec's mother, advertised in the local newspaper asking if anyone had heard news of her son in letters from their soldier relatives. She also asked if anyone was in correspondence with any soldier who had been taken prisoner at Neuve Chapelle, and to what camp in Germany they had been taken. Each year of the war, on the anniversary of Neuve Chapelle, she repeated her appeals but no news came of Alec.

In Hilmarton church there is a private memorial to Alec and his brother Keith who was to die one month later. The memorial states Keith was killed in action and Alec was wounded and missing, perhaps when the memorial was erected Nancie Atlay still had hope that one day Alec would return.

The Atlay brothers memorial in Hilmarton St. Laurence Church.

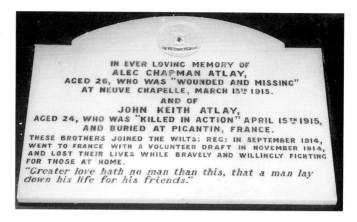

IN EVER LOVING MEMORY OF
ALEC CHAPMAN ATLAY,
AGED 26, WHO WAS "WOUNDED AND MISSING"
AT NEUVE CHAPELLE, MARCH 13TH 1915.
AND OF
JOHN KEITH ATLAY,
AGED 24, WHO WAS "KILLED IN ACTION" APRIL 15TH 1915,
AND BURIED AT PICANTIN, FRANCE.
THESE BROTHERS JOINED THE WILTS: REG: IN SEPTEMBER 1914,
WENT TO FRANCE WITH A VOLUNTEER DRAFT IN NOVEMBER 1914,
AND LOST THEIR LIVES WHILE BRAVELY AND WILLINGLY FIGHTING
FOR THOSE AT HOME.
"Greater love hath no man than this, that a man lay down his life for his friends."

Gunner Henry Newman Cole		*Royal Field Artillery*	
Service No.	65117	Age:	20
Place of Birth:	Calne, Wiltshire	Home Country:	England
Date of Death:	14/03/1915	Cause of death:	Died
Memorial:	Hilmarton		
War cemetery:	Brighton Bear Road Cemetery, Borough Cemetery		
Theatre of war:	Home		
Next of Kin:	Mary Anne Slade		
Address:	Rodwell Cottage, Hilmarton, Wiltshire		

At the age of twenty years and nine months Henry, a butcher by trade, enlisted in the army on Thursday 18th January 1915. He was sent for training at Hilsea in Hampshire. On 14th of February 1915 he was admitted to Brighton Borough Infection Hospital with Cerebo Spinal Fever where he died on Sunday 14th March 1915 and never saw active service.

Lance Sergeant John Keith Atlay		*2nd Bn Wiltshire Regiment*	
Service No.	11047	Age:	24
Place of Birth:	Lockington, Yorkshire	Home Country:	England
Date of Death:	15/04/1915	Cause of death:	Killed in action
Memorial:	Hilmarton & Melksham		
War cemetery:	Rue Du Bois Military Cemetery Fleurbaix		
Theatre of war:	France		
Next of Kin:	Thomas Ware and Nancie Atlay		
Address:	Hilmarton, Wiltshire		

John Keith Atlay, known as Keith, had followed his father and become a teacher, he had left Exeter Training College in 1913 and had taken a role as an Assistant Master in the Melksham Boys National School.

He had volunteered for service in September 1914 and arrived in France with his brother on Wednesday 11th November 1914. He and his family suffered the loss of his brother at Neuve Chapelle in March 1915. Keith was killed in action on Thursday 15th April 1915 in the trenches near La Gorgue, France

The Wiltshires war diary for the day states;

"A trench mortar fell in 'A' Company's trench about 8pm, killing 2 and wounding 4 . This trench was only 100yds from enemy's trench at this point".

Comrades from Hilmarton wrote home stating their regret at Keith's loss, one simply wrote to a relative;

"I saw Keith Atlay shot yesterday he took an hour to die."

Regular soldier, Lance Corporal William Rumming of the Coldstream Guards, son of Mrs W. Rumming of Highway, who survived the war wrote;

"I see in your local paper that a lot of chaps have enlisted and are out here. I have only met one man I knew (a Calne chap) all through the war, but should very much like to come across some of my schoolmates I was sorry to hear about poor Walter Rivers and Keith Atlay. I have had a few very narrow escapes myself, but I have managed to get through up till now. I have been in the trenches myself Knee deep with blood and water. It's not war, but murder! Hell let loose again!"

22ND APRIL 1915 - GERMANS USE CHLORINE GAS AT LANGEMARCK, BELGIUM

A Lieutenant serving in the Dorset Regiment wrote an account of his first experience of asphyxiating gas.

"I expect you have heard how the Germans on this 'Hill 60' played us the dirtiest trick that any British Regiment has had to put up with. The Canadians did not have it like we did, they had it from 400 to 500 yards away, whereas our trenches are at most 40 yards from the Germans. I saw more of the affair than anyone else, so I can tell you exactly what happened. At about seven o'clock I came out of my dug out and saw a hose sticking over the German parapet, which was starting to spout out a thick yellow cloud with a tinge of green in it. The gas came out with a hiss that you could hear quite plainly. I at once shouted to my men to put on respirators (bits of flannel), then I got mine and went and warned the Captain, who did not yet have his respirator on. The Huns began a terrible bombardment, not so much at us but at our supports and our dressing station.

British soldiers practice with early gas masks. The masks were soaked in urine and had to be wet to make them effective.
Soldiers often kept a bottle of urine in the trench in case of gas attacks.

Now, either they had miscalculated the direction of the wind or else it had changed, for the gas did not come directly toward us, but went slantwise, then our trench being so close the gas went into part of the German trenches as well as into ours. They bolted from theirs when they got a wiff of the filthy stuff, a few of our men staggered away down the hill, some got into a wood behind it and died there, as the ground was low and the gas followed them, others only got as far as the mine head and communication trenches. The company in support on my left moved up into the firing line, as did also half of my platoon, consequently, I was left with a few men to do all the rescue work.. My men were splendid; they all came with me into the gas, except the ones I ordered to stay behind, and we must have saved scores of lives. The men in most cases were lying insensible in the bottom of the trenches, and quite a number were in the mine head, which was the worst possible place. The best place after the first rush of gas was the firing line, being the highest point.

I was the only officer not in the firing line, and I should think quite 200 men passed through my hands, some died with me and some died on the way down. The Battalion had, I believe, 337 casualties. I can't understand how it was I was not knocked out; it must have been the work I had to do. I was simply mad with rage, seeing strong men drop to the ground and die in this way. They were in agonies. I had to argue with many of them as to whether they were dead or not. Why we got it so bad was because of our closeness of our tenches to the Germans, and this affair does away with the idea that it is not deadly. I saw two men staggering in over a field in our rear last night, and when I went to look for them this morning they were both dead. Altogether, I suppose 100 or 120 men and two or three officers are dead or will die of the stuff. I am absolutely sickened. Clean killing is at least comprehensible, but this murder by slow agony, it absolutely knocks me. The whole civilised world ought to rise up and exterminate those swine across the hill. "

British horse team struggles through the mud of Flanders.

3

BELGIUM - FRANCE
& TURKEY

On Sunday 25th April British forces were landed on the Gallipoli peninsula, the British and French Navy's had been attempting to force a passage through the Dardanelles Narrows with a view to put pressure on Germany's allies, Turkey, to aid Russia.

  The Ships were stopped by mines and the Turkish Forts that dominated the Dardanelles. A plan was conceived to Land British, Commonwealth and French troops on the Gallipoli Peninsula, to capture the forts and March North to Constantinople, Turkey's capital, knock the German allies out of the war and relieve pressure on Russia.

> *28th APRIL 1915 - FIRST BATTLE OF KRITHIA, GALLIPOLI, TURKEY*
> *6th MAY 1915 – SECOND BATTLE OF KRITHIA, GALLIPOLI, TURKEY*
> *9th MAY 1915 - THE BATTLE OF AUBERS RIDGE, FRANCE*

Engine Room Artificer Harry George Aspeck   *H.M.S. Victory Royal Navy*

Service No.	M/11034	Age:	23
Place of Birth:	Langley Burrell, Wiltshire	Home Country:	England
Date of Death:	06/05/1915	Cause of death:	Died
Memorial:	Bremhill- Foxham & East Tytherton Morovian Church		
War cemetery:	Haslar Royal Navel Cemetery		
Theatre of war:	Home		
Next of Kin:	Henry Louis & Kate Aspeck		
Address:	7, Charlcutt, Wiltshire		

Harry was a blacksmiths apprentice and he died most likely due to illness or disease at Haslar Military Hospital. He is buried in the cemetery of the same name.

Private Sidney Herbert Mathews   *1st Bn South Wales Borderers*

Service No.	14073	Age:	30
Place of Birth:	Bremhill, Wiltshire	Home Country:	England
Date of Death:	09/05/1915	Cause of death:	Killed in action
Memorial:	Not known		
War cemetery:	Bethune Town Cemetery		
Theatre of war:	France		
Next of Kin:	Elizabeth Mathews		

Address: Bremhill, Wiltshire.

Sidney arrived in France on 1st April 1915 and on Sunday 9th May 1915 he was in the British trenches facing the German positions on Aubers Ridge.

After the failures of Neuve Chapelle in March 1915, a new plan was made to take the German held Aubers Ridge, France. The attack was to fail and led to the resignation of Lord Kitchener as Minister of War, when the 1915 munitions scandal rocked the British government. The British had planned to precede the attack with a Bombardment that would cut the German wire and destroy the enemies trenches. Unfortunately many of the British artillery shells were duds: they did not explode, or worse they were what was known as shorts, which fell on the British trenches because there was not enough propellant in the shell.

At 4pm on the 9th of May the attack was not going well and orders were given that the assault was to be pressed *"At all costs"*. As soon as the 1st Battalion South Wales Borderers left the British trenches they were met by furious German machine gun fire. When the attack was about 100 yards into no mans land it was stopped in its tracks and the British soldiers were forced to take cover. By 4.20pm the attack was over, The South Wales Borderers had lost 9 officers and 224 men.

One of the dead was Sidney, he was probably killed close to the British trenches and his body recovered. He now lies in Bethune Town Cemetery, France.

Private John James Taylor   *Essex Yeomanry*
Service No.   1681   Age: 19
Place of Birth: Not known   Home Country: England
Date of Death: 14/05/1915   Cause of death: Killed in action
Memorial: Calne
War cemetery: Ypres Menin Gate
Theatre of war: Belgium
Next of Kin: Wiliam & Louisa Taylor
Address: The Cinema, Calne, Wiltshire

John was a soldier in the Essex Yeomanry, originally formed after the battle of Waterloo as a local cavalry force to defend Great Britain Homeland and to quell civil unrest. The Essex Yeomanry went to France in November 1914 as part of the 3rd Cavalry Division. John arrived in France on Saturday 27th of March 1915 and may have been the draft of 1 man and 22 horses that arrived at the Yemanry's HQ on the 12th April 1915, which is mentioned in the war diary.

The Essex Yeomanry were destined to take a dismounted role in the 2nd Battle of Ypres. On Thursday 13th May 1915 the regiment had a strength of 302 men & officers and were in a position east of Potiijze, Belgium. The British had been "shelled out of their trenches" by the German artillery and the Essex Yeomanry were ordered to counter attack and retake them. The assault commenced at 12.15am when the yeomanry made a bayonet charge at Frezenburg Ridge which recaptured the front line trenches. The Germans then bombarded the recaptured trenches until dark.

The Yeomanry's casualty list for 13th and 14th May 1915 was 33 killed, 100 wounded, 16 wounded & missing and 11 Missing. John was one of the missing, he was later presumed killed in action and never see again.

15th MAY 1915 - THE BATTLE OF FESTUBERT, BELGIUM

Private John Slade   *2nd Bn Wiltshire Regiment*

Service No.	13794	Age:	18
Place of Birth:	Barry, Glamorgan	Home Country:	Wales
Date of Death:	17/05/1915	Cause of death:	Killed in action
Memorial:	Calne & Calne Methodist		
War cemetery:	Pont Du Hem Military Cemetery La Gorgue		
Theatre of war:	France		
Next of Kin:	Henry & Hannah Slade - Adopted son of Mr & Mrs Hill		
Address:	Barry, Glamorganshire - The Marsh, Calne		

To serve in France from 1914 to the start of 1918 soldiers were supposed to be a minimum of 19 years of age. John Slade was only 18 years of age and therefore under age when he was killed at the Battle of Festubert, France. He was serving with the 2nd Battalion Wiltshire Regiment in the Rue De L'Epinette trenches. Furious and desperate fighting took place with bomb, shell, rifle, baynet and bare hands. The war diary states;

"The Commanding Officer when standing on the top of the parapet reconnoitering was knocked down by a high explosive shell which fell within three yards of him, but did no damage beyond shaking him badly. An officer of the Staffordshrie Regiment and two men were buried by this shell and had to be dug out."

John was one of thirteen members of the 2nd battalion Wiltshire regiment to be killed on that day and is buried in Pont Du Hem Military Cemetery, La Gorgue, France.

20th MAY 1915 - RMS LUSITANIA SUNK BY U-20 SUBMARINE
4th JUNE 1915 – THIRD BATTLE OF KRITHIA, GALLIPOLI, TURKEY

Private Albert Fry   *2nd Bn Wiltshire Regiment*

Service No.	5524	Age:	31
Place of Birth:	Castle Combe, Wiltshire	Home Country:	England
Date of Death:	15/06/1915	Cause of death:	Killed in action
Memorial:	Calne		
War cemetery:	Le Touret Memorial		
Theatre of war:	France		
Next of Kin:	Sarah Fry (wife); Isaac & Rhoda Fry (Parents)		
Address:	Calne, Wiltshire - Yatton Keynell, Wiltshire		

Albert married Sarah Bird in 1905 and at the outbreak of war they had 3 children. He had arrived in France on Monday 21st September 1914 and had been wounded twice previously. On Tuesday 15th of June he was in the trenches at Givenchy, France with the 2nd Battalion Wiltshire Regiment. As they left the trenches they were subjected to heavy fire from the front and the sides. The British reached a point 50 yards from the Germans trenches and in the leading Companies all but 1 officer were hit. At 9pm the Wiltshires were occupying an old

German trench and orders were received to make a further assault on the German lines at 9.15pm. The old German trench was not safe and was being fired upon by German Machine Guns from the side and because of this situation the attack was canceled. The war diary states;

"During the action of 15th and 16th, the Germans used incendiary bullets, and also sniped the wounded in front of their trenches."

In July Sarah received the news that Albert was missing and later it became known he had been killed along with 70 men of the 2nd Battalion Wiltshire Regiment. He has no known grave.

Private Oliver Arthur Henly		*2nd Bn Wiltshire Regiment*	
Service No.	18210	Age:	23
Place of Birth:	East Tytherton, Wiltshire	Home Country:	England
Date of Death:	15/06/1915	Cause of death:	Killed in action
Memorial:	Bremhill - Foxham - East Tytherton Morovian Church		
War cemetery:	Le Touret Memorial		
Theatre of war:	France		
Next of Kin:	Fanny Elizabeth Chivers		
Address:	East Tytherton, Wiltshire		

Oliver was a farm labourer. He volunteered for service and arrived in France on the 1st June 1915 joining the 2nd Battalion Wiltshire Regiment. Fourteen days later he took part in the action at Givenchy, France. In July 1915 he was listed as missing in action on Tuesday 15th June 1915 in a casualty return. Later it was reported that he had been killed in action on that day in the same action as Albert Fry. Oliver has no known grave.

Private Frank Stapleford		*2nd Bn Wiltshire Regiment*	
Service No.	13757	Age:	26
Place of Birth:	Calne, Wiltshire	Home Country:	England
Date of Death:	15/06/1915	Cause of death:	Killed in action
Memorial:	Calne & Derry Hill & Chippenham		
War cemetery:	Le Touret Memorial		
Theatre of war:	France		
Next of Kin:	George & Elizabeth Stapleford		
Address:	Studley, Wiltshire		

Frank arrived in France on Wednesday 24th March 1915 he fell in the same action as Albert Fry at Givenchy, France. News of his death reached home in early July 1915. Frank is remembered on the Le Touret Memorial, France, with over 13,000 men who fell in this area before 25 September 1915 and who have no known grave.

Private Francis James Wilkins		*2nd Bn Wiltshire Regiment*	
Service No.	11048	Age:	28
Place of Birth:	Hilmarton, Wiltshire	Home Country:	England
Date of Death:	15/06/1915	Cause of death:	Killed in action
Memorial:	Hilmarton		
War cemetery:	Le Touret Memorial		
Theatre of war:	France		

Next of Kin: James and Elizabeth Wilkins
Address: 13 Hilmarton, Hilmarton, Wiltshire

Frank was killed at Givenchy, France along with Albert Fry & Frank Stapleford. Frank had volunteered in September 1915 and arrived in France on Wednesday 24th March 1915. The first news of his death came from his brother Arthur who was also in the firing line, then hopes were raised with the arrival a day later of another letter. Arthur wrote that he had heard from a comrade that Frank was wounded. Hopes were dashed on the 1st July when the official notification from the War Office reached his parents. Frank was described as a promising and industrious young man with a genial courteous disposition. He has no known grave.

Private Harold John King   *2nd Wiltshire Regiment*
Service No.   13969   Age: 18
Place of Birth: Bremhill, Wiltshire   Home Country: England
Date of Death: 15/06/1915   Cause of death: Killed in action
Memorial: Bremhill - Foxham - East Tytherton Morovian Church
War cemetery: Le Touret Memorial
Theatre of war: France
Next of Kin: George & Florence King
Address: 10 Charlcutt, Charlcutt, Wiltshire

Eighteen year old Harold was under age to be serving in France when he arrived on Wednesday 24th March 1915. He was killed in action at Givenchy, France, in the same action as Albert Fry. Harold has no known grave.

Private Herbert John Butler   *1st Bn Wiltshire Regiment*
Service No.   13776   Age: 19
Place of Birth: Cherhill, Wiltshire   Home Country: England
Date of Death: 18/06/1915   Cause of death: Killed in action
Memorial: Calne & Cherhill
War cemetery: Bedford House Cemetery
Theatre of war: Belgium
Next of Kin: William & Mary Ann Butler
Address: Box Cottage, Cherhill, Wiltshire

Herbert, a farm labourer, volunteered for service and arrived on the continent at the start of April 1915. He was killed in action near Hooge Village, Belgium on Friday 18 June 1915. He is buried in Bedford House Cemetery.

Gunner Thomas Victor Cross   *Howitzer Bgd. Royal Marine Artillery*
Service No.   RMA/11310   Age: 27
Place of Birth: Calne, Wiltshire   Home Country: England
Date of Death: 20/06/1915   Cause of death: Died of wounds
Memorial: Trowbridge
War cemetery: Bully-Grenay Communal Cemetery French Extension
Theatre of war: France
Next of Kin: Lily Cross (wife); Thomas & Rosa Cross (parents)
Address: 37 Lower Bond Street, Trowbridge, Wiltshire

Above: British soldiers preparing to attack.

Right: Thomas Victor Cross of the Royal Marine Artillery.

Thomas was employed by the Great Western Railway at Bristol, he had left the Royal Marines in 1911 after 7 years service. He married Lily Elkins early in 1914 and as a reservist he rejoined his depot at Portsmouth at the commencement of hostilities. Thomas was sent to Coventry, where he watched the casting and making of some dozen big guns and in February 1915 he took the last of these guns to the continent. He was initially moved to Ostend, Belgium, then Dunkirk, France and then onto serve with the Marine Howitzer Brigade near Bethune, France.

Lily received a letter from Thomas in which he assured his wife that there was little chance of him being killed because he was so far behind the trenches. Shortly afterwards however, came the sad news from Eastney Barracks, that he had died of wounds at the Hospital at Le Brebis the previous day.

30th JUNE 1915 - ALLIED CASUALTIES AT GALLIPOLI REACH 42,434
25th JULY 1915 – NASRIYA IN MESOPOTAMIA IS CAPTURED BY BRITISH
30th JULY 1915 - GERMANS ATTACK WITH FLAMETHROWERS AT HOOGE
BELGIUM

Private Samuel Beer

Service No.	1236
Place of Birth:	Studley, Wiltshire
Date of Death:	01/08/1915
Memorial:	Calne
War cemetery:	Portianos Military Cemetery
Theatre of war:	Gallipoli
Next of Kin:	Frederick George & Thirza Beer
Address:	New Road, Studley, Wiltshire

6th Bn Royal Munster Fusiliers

Age:	23
Home Country:	England
Cause of death:	Died

It is likely that Samuel answered Kitchener's call for volunteers in 1914 and after being told the Wiltshire Regiment was full was enlisted in the 6th Battalion Royal Munster Fusiliers. He would have joined his regiment in May 1915, when they were based near Basingstoke for war training. On July 1st 1915 it was confirmed that Samuel's unit were to prepare for service at Gallipoli and he was issued with sun helmet and khaki drill clothing.

On Monday 18th July Samuel had reached the Greek Island of Lemnos, which was a supply base for the operations on the Gallipoli peninsular. It was here on Sunday 1st August 1915 Samuel succumbed to illness. He had been in the army just eleven months and never saw the enemy.

He is buried at Portianos Military Cemetery, on the west side of Murdos Bay, Lemnos, Greece.

6th AUGUST 1915 - BATTLE OF SARI BAIR AND LANDINGS AT SUVLA BAY AND ACHI BABA, GALLIPOLI, TURKEY

5th Wiltshire Regiment Almost Annihilated

In January 1916 a report in the local paper lead with the headline "5th Wilts Almost Annihilated".

It referred to Sir Ian Hamiltons' (who had been the commander of the Gallipoli Peninsula Operations), dispatches describing the events of the 6th to 10th August 1915 when a great attack had taken place from the ANZAC area.

The aims were to break out of ANZAC and cut off the bulk of the Turkish forces on the peninsula from Constantinople and to gain a commanding position for the artillery to cut off the Turkish army with sea traffic.

The 5th Wiltshire Regiment were part of the left covering column and were to march northwards along the beach and seize a hill called Damakjelik Bair some 1400 yards north of Table Top. This would enable 9th corps to be aided as it landed south of Nibrunei Point, while protecting the flank of the other assaulting columns.

During the main attack hill Chunuk Bair had been taken and on the night of Monday 9th and Tuesday 10th August 1915 the 5th Battalion Wiltshire Regiment and the 6th Loyal North Lancashire Regiment were chosen to hold this position. The Loyal North Lancashire's arrived first and their commanding officer, even though it was dark, recognised how danger-ously the trenches were sited. He at once ordered that observation posts were dug on the actual crest of the hill.

The Wiltshire's were delayed by the rough terrain of the intricate country and did not reach the position until 4a.m. The war diary disagrees with this time stating that the Wiltshire's arrived at 3a.m. and lays the blame on a New Zealand officer who was their guide. When the Wiltshire's did arrive they were told to lie down in what was believed, erroneously, to be a covered and safe position.

At daybreak on Tuesday 10th August the Turks delivered a grand attack from the line at Chunuk Bair Hill against the Wiltshire's and the Loyal North Lancashire's, which were already weakened in numbers by previous fighting. First the British were shelled and then at 5.30am they were assaulted by a huge column, consisting of a division plus a regiment and three battalions. The Loyal North Lancashire Regiment were overwhelmed in their shallow trenches by the sheer weight of the Turkish attack while the Wilts Regiment were caught out in the open and were almost annihilated. The War diary for the Wiltshire states the Turks attacked 15 minutes after machine guns opened fire at 4.30a.m. It also gives an indication of how desperate the British were to escape from the fighting and during the desperate fighting Lieutenant Colonel J. Carden commanding the 5th Wiltshire's was killed.

Another account is given from Captain (then Lieutenant) Bush who was honoured for his conspicuous service during the Gallipoli campaign. According to the dispatches, the Wiltshire's and another regiment had a whole division of Turks and two other Battalions against them on August 10th, 1915. Fire was opened on them at dawn with terrible results. Those who could, retired down a narrow gully, only to come under fire from more machine guns, and here, the two remaining senior officers being killed, Lieutenant Bush found himself left in command. He immediately, with the help of two sergeants, rallied the men and lined them against the side of the gully just out of reach of the machine guns. He, himself, went up and across the gully, finding a fairly practicable though terribly steep way up, got the men across by twos and threes, and led them to a place of safety under the top of the cliffs. Leaving them with the two remaining subalterns with orders not to move till after dark if he did not return, and then to make their way to the beach, he went across the open, under machine gun and rifle fire about 300 yards, finally reaching a New Zealand trench. From there he was passed down to Headquarters, and was able to pass word along the line to look out for the men as they came in after dark. A party was sent out to clear the bottom of the gully - about 150 to 200 men came in that night. Lieutenant Bush was invalided home about 10 days afterwards, with dysentery.

Some of the men of the 5th Wiltshire's lay hidden and survived the attack returning to their unit as late as the 26th August 1914.

Almost 150 members of the 5th Wiltshire's were killed on Tuesday 10th August 1915 the majority have no known grave and are remembered on Helles Memorial.

Lieutenant Geoffrey Peter Guillebaud		6th Loyal North Lancashire Regiment	
Service No.	N/A	Age:	20
Place of Birth:	Southill, Bedfordshire	Home Country:	England
Date of Death:	10/08/1915	Cause of death:	Killed in action
Memorial:	Yatesbury		
War cemetery:	Helles Memorial		
Theatre of war:	Gallipoli		
Next of Kin:	Rev. John Alex & Sarah Helena Guillebaud		
Address:	Yatesbury, Wiltshire		

Twenty year old Geoffrey was educated at Marlborough College and a Scholar of Queen's College, Oxford. He received a commission in the 6th Battalion Loyal North Lancashire Regiment which was a service battalion, one part of the armies that Lord Kitchener had appealed for at the outbreak of war and were in service for the duration of the war. The 6th LNL were formed at Preston, Lancashire in August 1914, and in June they were informed that they were to make ready for service in the Mediterranean.

The 6th LNL sailed from Avonmouth on the 13th June and arrived in Murdos on the island of Lemnos on the 4th July. Geoffrey and his Battalion landed at Anzac Cove, Gallipoli on 4th August 1915. By Tuesday 10th August the 6th LNL had moved to Chunuk Bair. As soon as they arrived they realized there was a problem, the war diary states;

"The Loyal North Lancashire's arrived first and their commanding officer, even though it was dark, recognised how dangerously the trenches were sited. He at once ordered that observation posts were dug on the actual crest of the hill".

In the early hours of the morning the Turkish forces attack with a vastly superior force, the war diary continues;

"The Loyal North Lancashire Regiment were overwhelmed in their shallow trenches by the sheer weight of the Turkish attack".

Geoffrey was reported as missing, his body was never found and he is remembered on Helles Memorial

Private Arthur Edward Strange		*7th Bn Bedfordshire Regiment*	
Service No.	19791	Age:	21
Place of Birth:	Calne, Wiltshire	Home Country:	England
Date of Death:	20/09/1915	Cause of death:	Killed in action
Memorial:	Calne		
War cemetery:	Dartmoor Cemetery Becordel Becourt		
Theatre of war:	France		
Next of Kin:	James & Kate Strange		
Address:	Quemerford, Calne, Wiltshire		

Arthur volunteered for service hand arrived in France on 26th July 1915 with the Bedfords. They were sent to the Somme which at that time was a quieter area of the Front and an ideal area to "wear in" the new divisions of Kitcheners army. He was killed in action, probably on a normal tour in the trenches. A year later his brother, Henry Herbert Strange, was killed in the Battle of the Somme in October 1916.

21st AUGUST 1915 - ANZAC ATTACK AT ANAFARTA, SUVLA BAY AND THE START OF THE BATTLE OF SCIMITAR HILL, GALLIPOLI, TURKEY

Lance Corporal Harry Thomas		*9th Bn Sherwood Foresters*	
Service No.	12503	Age:	20
Place of Birth:	Norton in Hales, Shropshire	Home Country:	England
Date of Death:	21/08/1915	Cause of death:	Killed in action
Memorial:	Hilmarton		
War cemetery:	Helles Memorial		
Theatre of war:	Gallipoli		
Next of Kin:	Benjamin and Hannah Thomas		
Address:	Lyneham, Wiltshire		

Thomas volunteered at the outbreak of war and joined the 9th Service Battalion the Sherwood Foresters who were formed in August 1914 at Derby. The Sherwood Foresters landed at Suvla Bay Gallipoli on 6th August 1915 and were part of a force that failed in nearly all its objectives which, in December 1915, led to the start of the evacuation. Thomas was killed in action on Saturday 21st August, just fifteen days after he had set foot on the Gallipoli peninsular. He has no known grave.

31st AUGUST 1915 - THE ALLIES LOSSES IN GALLIPOLI DURING AUGUST NUMBER 40,000 SOLDIERS, FROM DEATH DUE TO FIGHTING OR THROUGH DYSENTERY OR OTHER DISEASES

4

LOOS

This was to be the biggest British offensive to date in the First World War and involved 6 Divisions. It was the first time that poison gas was used by the British, the battle began on Sunday 25th September.

  Gas was released early on the of 25th September and in some places hung where it had been released. Though the battle was successful, heavy casualties were inflicted on the British and Commonwealth Forces.

Lance Coporal Victor Mepham   *6th Bn Wiltshire Regiment*

Service No.	13694	Age:	23
Place of Birth:	Burwash, Sussex	Home Country:	England
Date of Death:	25/09/1915	Cause of death:	Killed in action
Memorial:	Calne		
War cemetery:	Cabaret Rouge British Cemetery Souchez		
Theatre of war:	France		
Next of Kin:	Mr George & Fanny Mepham		
Address:	Lower Gates, Burwash, Sussex		

The 6th Service Battalion Wiltshire Regiment were formed in September 1914 at Devizes. Victor had volunteered and arrived in France on the 19th July 1915. On Saturday 25th September Victor was in the trenches at Rue de Callioux, near Loos and was to witness the first use of asphyxiating gas to be used by the British in the Great War.

  At 5.15am an order was received that the attack would commence at 5.50am with asphyxiating gas and smoke candles. The assault signal was given at 5.30 by rocket from Brigade H.Q. the objective was the German lines to the front and rear of Rue d'Auvert. The Wiltshires advanced through some saps which were trenches leading into no mans land but were soon fired upon from the side and the saps (trenches extending toward the German front line), were soon full of German soldiers and the British attack was repulsed. D Company got out of the trenches and attacked but were held up by heavy German fire and eventually were forced to retire. Casualties were 19 killed, 17 missing and 48 wounded. The war diary states;

"Owing to the wet weather considerable difficulty was experienced in bringing back the wounded and clearing up the trenches."

  Victor was one of those killed in action. He is buried in Cabaret Rouge British Cemetery Souchez, France

Aerial view of a gas attack.

Private Edward John Dash   *2nd Bn Wiltshire Regiment*
Service No.   18459   Age: 30
Place of Birth: Hilmarton, Wiltshire   Home Country: England
Date of Death: 25/09/1915   Cause of death: Died of wounds
Memorial: Hilmarton
War cemetery: Loos Memorial
Theatre of war: France
Next of Kin: George & Amy Dash
Address: 28, Hilmarton, Wiltshire

Edward, known as John, was the youngest son of George Dash, he was an esteemed employee at the gardens of Compton Bassett House for nearly nine years. He had volunteered for service on the 4th September 1914 and arrived in France on Wednesday 24th March 1915. While serving as part of C Coy of the 2nd Battalion Wiltshire Regiment, he wrote home about his experiences of being abroad for the first time;

"We are having a rest and just enjoying some lovely weather, hoping it will continue. Everything looks very nice out here, the trees are simply covered in flowers and the fruit trees are loaded, especially the pears. This is really a very nice country, so nice and level; it must have been a picture before the war started. But some of the buildings have now gone to ruin, and it seems such a pity. You see some very funny things out here. They have small farms, work the milking-cows on the land, and also have dogs in harness drawing about trucks. You seldom see the French horses except grey ones, and they look well. The women work very hard, start about three in the morning and work until dark at night, and the girls do hoeing on the ground. They grow a lot of teas and rye. Nearly all their husbands are fighting. They go into the cowsheds and throw a rope round the cows' horns and lead them to the ponds for

water. This seems very peculiar, not seeing anything like it in England. They have machines for nearly every purpose. I saw two cows at drill today. Are the potatoes up yet? They are in row lovely out here. The last time we went into the trenches we had rather a warm time of it. A.Wilkins is still at base. You know we have two of our boys wounded. It was so sad about poor Keith (Atlay) and Walter (Rivers), and if we are spared to return I shall miss them so much. I trust, please God, the rest of us boys will be spared to return to you. Fondest love and remembrances to all friends from all the Hilmarton lads at the front."

John did not return to Hilmarton. He was shot through the temple and died instantaneously while attacking Cite St Elise at the battle of Loos, France.

The British wore cloth caps and many soldiers were killed by head injuries, at the end of 1915 the first steel helmets were introduced.

A comrade writing to friends described John as:

"A good man and a good soldier".

Private Frederick Bull   *1st Bn Wiltshire Regiment*

Service No.	10952	Age:	39
Place of Birth:	Pewsham, Wiltshire	Home Country:	England
Date of Death:	25/09/1915	Cause of death:	Killed in action
Memorial:	Derry Hill		
War cemetery:	Ypres Menin Gate		
Theatre of war:	Belgium		
Next of Kin:	Emily Bull		
Address:	Studley, Wiltshire		

Frederick was a farmer, he married Emily Hillier in 1902 and they had four children. He had volunteered for service and had arrived in France on 17th January 1915.

While the Battle of Loos was taking place the 1st Battalion Wiltshire Regiment were in support trenches as an attack was prepared at Hooge, Belgium. At 3.50am the British bombardment commenced while the Wiltshires waited in the trenches. Thirty seconds later the Germans replied raking the British trenches with high explosive and shrapnel shells; a shrapnel shell consisted of a thin canister filled with hundreds of ball bearings which usually exploded in the air showering the area in deadly pellets. The British lost communication as all telephone wires were cut. It was believed the British had captured the German trenches but it had been observed that soldiers had been seen retiring from the German lines.

At 7.30am the Wiltshires were ordered to move to the fire trenches, the war diary describes the state of the trenches;

"The fire trenches especially on the right were found to be in a very demolished condition and the line in front practically destroyed and many dead were lying about, a large number of bombs were buried and others rendered unserviceable".

By the end of the day the Wiltshire were in an exhausted condition, there had been little opportunity to get any sleep during the passed week. Their casualties were 16 killed and 54 wounded. One of those killed was Frederick, he has no known grave.

Private Joseph Richard Brazier   *1st Middlesex Regiment*

Service No.	G/11046	Age:	20
Place of Birth:	Sunningdale, Berkshire	Home Country:	England
Date of Death:	25/09/1915	Cause of death:	Killed in action
Memorial:	Heddington		
War cemetery:	Cambrin Churchyard Extension		
Theatre of war:	France		
Next of Kin:	Richard & Mary A Brazier		
Address:	Fobdown Farm, Arlesford, Hampshire.		

Joseph, known as Richard, was a jockey before the Great War and lodged at Splatts Cottage in Heddington. He volunteered for service on 29th August 1914 and originally joined the cavalry but was transferred to the 1st Middlesex Regiment at the beginning of June 1915. He arrived in France on the 29th June 1915.

He is buried in Cambrin Churchyard Extension and lies with 115 soldiers of the 1st Middlesex in row H, all of whom were killed on Saturday 25th September 1915, the first day of the Battle of Loos.

26th SEPTEMBER 1915 – SUCCESSFUL FRENCH ATTACKS IN CHAMPAGNE
16,000 GERMAN PRISONERS CAPTURED

Rifleman John Henry Pearce   *1st Bn Kings Royal Rifle Corps*

Service No.	R/8290	Age:	37
Place of Birth:	Berwick Bassett, Wiltshire	Home Country:	England
Date of Death:	26/09/1915	Cause of death:	Died of wounds
Memorial:	Not known		
War cemetery:	Loos Memorial		
Theatre of war:	France		
Next of Kin:	Lilian Emily Pearce (wife); Jacob and Mary Pearce (parents)		
Address:	188, Winterbourne Monkton, Wiltshire; The Common, Heddington		

John was a shepherd and had married Lilian Emily Bull in 1909. At the start of hostilities he volunteered for service and after completing his training he arrived in France on 25th March 1915. He was killed in action at the Battle of Loos on Sunday 26th September 1915. The 1st KRRC had been ordered to re-capture a position called the quarries which had been lost in the previous days fighting. They had waited most of the day in reserve trenches but reached the front line during the afternoon. The area was covered with dead men and horses from the previous days fighting. The 1st KRRC were ordered to fix bayonets and as they left the trenches there was a lull in the German machine gun fire which had been concentrating on the British parapet. The German trenches were about 400 yards away and as the 1st KRRC got about half way they came across a barbed wire barrier which the British barrage had failed to destroy. The 1st KRRC were to go through the obstacle in single file and it was then that the Germans opened fire with murderous results. It is likely John was killed at this point of the attack, his body was never recovered and he has no known grave.

27th SEPTEMBER 1915 – BRITISH GUARDS DIVISION CAPTURE HILL 70 AT LOOS, FRANCE

Private Frederick Herbert Summers   *1st Bn Wiltshire Regiment*
Service No.   13971   Age: 18
Place of Birth: Calne, Wiltshire   Home Country: England
Date of Death: 27/09/1915   Cause of death: Died of wounds
Memorial: Calne & Bremhill
War cemetery: Lijssenthoek Military Cemetery
Theatre of war: Belgium
Next of Kin: Frederick & Elizabeth Summers
Address: Ratford Bridge, Bremhill, Wiltshire

Eighteen year old volunteer Frederick was under age when he arrived in France on the 19th January 1915. It is likely he was wounded around the 24th/25th September at Hooge, Belgium. He was evacuated to Lijssenthoek village, west of Ypres, to a casualty clearing station where he was to die of his wounds. At the end of August 1918 the following memoriam appeared in the local paper.

"In ever loving memory of our dear son and brother died of wounds received at the Battle of Loos 25th and 27th September 1915 Never forgotten by his loving Mother and sisters Lil & Nell, Ratford Bridge, Calne"

If we could have raised his dying head
or heard his last farewell
His memory would not be so hard
From those who loved him well
No one knows the heartache only those can tell
who have lost their loved and dearest
Without saying Farewell

It is interesting to note that Frederick's family believed he had died from wounds received at the battle of Loos. While Loos was well reported and documented, it overshadowed other events that took place in September 1915.

Private Charles Ponting   *5th Bn Wiltshire Regiment*
Service No.   9956   Age: 27
Place of Birth: Bremhill, Wiltshire   Home Country: England
Date of Death: 22/10/1915   Cause of death: Died of wounds
Memorial: Hilmarton
War cemetery: East Mudros Military Cemetery
Theatre of war: Gallipoli
Next of Kin: Joseph & Emily Ponting
Address: Cowage, Hilmarton, Wiltshire

Charles arrived in Gallipoli in July 1915. He was wounded in subsequent fighting and evacuated to one of the military hospitals at Mudros on the Island of Lemnos, Greece, where he died of his wounds on Friday 22nd October 1915.

A postcard depicting the death of Edith Cavell, executed by the Germans. It is interesting to note Edith is portrayed in white for good, while the dastardly German is portrayed in black for evil, part of the propaganda war that war in operation on both sides.

5th OCTOBER 1915 – A BRITISH AND FRENCH FORCE LANDS AT SALONIKA GREECE, TO SUPPORT SERBIA
12th OCTOBER 1915 -ENGLISH NURSE EDITH CAVELL WAS SHOT BY THE GERMANS FOR HELPING BRITISH PRISONERS OF WAR TO ESCAPE FROM BELGIUM INTO HOLLAND

Saddler Henry Richard Cleverly *29th Div Royal Field Artillery*

Service No.	16073	Age:	21
Place of Birth:	Calne, Wiltshire	Home Country:	England
Date of Death:	23/10/1915	Cause of death:	Died
Memorial:	Calne - Blacklands & Calstone		
War cemetery:	Mikra Memorial		
Theatre of war:	At Sea		
Next of Kin:	James Henry & Ellen Cleverly		
Address:	Dykes Farm, Blacklands, Calne, Wiltshire.		

One of the reasons Henry had enlisted in the Royal Artillery was because he had grown up on a farm and was used to dealing with working horses.

In October 1915 Henry was aboard the H.T. Marquette bound for Salonika, Greece where the French and British were fighting the Bulgarians. The Marquette was launched in 1897 and had originally been named the SS Bodicea but was renamed in 1898. The ship set off from Alexandria, Egypt on 19th October 1915. On board were 22 officers and 588 other ranks of the 29th Division Ammunition Column, Royal Field Artillery with it's vehicles and animals. Also on board were 8 officers, 9 NCO's and 77 other ranks of the New Zealand

Anvers
S. S. „Marquette" de la Red Star Line

H.T. Marquette sunk by the German sub- marine U35..

Medical Corps, and the equipment and stores of No.1 New Zealand Stationary Hospital, including thirty-six nurses.

At 9.15am on Saturday 23ʳᵈ October 1915 without warning the HT Marquette was struck by a torpedo from the German submarine U35 and sank in 13 minutes with the loss of 167 lives. The U35 was the most successful German submarine in the Great War sinking more tonnage in ships than any other.

Henry was lost in the sinking. He may have been trying to calm the horse with whom he worked so closely

Corporal Walter Alfred Hillier   *1st Bn Wiltshire Regiment*
Service No.   7301   Age: 30
Place of Birth: Stockham Marsh, Wiltshire   Home Country: England
Date of Death: 02/11/1915   Cause of death: Killed
Memorial: Hilmarton
War cemetery: Ploegsteert Wood Military Cemetery
Theatre of war: Belgium
Next of Kin: James & Eliza Bradfield (parents)
Address: Cliffansty, Wiltshire

Walter had a long military career, he had enlisted in the militia on the 1ˢᵗ February 1904, aged 18 years 7 months. He had arrived in France with the 1ˢᵗ Battalion Wiltshire Regiment on the 14ᵗʰ of August 1914 and served through all the initial actions the Wiltshires were involved in. He died at Ploegsteert Wood, Belgium and was buried alive when a dugout collapsed after heavy rain. The war diary states;

"Heavy rain all day, trenches and communication trenches falling in. Corporal Hillier who came out with the Battalion killed owing to dugout falling in."

22ⁿᵈ NOVEMBER 1915 – BATTLE OF CTESIPHON, MESOPOTAMIA

Private Herbert John Gunning   *5th Bn Wiltshire Regiment*

Service No.	18804	Age:	19
Place of Birth:	Calne, Wiltshire	Home Country:	England
Date of Death:	29/11/1915	Cause of death:	Died
Memorial:	Calne		
War cemetery:	Hill 10 Cemetery		
Theatre of war:	Gallipoli		
Next of Kin:	Herbert E & Maria Gunning		
Address:	25 High Street, Calne, Wiltshire		

Eighteen year old Herbert was under age when he volunteered to serve. He arrived at Gallipoli on Saturday 4th September 1915 as a replacement for the troops lost in the previous fighting.

On Friday 26th November as winter arrived in Gallipoli, the men of the 5th Battalion Wiltshire Regiment were at Suvla Bay. They were dressed in their thin war climate uniforms and had little protection from what was to come. During the night there was a tremendous thunder storm. Water rushed into the trenches destroying parapets and washing away the soldier's kit, blankets and other equipment. After the rain stopped the night was bitterly cold and the Wiltshires attempted to repair the trenches. At dawn the trenches were full of deep water, the cook house was flooded and with no fires conditions were described as deplorable.

The following day the rain continued and orders were received to evacuate any unfit men. Unfortunately the roads were flooded and the unfit men had to remain. As night fell the rain turned to snow and the Turks fired artillery shells at the British positions.

On Sunday 28th November there was a heavy blizzard. The Wiltshires were in the fire trenches huddling around braziers and biscuit tins trying to keep the fires burning. One man died of exposure and some were described as comatose. The war diary states;

"The majority kept up their spirits admirably and continued rifle and machine gun fire during night."

The following day, Monday 29th November, the Wiltshires were still in the fire trenches, the war diary states;

"Two of the sick awaiting removal on stretchers which did not arrive from ambulance died and then 3 others were found dead from exhaustion in the trenches. Frost began to dry trenches and conditions improved, fires being started and cookhouses in good working order. Extra issues of rum during these days of bitter cold were much appreciated. Unfit men still awaiting embarkation."

Herbert, an under age soldier with inadequate clothing, died of exposure at Suvla Bay, Gallipoli and was buried at Hill 10 Cemetery on the peninsular. By the 9th January 1916 the British & Anzac Force had left Gallipoli and the mission that was believed would end the war, was a failure.

5th DECEMBER 1915 – BRITISH FORCES IN KUT, MESOPOTAMIA ARE SURROUNDED BY TURKISH TROOPS
8th DECEMBER 1915 – EVACUATION OF GALLIPOLI BEGINS

Stoker 1st Class Edward Drew   *H.M.S. Royal Navy*
Service No.   K/18191   Age: 22
Place of Birth: Calne, Wiltshire   Home Country: England
Date of Death: 09/12/1915   Cause of death: Accident
Memorial: Bishops Cannings
War cemetery: Ford Park Cemetery (Plymouth Old Cemetery) Pennyco
Theatre of war: Home
Next of Kin: Joseph & Harriett Drew
Address: Bishops Cannings, Wiltshire.

In January 1916 the body of twenty two year old Edward was found in the sea near Devonport dockyard. It was believed he had fallen overboard while passing from a destroyer to another vessel on Thursday 9th December 1915. After it was discovered he was missing a search was made without success. The body that was recovered could not be identified by the clothing as the body was so badly decomposed, but no other stoker had been reported drowned in the area. The Fleet surgeon states that the decomposition was in line with a body that had been in the water that length of time. Edwards father, Joseph, had no doubt that the body was his sons and identified a heart tattoo and they shared the same shoe size. Joseph Drew was described as a lonely man, his wife was in an asylum and his other son was a prisoner of war in Germany. Edward was buried at Plymouth with full Naval honours.

Private Frederick Elms   *5th Wiltshire Regiment*
Service No.   9262   Age: 25
Place of Birth: Calne, Wiltshire   Home Country: England
Date of Death: 09/12/1915   Cause of death: Died
Memorial: Not known
War cemetery: Helles Memorial
Theatre of war: Gallipoli
Next of Kin: Joseph & Elizabeth Elms
Address: Quemerford, Calne, Wiltshire.

Frederick had arrived at Gallipoli at the end of June 1915, he died, most likely of illness, on Thursday 9th December 1915, just one month before Gallipoli was evacuated.

4th JANUARY 1916 – THE BATTLE OF SHEIK SA'AD, MESOPOTAMIA – AN ATTEMPT TO RELIEVE THE BRITISH GARRISON IN KUT
9th JANUARY 1916 - GALLIPOLI EVACUATION COMPLETED

Gunner William Sinclair   *Royal Garrison Artillery*
Service No.   446   Age: 37
Place of Birth: Tillcoultry, Clackmannan   Home Country: Scotland
Date of Death: 18/01/1916   Cause of death: Died
Memorial: Not known
War cemetery: Calne Holy Trinity Churchyard
Theatre of war: Home
Next of Kin: Alexander & Jane Sinclair
Address: 1 Albion Road, Edinburgh

VOLUNTARY ATTESTATION.

CLOSING OF GROUPS

Except in the case of men who have claimed exception from the Military Service Act, 1916, on the grounds of medical rejection

The Married Groups
(24 to 46.)

will be closed at Midnight on the 7th June, 1916.
AND

The Single Groups
(1 to 23)

Now open for single men who are otherwise excepted from the Military Service Act, will also be closed at Midnight on the 7th June, 1916

Group "A"

For single and married men born in 1898, will be closed at Midnight on the 7th June, 1916, for any man who has then attained his 18th birthday, and will thereafter be closed to men individually as they attain their 18th birthdays

CAUTION.
   It should be realised that only a certain number of men can be dealt with each day at Recruiting Offices, and therefore if many men wait until the last moment, it may not be possible to attest all who apply on June 7th

Left: The grave of William Sinclair the first soldier to die at Calne's Red Cross hospital at the pavilion.

Right: A poster stating the end of voluntary attestation, conscription would commence in England.

William was the first soldier to die at Calne's Red Cross Hospital at the Pavilion. He was a member of the Artillery section attached to the 486 Company Royal Army Service Corps.

   William had taken part in the fighting on the Continent and had been evacuated with trench fever. When he reached Calne he was not fully recovered and was admitted to the hospital on 20th October 1915 with disease of the liver. After an operation it was hoped that he would make a full recovery but a few weeks later became unconscious and fell into a coma. He died on Tuesday 18th January 1916.

   William had served 12 years in the army and rejoined the colours at the outbreak of the war and had recently lost a brother in the fighting. He was buried in Calne with full Military honours.

24th JANUARY 1916 - THE MILITARY SERVICE ACT IS PASSED IN PARLIAMENT
CONSCRIPTION WOULD COMMENCE IN MAY 1916

Private Lewin Blackford   *2nd Wiltshire Regiment*

Service No.	10406	Age:	27
Place of Birth:	Calne, Wiltshire	Home Country:	England
Date of Death:	15/02/1916	Cause of death:	Killed in action
Memorial:	Calne		
War cemetery:	Carnoy Military Cemetery		
Theatre of war:	France		
Next of Kin:	Violet Maude Blackford		

Address: 22 London Road, Calne, Wiltshire.

Lewin arrived in France on the 11th November 1914. He was wounded during fighting in May 1915 in France and after his recovery he returned to the 2nd Battalion Wiltshire Regiment. He was subsequently killed in action on Tuesday 15th February near Carnoy, France. The war diary for the day makes no mention of his death it simply states;

"The day was very quiet. The weather was very bad."

Private Herbert Ernest Archard   *70th Coy Machine Gun Corps*
Service No.   6892   Age: 24
Place of Birth: Calne, Wiltshire   Home Country: England
Date of Death: 29/03/1916   Cause of death: Killed in action
Memorial: Calne & Devizes Odd Fellows
War cemetery: Ecoivres Military Cemetery Mont St Eloi
Theatre of war: France
Next of Kin: Albert E & Sarah A Archard
Address: 3 Oxford Villas, Calne, Wiltshire

At the outbreak of the Great War each Battalion in the British army had two machine guns. This was soon found to be inadequate and the number of machine guns was increased to 4 per battalion. It was also found that to operate machine guns effectively it was necessary to have a certain amount of expertise. The Machine Gun corps was formed in October 1915 and after volunteering to join the army Herbert transferred to the 70th Company Machine Gun Corps. He was killed in action on Wednesday 29th March 1916 near Mont-St. Eloi, France. Herbert was a Member of the Odd Fellows Friendly Society and his name appears on the Odd Fellows memorial in Devizes. On the anniversary of Herbert's death, his parents inserted the following Memoriam in the local paper.

"In fond remembrance of Herbert Archard who fell in France.
Goodnight be loved not farewell from his loving Mum and Dad & Vic."

5th APRIL 1916 – FIRST BATTLE OF KUT, MESOPOTAMIA

Private George Gingell   *5th Bn Wiltshire Regiment*
Service No.   18790   Age: 24
Place of Birth: Calne, Wiltshire   Home Country: England
Date of Death: 09/04/1916   Cause of death: Killed in action
Memorial: Calne
War cemetery: Basra Memorial
Theatre of war: Mesopotamia
Next of Kin: Jonas & Eliza Gingell
Address: Calne, Wiltshire.

After the evacuation of Gallipoli in January 1916 the 5th Battalion Wiltshire Regiment were moved to Mesopotamia, which is modern day Iraq. British and Common Wealth landed in Mesopotamia, which was part of the Turkish Ottoman empire, to protect their oil interests. The Royal Navy had just begun to convert its fleet from coal to oil fired engines.

George had served with the 5th battalion Wiltshire Regiment at Gallipoli since October 1915, after the evacuation the Wiltshires were first moved to Egypt, and then in February 1916 landed in Mesopotamia.

On Sunday 9th April 1916 at 4.20am the Wilshires were at Sannaiyat, Iraq, advancing toward the Turkish positions. The Wiltshires found that in the dark they kept losing direction, the Turkish forces were continually sniping and sending starlights, (flares). There was confusion and the British lost their bearing after the Turks opened fire and eventually the Wiltshires dug in 650 yard from the enemies positions.

During the advance the Wiltshires commanding officer, Lieutenant Colonel Throckmorton was killed and the overall casualties were 23 killed, 163 wounded and 40 missing. Many of the wounded crawled in and many were collected. Two soldiers were recommended for the DCM for collecting and evacuating the wounded.

George was killed in action and if he was buried the grave was lost. Local Arabs were known to dig up soldiers graves and strip the bodies removing all clothes and possessions. He is remembered on the Basra Memorial, Iraq, with over 40,000 members of the Common forces who died in Mesopotamia and have no known grave.

Private Sidney Selman   *5th Bn Wiltshire Regiment*

Service No.	18161	Age	30
Place of Birth:	Bushton, Wiltshire	Home Country:	England
Date of Death:	09/04/1916	Cause of death:	Killed in action
Memorial:	Bremhill - Foxham - East Tytherton Morovian Church		
War cemetery:	Basra Memorial		
Theatre of war:	Mesopotamia		
Next of Kin:	Luke & Louisa Selman		
Address:,	Clyffe Pypard, Wiltshire		

Sidney was a farm labourer. He volunteered for service at the out break of hostilities and arrived at Gallipoli on the 4th December 1915. After the evacuation of Gallipoli in January 1916 the 5th Battalion Wiltshire Regiment were sent to Mesopotamia.

Sidney was killed in the same action as George Gingell. He is remembered on the Basra Memorial and has no known grave.

Private Frederick Goddard   *5th Bn Wiltshire Regiment*

Service No.	19446	Age:	21
Place of Birth:	Stamford in the Vale, Berkshire	Home Country:	England
Date of Death:	18/04/1916	Cause of death:	Killed in action
Memorial:	Yatesbury		
War cemetery:	Basra Memorial		
Theatre of war:	Mesopotamia		
Next of Kin:	James & Ruth Goddard		
Address:	33, Yatesbury, Wiltshire		

Frederick was another volunteer and a survivor of Gallipoli where he had arrived in October 1915. He was killed in action on Tuesday 18th April 1916 during a Turkish counter attack at Beit Aiessa, Iraq.

He is remembered on the Basra Memorial and has no known grave.

After the surrender of Kut British troops were marched into captivity by the Turks. Many were never to see England again.

29th APRIL 1916 – BRITISH FORCES AT KUT EL AMARA SURRENDER TO TURKISH FORCES

Private Ernest Frederick Wild   *5th Bn Wiltshire Regiment*

Service No.	5717	Age:	33
Place of Birth:	Clapham, London	Home Country:	England
Date of Death:	10/05/1916	Cause of death:	Died of wounds

Memorial: Calne
War cemetery: Kirkee 1914-1918 Memorial
Theatre of war: Mesopotamia
Next of Kin: Sarah Anne Wild (wife); Frederick & Sarah Wild (parents)
Address: Highway Common, Highway, Wiltshire

Ernest married Sarah Anne Reeves in 1909 and five years later, in October 1914, he was in France with the 1st Battalion Wiltshire Regiment. It is likely he was wounded and after his recovery transferred to the 5th Battalion Wiltshire Regiment. He was probably wounded in the fighting in Mesopotamia in April 1914 and evacuated to India. News reached Rodwell, Hilmaton where his wife was living that he had died but this was hoped to be untrue when a letter arrived from Ernest, unfortunately it was found he had succumbed to his wounds.

He is buried in India and as the Common Wealth War Graves Commission can no longer be properly maintained many of the graves are unkept. He is remembered on the Kirkee 1914-1918 Memorial. The memorial commemorates 1800 soldiers killed during the Great War who are buried throughout India and Pakistan.

Private Lionel Frank Henly   *16th Bn Manitoba Regiment*

Service No.	442682	Age:	32
Place of Birth:	Calne, Wiltshire	Home Country:	Canada
Date of Death:	11/05/1916	Cause of death:	Killed in action
Memorial:	Calne		
War cemetery:	Larch Wood Railway Cutting Cemetery		
Theatre of war:	Belgium		
Next of Kin:	Henry & Emily M Henly		
Address:	2 Market Hill, Calne, Wiltshire		

Lionel, known as Frank, was born in Calne and emigrated to Canada prior to the Great War. He enlisted on 17th August 1915 at Vernon, British Columbia and his occupation is detailed as a Rancher. He was killed in action in the trenches while preparing for attack on Hooge, Belgium. It is likely he was originally buried in Handzaeme German Cemetery and his remains removed to Larch Wood Railway Cutting Cemetery at the end of the war. He is also remembered on the Nelson, British Columbia Cenotaph, Canada

Private John Taylor   *5th Bn Wiltshire Regiment*

Service No.	11037	Age:	36
Place of Birth:	Hilmarton, Wiltshire	Home Country:	England
Date of Death:	12/05/1916	Cause of death:	Died of wounds
Memorial:	Hilmarton		
War cemetery:	Kirkee 1914-1918 Memorial		
Theatre of war:	Mesopotamia		
Next of Kin:	James and Elizabeth Taylor		
Address:	Rose Cottage, Goatacre, Wiltshire		

John was the eldest son of James and Elizabeth Taylor. Prior to the war John was employed by Mr Brinkworth, baker and grocer of Landsend, Chippenham and for many years at Lord Islington's estate in Hilmarton. He had volunteered for service in September 1914 and had originally served in France in April 1915. He was wounded and invalided home mid 1915 and after his recovery transferred to the 5th Battalion Wiltshire Regiment. He received a gun shot wound to the head and was evacuated to India. He died at Calaba Military Hospital, Bombay, India on Friday 12th May 1916 and was buried at a local cemetery. He is remembered on the Kirkee 1914-1918 Memorial. His brother Tom Taylor was to be killed in France in 1917.

Left: John Taylor wounded in Mesopotamia subsequently died in India.

Below : British soldiers in the trenches.

5
THE SOMME

Private William George Robinson
Service No.   PO/1752
Place of Birth: Henley on Thames, Oxfordshire
Date of Death: 31/05/1916
Memorial: Hilmarton
War cemetery: Portsmouth Navel Memorial
Theatre of war: At Sea
Next of Kin: George Phillip and Lucy Robinson
Address: Northcote Lichill, Calne, Wiltshire

Royal Marine Light Infantry
Age: 19
Home Country: England
Cause of death: Killed in action

William was a cook and gardener at the outbreak of hostilities. He volunteered for service and enlisted in the Royal Marine Light Infantry on 17th September 1914. After completing his training he was posted to H.M.S.Black Prince.

The first and biggest naval engagement of the Great War took place off the Danish coast on Wednesday 31st May 1916 and came to be known as Jutland. It was the first time the British and German Fleets had met in battle and was to lead to both sides claiming victory. It would also be the last time the German Fleet would put to sea during the Great War.

During the dark hours of 31st May it is thought H.M.S. Black Prince mistook some of the German Fleet for the British ships. As she passed the German Fleet the British armoured cruiser was suddenly illuminated by search lights and she was raked from stern to stem by German gunfire. As she drifted helpless and unable to fire the Black Prince blew up and vanished below the waves with all hands with her.

Nineteen year old William was one of 857 crew to be lost, the following day H.M.S. Oak found some of the Black Princes life belts.

The total British casualties for the battle was, killed 6,094, wounded 614, prisoners 177. They had also lost the Battle Cruisers Queen Mary, Indefatigable, Invincible and the sister ship to the armoured cruiser Black Prince, the Defence.

2nd JUNE 1916 – THIRD BATTLE OF YPRES, BELGIUM

Private William Henry Watkins
Service No.   G/4530
Place of Birth: Calne, Wiltshire
Date of Death: 03/06/1916
Memorial: Calne
War cemetery: Calne Holy Trinity Churchyard
Theatre of war: Home
Next of Kin: William & Emma Watkins
Address: Hunger Row, Curzon Street, Calne, Wiltshire

13th Bn Middlesex Regiment
Age: 18
Home Country: England
Cause of death: Died of wounds

Far left: The grave of William Watkins in Calne Holy Trinity Churchyard.

Left: Arthur Weston killed during the 7 day bombardment before the Battle of the Somme.

Eighteen year old William was under age when he volunteered for service with the Middlesex Regiment, a service battalion. He arrived in France on 1st September 1915. It is likely he was wounded during fighting at Wulverghem, Belgium, at the end of April 1915 when 25th Division, of which he was a part, was subject to a major gas attack. He was taken to a base hospital on the continent and then removed to the hospital at Leicester where he later died from his wounds.

William's body was brought to Calne by rail and was buried with full military honours. The coffin was covered with the Union Jack from the Boys' school where he had been educated. The pupils of the Boys School lined up on each side between the grave and the gate and hundreds of people including the Mayor paid their last respects. At the close of the service the choir sang "Abide with me", volleys were fired and the "Last post was sounded".

5th JUNE 1916 – LORD KITCHENER DIES AFTER HMS HAMPSHIRE SINKS AFTER HITTING A MINE IN THE NORTH SEA

Private Ernest William Hillier
Service No.   18015
Place of Birth: Goatacre, Wiltshire
Date of Death: 17/06/1916
Memorial: Hilmarton
War cemetery: St Sever Cemetery Rouen
Theatre of war: France
Next of Kin: Francis and Augusta Ann Hillier
Address: 77 Curzon Street, Calne, Wiltshire

1st Bn Wiltshire Regiment
Age: 23
Home Country: England
Cause of death: Died of wounds

Ernest had volunteered for service and arrived in Gallipoli on the 12th July 1915. He was evacuated back to England after either being wounded or through disease. He was then transferred to the 1st Battalion Wiltshire Regiment, initially he was reported wounded but in July 1916 news reached Hilmarton that he had died of his wounds. Rouen, being a port, was a major base for the British and it included eight general, five stationary, one British Red Cross and one labour hospital. Ernest is buried in the St Sever Cemetery Rouen with over 3.00 casualties from the Great War.

Private Arthur Weston   *2nd Bn Wiltshire Regiment*

Service No.	3/23	Age:	26
Place of Birth:	Calne, Wiltshire	Home Country:	England
Date of Death:	29/06/1916	Cause of death:	Killed in action
Memorial:	Calne - Calstone & Blacklands		
War cemetery:	Perrone Road Cemetery Maricourt		
Theatre of war:	France		
Next of Kin:	Walter & Mary Weston		
Address:	Hayle Cottages, Calne, Wiltshire		

Arthur had originally arrived in France in November 1914. He was killed during the 7 day bombardment that preceded the battle of the Somme. The bombardment commenced on the 25th June 1916 and the 2nd Battalion Wiltshire Regiment were in the trenches opposite the German held Montauban. It is likely he was killed when the Germans retaliated by shelling the British positions.

Guardsman Henry Short   *3rd Bn Grenadier Guards*

Service No.	21304	Age:	22
Place of Birth:	Calne, Wiltshire	Home Country:	England
Date of Death:	30/06/1916	Cause of death:	Died of wounds
Memorial:	Derry Hill		
War cemetery:	Ferme-Olivier Cemetery		
Theatre of war:	Belgium		
Next of Kin:	Henry & Isobel Short		
Address:	Not known		

Henry had been a domestic gardener prior to the Great War and had arrived in France on the 26 July 1915. The twenty two year old died of wounds probably due to German shell fire on Friday 30th June 1916 at one of the field hospitals at Ferme-Olivier which lies north west of the Belgium town of Ypres. He is buried in Ferme-Olivier Cemetery with over 400 casualties from the Great War

24th JUNE 1916 – A WEEK LONG BRITISH ARTILLERY BOMBARDMENT COMMENCED AT THE SOMME

Lance Corporal Edward Slade   *1st Bn Wiltshire Regiment*

Service No.	11042	Age:	29
Place of Birth:	Hilmarton, Wiltshire	Home Country:	England
Date of Death:	08/07/1916	Cause of death:	Died of wounds
Memorial:	Hilmarton		
War cemetery:	Authuile Military Cemetery		
Theatre of war:	France		
Next of Kin:	Robert & Emily Slade		
Address:	Cowage, Hilmarton, Wiltshire		

Edward had volunteered for service with his brothers Jack and Herbert in September 1914 and all had been sent to France. Prior to the war he lived at Cowage with his parents where he was employed as a ploughman. It is likely that Edward was wounded during the initial stages of the battle of the Somme when the 1st Battalion Wiltshire Regiment attacked the German position at Leipzig Salient. He was evacuated to one of the Field Ambulances at

Above: British burials in France.

Left: Edward Slade.

Authulie, a village but at this stage of the war it was just ruins. He died of his wounds on Saturday 8th July 1916 and was buried in Authuile Military Cemetery.

Of his brothers, Herbert Slade died in October 1916 after being wounded at the Somme and Jack, who survived the war, was wounded in 1915 and evacuated to England and was serving in India when his brothers were killed.

On the anniversary of his death in 1918, Edward's Parents inserted the following memoriam;

"In loving memory of Corporal Edward Slade of Hilmarton

If we could have raised his dying head
Or heard his last farewell
His memory would not be so hard
From us who loved him well
No one knows the silent heartache
Only those can tell
Who have lost their loved and dearest
Without saying Farewell
From Father, Mother, Brother and Sisters".

Major William Pyt Bennett　　　　　　*Royal Garrison Artillery*

Service No.	N/A	Age:	36
Place of Birth:	Calne, Wiltshire	Home Country:	England
Date of Death:	15/07/1916	Cause of death:	Killed in action
Memorial:	Not known		
War cemetery:	Dartmoor Cemetery Becordel Becourt		
Theatre of war:	France		
Next of Kin:	Mrs Bennett		
Address:	Ballykeel Cowley, Exeter, Devon		

William was the only surviving son of late William Stephenson Bennett of Tower house, Slough, and of Fanny Bennett, Wood Norton, Fleet, and the grandson of the late Rev. William Coles Bennett, for many years the Rector of Corsham, Wiltshire. Major Bennett was

36 years of age and was educated at Marlborough and Woolwich. He served at Gibraltar, Malta and India and went through the Tibet Expedition. He left a widow and one son. On his death he left an estate of £24,299. He left £250 each to; Dr Barnardo's Homes, Marlborough College Mission, Hospital for sick children Great Ormond street, National Home for Homeless and Destitute Children, the Royal Artillery Charities, the Poor Clergy Relief Corporation, the School for Daughters of Officers and the London Hospital.

William was killed in action on Saturday 15th July 1916, most likely due to German Bombardment on the British Artillery positions at the Somme.

Private Jesse Edward Lewis   *23rd Bn Australian Infantry AIF*
Service No.   3564   Age: 26
Place of Birth:,   Avon, Wiltshire   Home Country: Australia
Date of Death: 28/07/1916   Cause of death: Killed in action
Memorial: Bremhill - Foxham - East Tytherton Morovian Church
War cemetery: Serre Road Cemetery No 2
Theatre of war: France
Next of Kin: John & Mary Lewis
Address: 52 Wick Hill, Bremhill, Wiltshire

Jesse, a wagon driver, had traveled to Australia with Charles Fortune before the Great War and enlisted with his friend in the Australian Army on the 16th August 1915. After completing his training he sailed from Melbourne on the 5th January 1916 and after changing ships at Alexandria in Egypt on the 19th March 1916 he arrived at Marsielles, France on the 26th March 1916. He was reported missing in action Friday 27th July 1916 during fighting near the Baupaume road. In December 1917 he was reported to have been killed in action on the same day. In 1928 Jesse's remains were exhumed and relocated to Serre Road Cemetery No 2 because there was a policy to relocate scattered graves to larger cemeteries. His friend Charles Fortune was to die of wounds on the 7th August 1916.

Private George Bruce Fletcher Hunt   *17th Bn Australian Infantry AIF*
Service No.   2672   Age: 19
Place of Birth: Dandaloo, New South Wales   Home Country: Australia
Date of Death: 02/08/1916   Cause of death: Killed in action
Memorial: Private Memorial on Alfred Stanley Hunt's grave, Yatesbury
War cemetery: Gordon Dump Cemetery Ovillers La Boisselle
Theatre of war: France
Next of Kin: Alfred Edgar & Sarah Ruth Hunt
Address: Robel, Rangers Avenue, Mosman, New South Wales.

George enlisted in the Australian army on the 4th August 1915, one year after the British Empire had declared war on Germany, at the age of eighteen years and one month.

He left Sydney on the troopship "Euripides" on the 2nd November 1915 and after a month in Egypt arrived in Marseilles, France on the 23rd March 1916. He was killed in action at the Somme, probably near Muster Alley a trench to the east of Pozieres, France.

George was missing and his date of death was initially listed between 26th July and 7th August. He was buried at Gordon's Dump Cemetery, Sausage Valley, but records can only tell us he was buried between 31st July and 3rd August. One of the reasons for this confusion was the number of dead the burial party had interred.

His personal possessions were sent to his parents and consisted of;

"Safety razor in case with strop. Bag, Waterproof, wallet"

In April 1917 George's father wrote to the Army asking why his sons wallet watch and number identity disc were not return and it was found that these were not on the body when he was buried. No explanation was give to what had happened to these items. Perhaps his parents were hoping that because his identity disc was not recovered George was still alive.

Alfred Stanley Hunt, George's brother, was to be killed in a flying accident at Yatesbury one year later in August 1917. Both are remembered on Alfred's grave at Yatesbury.

Private Charles Fortune		*23rd Bn Australian Infantry AIF*	
Service No.	3525	Age:	26
Place of Birth:	Avon, Wiltshire	Home Country:	Australia
Date of Death:	07/08/1916	Cause of death:	Died of wounds
Memorial:	Bremhill - Foxham - East Tytherton Morovian Church		
War cemetery:	Puchevillers British Cemetery		
Theatre of war:	France		
Next of Kin:	William James & Elizabeth Fortune		
Address:	Foxham, Wiltshire		

Charles, a labourer, had traveled to Australia with Jesse Lewis before the Great War. He enlisted with his friend in the Australian Army on the 16th August 1915. After completing his training he sailed from Melbourne on 5th January 1916 on the troop ship Africa and after changing ships at Alexandria in Egypt on 14th March 1916 arrived at Marsielles, France on 19th March 1916. He was involved in fighting at the Somme, between the Baupaume Road and the track to Courcelette.

The 23rd Battalion were held up by a German machine gun and it is likely Charles was wounded in an attack on this position on Saturday 5th August 1916. He was admitted to the 3rd Casualty Clearing Station with gunshot wounds to the leg and buttock and succumbed to his wounds on Monday 7th August 1916. He was buried at Puchevillers British Cemetery on the 12th August 1916 and the ceremony was conducted by The Rev. A.H. Broughton. His personal property was returned to his father, it consisted of - Identity disc, Testament, French Book, Letter Cards, Scarf, 2 Brushes, Razor, Strop, Rubber stamp, Shaving brush, Cigarrette lighter, Celluloid case and a pencil. Charles's friend, Jesse Lewis, was listed as killed in action at the Somme on the 28th July 1916.

Private Frederick Edward George Angell		*1/8th Royal Warwickshire Regiment*	
Service No.	5290	Age:	19
Place of Birth:	Calne, Wiltshire	Home Country:	England
Date of Death:	27/08/1916	Cause of death:	Killed in action
Memorial:	Calne & Calne Methodist		
War cemetery:	Thiepval Memorial		
Theatre of war:	France		
Next of Kin:	William Henry & Annie Angell		
Address:	27 Shelburne Road, Calne, Wiltshire		

Frederick enlisted in the Royal Warwickshire Regiment on the 5th December 1915 at eighteen years and nine months and he had been employed as a printer. He arrived in France in May 1916 and on Sunday 27th August 1916 he was at the Somme near Mouquet Farm, known as Mucky Farm to the British, near the village of Thiepval.

At 7pm the Warwicks assaulted part of Constance trench either side of Pole trench . They were following a Creeping Barrage, the British Artillery would gradually lift the trajectory of the guns and the infantry would follow behind a screen of shells which would hopefully prevent the Germans leaving their dugouts and manning their trenches. Unfortunately the Warwicks moved forward too quickly and ran into the screen of shells and were forced to withdraw.

Nineteen year old Frederick was listed as missing. His remains were never found and it is likely he was one of those killed when the Warwicks ran into the British barrage. He is remembered on the Thiepval Memorial with over 70,000 soldiers who died in the Somme area before 20 March 1918 and have no known grave.

Private Herbert William Green   *1/8th Royal Warwickshire Regiment*
Service No.   306659   Age: 34
Place of Birth: Calne, Wiltshire   Home Country: England
Date of Death: 27/08/1916   Cause of death: Killed in action
Memorial: Calne - Calstone & Blacklands
War cemetery: London Cemetery and Extension Longueval
Theatre of war: France
Next of Kin: Clare Green & Emma Green
Address: Waggon & Horses, Calne, Wiltshire

Herbert was an agricultural labourer and lived at Blacklands. He had probably enlisted around the same time as Frederick Angell. He was killed in the action on the same day as the Warwicks ran into the British barrage near Thiepval on Sunday 27th August 1916.

His body was buried at London Cemetery and Extension, Longueval, one of five cemeteries in the immediate vicinity of Longueval which together contain more than 15,000 graves.

Private Frank Atwood   *1/8th Royal Warwickshire Regiment*
Service No.   306674   Age: 40
Place of Birth: Not Known   Home Country: England
Date of Death: 27/08/1916   Cause of death: Killed in action
Memorial: Derry Hill
War cemetery: Thiepval Memorial
Theatre of war: France
Next of Kin: Isobella Atwood (stepmother)
Address: Minehead, Somerset

Frank was a cowman, he lived at Forest Gate, Pewsham and it is likely he was employed at the Bowood Estate. He enlisted on 15th December 1915 at the age of 39 years and 10months. He is listed as wounded and missing on Sunday 27th August 1916, likely wounded when the Warwicks ran into the British barrage near Thiepval. His body was never found and in October 1916 he was assumed to have died on the day he was declared missing. He has no known grave.

Private Albert George Daniels   *1st/1st Royal East Kent Yeomanry*

Service No.	1754	Age:	20
Place of Birth:	Hardenhuish, Wiltshire	Home Country:	England
Date of Death:	30/08/1916	Cause of death:	Died
Memorial:	Derry Hill		
War cemetery:	Alexandria Hadra War Memorial Cemetery		
Theatre of war:	Egypt		
Next of Kin:	Tom and Louisa Daniels		
Address:	Derry Hill, Wiltshire.		

Albert arrived in Egypt in October 1915 and it is likely he served in Gallipoli with the East Kent Yeomanry in a dismounted role. After the evacuation of Gallipoli in January 1916 he returned to Egypt. He died most likely of disease on Wednesday 30th August 1916. He was buried in Alexandria Hadra War Memorial Cemetery, with 1700 other soldiers who died during the Great War.

Corporal Charles John James   *1st Bn Wiltshire Regiment*

Service No.	10466	Age:	23
Place of Birth:	Calstone, Wiltshire	Home Country:	England
Date of Death:	03/09/1916	Cause of death:	Killed in action
Memorial:	Calne & Calstone & Blacklands		
War cemetery:	Lonsdale Cemetery Authuile		
Theatre of war:	France		
Next of Kin:	Thomas & Harriet James		
Address:	18 Calstone, Calne, Wiltshire		

Charles had volunteered for service and arrived in France on 28th November 1915. On Sunday 3rd September 1916 at 2.30am the 1st Battalion Wiltshire Regiment had just arrived at the Leipzig Salient, the front line at the battle of the Somme.

   As they made their way to the front they had been heavily shelled but were lucky and sustained no casualties.

   The Wiltshires were preparing to attack and at 5.10am as they left their trenches they were met by heavy "Whizbang" fire and at the same time German machine guns opened fire from the sides. On the right D company were wiped out by the British barrage which did not lift in time. By the time the rest of the Wiltshires reached the enemy trenches their losses were so great that they were forced to retire. Back at the British front line it was not known what was happening and the reserve company was sent to strengthen the attack. The reserve company now suffered at the hands of the German machine guns.

   Charles was one of those killed in the attack. He is buried in Lonsdale Cemetery Authuile.

Rifleman Arthur Robert Summers   *10th Bn Kings Royal Rifle Corps*

Service No.	R/1771	Age:	25
Place of Birth:	Reading, Berkshire	Home Country:	England
Date of Death:	03/09/1916	Cause of death:	Killed in action
Memorial:	Calne		
War cemetery:	Thiepval Memorial		
Theatre of war	France		
Next of Kin:	Alfred & Annie Summers		
Address:	Swerves Farm, Calne, Wiltshire		

Arthur had volunteered with the 10th Service Battalion the Kings Royal Rifle Corps and arrived in France on the 21st July 1915.

On Sunday 3rd September 1916 the 10th KRRC were attacking German held Guillemont Village at the Somme. The KRRC were able to keep close to the British Barrage and were able to surprise the Germans. They reached their objective on the Hardecourt Road and the 10th KRRC then mopped up to check there was no German resistance behind them.

Arthur was one of 60 men of the 10th KRRC to be killed on that day. He is remembered on the Thiepval memorial and has no known grave.

Private William George Leonard Marshman   *1/4th Bn TF Wiltshire Regiment*
Service No.   2885   Age: 42
Place of Birth: Calne, Wiltshire   Home Country: England
Date of Death: 11/09/1916   Cause of death: Died
Memorial: Not known
War cemetery: Kirkee 1914-1918 Memorial
Theatre of war   India
Next of Kin: Annie Maria Marshman
Address: London Road, Calne, Wiltshire

During the Great War the 1/4th Wiltshire Regiment was on Garrison duty in India. Many older soldiers or soldiers who were wounded and not fit to fight were sent for Service. Forty two year old William died of malaria, a Wiltshire officer said at the time that all the soldiers suffered from malaria but some were worse than others.

William was buried in India, and is remembered on the Kirkee 1914-1918 Memorial.

Private George Charles Chubb   *1st Bn Wiltshire Regiment*
Service No.   24176   Age: 32
Place of Birth: Bremhill, Wiltshire   Home Country   England
Date of Death: 12/09/1916   Cause of death: Died of wounds
Memorial: Bremhill - Foxham - East Tytherton Morovian Church
War cemetery: Bremhill St Martin Churchyard
Theatre of war: Home

Left: The grave of George Chubb in Bremhill St. Martin Churchyard.

Below: A British Tank in action.

Next of Kin: Isaac & Sarah Jane Chubb
Address: 23, Bremhill, Wiltshire

George was a farm labourer. He was wounded in the fighting in France, probably at the Battle of the Somme, and evacuated back to England. He died at Chichester on Tuesday 12th September 1916.

15th SEPTEMBER 1916 – FIRST USE OF THE BRITISH SECRET WEAPON THE 'TANK'- GREAT ADVANCES MADE AND A TANK DROVE DOWN THE MAIN STREET OF FLERS

Private Percy Gordon Bridges   *43rd Bn Manitoba Regiment*
Service No.   424606   Age: 31
Place of Birth: Calne, Wiltshire   Home Country: Canada
Date of Death: 22/09/1916   Cause of death: Died of wounds
Memorial: Calne
War cemetery: Albert Communal Cemetery Extension
Theatre of war: France
Next of Kin: John & Mary Bridges
Address: Rough Leaze Farm, Calne, Wiltshire

Percy was a farm labourer and had emigrated to Canada before the Great War, like many others British émigré's he had answered the call to fight for King, Country and Empire. He enlisted on 4th September 1915. On Friday 22nd September 1916 he found himself at the Battle of the Somme. The 1st Canadian Division had occupied trenches around the village of Coucelette, France. It is likely Percy was wounded in this area and evacuated to one of the Field Ambulances in the Albert area where he later died.

Private William Ernest Rose   *2nd Bn Wiltshire Regiment*
Service No   10978   Age: 22
Place of Birth: Calne, Wiltshire   Home Country: England
Date of Death: 17/10/1916   Cause of death: Killed in action
Memorial: Not known
War cemetery: Thiepval Memorial
Theatre of war: France
Next of Kin: Joseph & Anne Rose
Address: Chippenham, Wiltshire

Twenty two year old William who was a labourer, arrived in France on the 11th December 1914 with the 2nd Battalion Wiltshire Regiment. On Tuesday 17th October 1916 he was taking part in 'the big push', the battle of the Somme now being in its fourth month. The Wiltshires were in the trenches at Flers France, Flers had been made famous in England when a journalist made a report of the new wonder weapon the Tank - he had seen this marvel rolling through the centre of the French town.
   In October the weather was described as awful and all the Wiltshires were soaked. The German shelling was very active and it is likely William was killed during this bombardment. He may have been one of the rations party that was shelled on that day and is recorded in the war diary. William has no known grave and is remembered on the Thiepval Memorial.

Above: Henry Herbert Strange, missing.

Left: Thiepval Memorial.

18th SEPTEMBER 1916 – THE END OF THE BATTLE OF THE SOMME

Corporal Henry Herbert Strange
Service No.   18463
Place of Birth: Calne, Wiltshire
Date of Death: 18/10/1916
Memorial: Calne
War cemetery: Thiepval Memorial
Theatre of war: France
Next of Kin: James & Kate Strange
Address: Quemerford, Calne, Wiltshire

2nd Bn Wiltshire Regiment
Age: 31
Home Country: England
Cause of death: Killed in action

Henry, a volunteer, had arrived in France on the 8th June 1916 as part of a replacement draft for the 2nd Battalion Wiltshire Regiment. On Wednesday 18th October 1916 the Wiltshires were making a frontal attack on German positions at Flers, France. The British had first bombarded the German positions during the early hours of the morning and at 3.40am the attack commenced.

The Wiltshires managed to get into the German trenches and after fierce close quarter fighting with bombs and hand grenades, they managed to consolidate the position making a block across the German trench. Information then arrived that although the Wiltshires had managed to capture the German trench the attack as a whole had failed. Two tanks which were supposed to take part in the attack had broken down at Flers; at 8am when the fighting had died down one of the tanks went forward but by this time the infantry were so exhausted and in disorder that no advantage could be made. The Wiltshires casualties for the day were 14 officers and 350 other ranks killed, wounded or missing. One of the missing was Henry.

In November Henry's brothers and sister put a picture in the local paper asking for information concerning their lost brother. Later he was listed as killed in action and is remembered on the Thiepval Memorial.

Private Ernest William Hacker   *7th Bn Royal West Surrey Regiment*
Service No.   G/21764   Age: 25
Place of Birth: Hilmarton, Wiltshire   Home Country: England
Date of Death: 26/10/1916   Cause of death: Killed in action
Memorial: Nettleton
War cemetery: Thiepval Memorial
Theatre of war: France
Next of Kin: Eli Henry & Elizabeth E Hacker
Address: The Keeper's Lodge, Nettleton, Wiltshire

On Thursday 26th October 1916 Ernest was in Fabick Trench, east of Mouquet Farm on the Somme; the weather was showery. The previous day they had been under intense German bombardment and the war diary states Thursday was a "quiet day". Their Casualties for the four day tour in the trenches was killed 15, wounded 98 and missing 1.

   Ernest was probably killed by German shell fire. He is remembered on the Thiepval memorial and has no known grave. His brother Percival John Hacker was to be killed in Belgium in November 1917.

Lance Coporal Henry Herbert Slade   *1st Bn Wiltshire Regiment*
Service No.   11123   Age: 21
Place of Birth: Hilmarton, Wiltshire   Home Country: England
Date of Death: 30/10/1916   Cause of death: Died of wounds
Memorial: Hilmarton
War cemetery: Wimereux Communal Cemetery
Theatre of war: France
Next of Kin: Robert and Emily Slade
Address: Cowage, Hilmarton, Wiltshire.

Henry, known as Bert, had volunteered with his brothers in September 1914 and had arrived in France in early 1916. He had fought through many engagements and by 1916 he would have been described as a veteran. His brother Edward had been killed at the opening stages of the Battle of the Somme which must have been a great blow to him.

   On Wednesday 23rd August 1916, at Leipzig Salient, the Wiltshires were in the front line trenches, the British artillery was bombarding the German front and the Germans were retaliating by shelling the British front. Bert was awarded the Military Medal as the following citation describes;

11123 L/Cpl Slade, Herbert.

"This NCO acted as an orderly throughout the operations at Leipzig Salient from Aug 23rd to Aug 26th, and continuously carried messages under terrific shell-fire and would always volunteer, whether it was his turn or not. He has taken part as orderly in all the operations of Regt since the beginning of July".

Military Medal.

On the 20th October 1916 the Wiltshires were back in the front line, the war diary describes the day;

"The weather had cleared and was then frost and sunny. The day was quiet on the whole."

Right: The Military Medal.

Far right: Bert Slade, won his Military Medal for bravery at the Somme.

Even though it was described as a quiet day, Bert was wounded in the leg so seriously that it was necessary to evacuate him to one of the field hospitals at Wimereux, France and his condition was so serious that his leg was amputated. Bert succumbed to his wounds on Monday 30th October 1916 and he was buried in Wimereux Communal Cemetery.

Private Edward Andrews   *6th Bn Wiltshire Regiment*

Service No.	18810	Age: 29
Place of Birth:	Spirthill, Wiltshire	Home Country: England
Date of Death:	24/11/1916	Cause of death: Died of wounds
Memorial:	Calne	
War cemetery:	St Sever Cemetery Extension Rouen	
Theatre of war:	France	
Next of Kin:	Henry & Emily Andrews	
Address:	Spirthill, Wiltshire	

Edward was a coachman and groom. It is likely he either joined the army under the Derby Scheme or was conscripted. By Autumn 1915 recruitment was at an all time low and men were desperately needed for the armed forces.

Edward was wounded during the fighting at the battle of the Somme and evacuated to one of the base hospitals at Rouen where he died on Friday 24th November 1916.

Private Percy George Weaver   *1st Bn Gloucestershire Regiment*

Service No.	22440	Age: 22
Place of Birth:	Calne, Wiltshire	Home Country: England
Date of Death:	30/11/1916	Cause of death: Killed in action
Memorial:	Not known	
War cemetery:	Thiepval Memorial	
Theatre of war:	France	
Next of Kin:	Samuel & Eliza Weaver	
Address:	Calne, Wiltshire	

Percy had been in the Army prior to the war with the cavalry. As a reservist he would have been called up immediately and enlisted with the Gloucestershire Regiment at Birmingham. He arrived at Gallipoli in September 1915 and was evacuated either due to being wounded or through sickness. He was then posted to the 1st Battalion Gloucestershire Regiment and took part in the Battle of the Somme. The casualties for five months fighting at the Somme was around 1.1million British, French and German soldiers killed and wounded. The battle officially ended on 18th November 1916.

Percy was killed in action on Thursday 30th November 1916. He is remembered on the Thiepval memorial and has no known grave.

Private Edward Chandler		*1/6th Bn Hampshire Regiment*	
Service No.	2022	Age:	44
Place of Birth:	Yatesbury,	Home Country:	England
Date of Death:	12/12/1916	Cause of death:	Died
Memorial:	Not known		
War cemetery:	Kirkee 1914-1918 Memorial		
Theatre of war:	India		
Next of Kin:	Mary Jane Chandler		
Address:	Not known		

Before the war Edward had worked on a barge transporting freight by canal. Edward was on garrison duties in France when he died of disease and was buried in India. He is remembered on the Kirkee 1914-1918 Memorial. It is not known why, but his medals were not collected at the end of the war. It is possible his wife lived on a barge and had no fixed address but in December 1922 the Army records office in Exeter made an application for the disposal of his medals.

Kings Regulation 8071 states medals returned under paragraph 1743 of King's Regulations. "Medals which at the end of 10 years, still remain unclaimed will be sent to the deputy director of ordnance stores, Royal Dockyard, (Medal Branch), Woolwich (if granted for other service) to be broken up.

Medals that could not be issued to the next of kin were returned and it is believed that if they were not claimed within ten years were scrapped. It is not known at this time how many medals were disposed of in this way.

Private Ernest Bennett		*1st Bn Wiltshire Regiment*	
Service No.	10078	Age:	30
Place of Birth:	Calne, Wiltshire	Home Country:	England
Date of Death:	25/12/1916	Cause of death:	Died
Memorial:	Trowbridge		
War cemetery:	Trowbridge Cemetery		
Theatre of war:	Home		
Next of Kin:	Emily Bennett (wife); Henry & Elizabeth Bennett (parents)		
Address:	9 Mortimer Street, Trowbridge, Wiltshire; Calne		

Ernest was carter and had married Emily Hitchens on the 6th December 1913. He volunteered for service on the outbreak of hostilities and arrived in France on the 28th November 1914. In February 1915 he was evacuated from France and sent to Liverpool Hospital suffering from frost-bite and rheumatism and after several months' treatment he was discharged from the army. He died at his home on Christmas morning 1916 leaving a widow and two small children. He was buried in Trowbridge Cemetery with full military honours. He is not listed on the Commonwealth War Graves Commission web site or in the soldiers died in the Great War listing.

DECEMBER 1916 – ARRIVAL OF GERMAN PRISONERS OF WAR IN CALNE

In December 1916 about 200 German prisoners arrive in Calne on a special train from a camp at Blandford in Dorset. The men appeared to be well fed and clothed and were in the best of spirits. One was no stranger to the district, having visited Calne a few years previously, with a cheap bazaar which was located tin the White Hart Yard. Another was employed for some time as a leather cutter at Devizes. One of the party carried a model aeroplane, of which he was was very proud as an exhibition of his skill. Under a strong guard they were marched to the camp at Yatesbury where they were to be engaged in such useful work as road making and drainage. The arrival of the men excited much curiosity, and their progress through the town singing "Wacht am Rhein" was witnessed by large crowds, who displayed no ill feeling towards the prisoners.

Top left: German prisoners marching to a camp in England.   *Top right: Ernest Bennett.*

Above: Engraving by a prisoner of war (Ruger) of the camp at Yatesbury, can be seen in Calne Heritage Centre.

6
1917

Private George Victor Jim Elmes   *F Bn Tank Corps*

Service No.	6921	Age:	19
Place of Birth:	Derry Hill, Wiltshire	Home Country:	England
Date of Death:	03/01/1917	Cause of death:	Died
Memorial:	Chippenham		
War cemetery:	Trowbridge Cemetery		
Theatre of war:	Home		
Next of Kin:	Nelson Jim & Hannah Elmes		
Address:	6 Park Lane, Chippenham, Wiltshire		

George was a member of the newly formed Tank Corps originally named the Machine Gun Corps Heavy. He was a new recruit and in training at Bovington, Dorset (which later became home of the Tank Corps). He was taken ill on New Years Day 1917 while traveling to his home from Bovington to visit his mother. At Trowbridge he was found to be so seriously ill that he was admitted to the Red Cross hospital where he died two days later of illness. He was buried with full military honors at Trowbridge cemetery.

Major Frederic George Greenstreet   *105th Bn Mahratta Light Infantry*

Service No.	N/A	Age:	36
Place of Birth:	London	Home Country:	India
Date of Death:	09/01/1917	Cause of death:	Killed in action
Memorial:	Compton Bassett & Pattingham		
War cemetery:	Basra Memorial		
Theatre of war:	Mesopotamia		
Next of Kin:	Col W L & Maude Greenstreet		
Address:	The Rectory, Compton Bassett, Wiltshire		

In April 1916 the British and Commonwealth Garrison at the City of Kut, which consisted of a force of over 13,000 men, had surrendered to the Turkish forces and were marched north through the desert as prisoners of war, many of whom were never to return to their homes.

Frederic had started his military career with the Gloucestershire regiment but transferred to the Indian Army. The Indian Government had taken charge of operations in Mesopotamia. To avenge Kut, British and Commonwealth forces were fighting their way along the River Tigris in modern day Iraq. At that time there were very few roads in Mesopotamia and the quickest way to transport both men and supplies was via the rivers, along which the Turkish forces had defensive positions.

On Tuesday 9th January 1917 the British and Commonwealth forces were attacking Turkish positions at Abdul Hassan bend. The initial attack went very well and the British and Commonwealth forces captured the western end of the Turkish positions. The day was very misty and under cover of the mist the Turkish forces counter attacked. A very fierce fight took place which included a great deal of hand to hand fighting. At the end of the day the British and Common wealth forces had won the position but at a cost of 700 casualties. One of the dead was Frederic, he has no known grave.

Private Arthur George James Freegard · *7th Bn Wiltshire Regiment*

Service No.	12415
Place of Birth:	Stroud, Gloucestershire
Date of Death:	19/01/1917
Memorial:	Calne
War cemetery:	Salonika Lembet Road Military Cemetery
Theatre of war:	Salonika
Next of Kin:	Frederick & Mary Freegard
Address:	Old Road, Studley, Wiltshire

Age: 27
Home Country: England
Cause of death: Died of wounds

In October 1915 a British and French force landed at Salonika, Greece at the request of the Greek Prime Minster. Originally it was planned they would support the Serbs who were in conflict with the Bulgarians, but the force arrived too late and the Serbs had been beaten. It was decided that the force would remain in Salonika for future operations. During the Salonika campaign, for every casualty of battle three died from disease.

Arthur had volunteered and enlisted in the 7th Service Battalion Wiltshire Regiment. He had arrived in France on 21st September 1915. In November 1915 the 7th Wiltshires were moved to Salonika, Greece. On Christmas Eve 1916 the Wiltshires were in trenches on the Doiran sector of the front. At midnight a raid was sent out to the Bulgarian trenches to get information concerning their defensive positions, during this raid Arthur was wounded. He was taken back to the British trenches and evacuated to No 4 Canadian General Hospital were he succumbed to his wounds and died on Friday 19th January 1917.

Sergeant George Brewer · *5th Bn Wiltshire Regiment*

Service No.	18792
Place of Birth:	Calne, Wiltshire
Date of Death:	26/01/1917
Memorial:	Calne
War cemetery:	Amara War Cemetery
Theatre of war:	Mesopotamia
Next of Kin:	William & Sarah Brewer
Address:	London Road, Calne, Wiltshire

Age: 32
Home Country: England
Cause of death: Died of wounds

Prior to the Great War George was employed at the Post Office, was a member of the Constitutional Club and had been one of the foremost members of the Town football club eleven.

He joined the army with his brother Bert in January 1915, and immediately went into training. The two brothers were together, and step by step rose to the rank of sergeant, becoming full sergeants in January 1916. On the 4th May 1916, Bert, the elder brother, was sent to Mesopotamia, and for the first time the brothers were parted. George sought the first opportunity of joining him, and a few months later on the 3rd September he was drafted there

Above left: Burials in the Dessert.

Above right: George Brewer remembered on a grave in Calne Holy Trinity Churchyard.

himself. One of the first persons he saw upon landing was his brother on duty at the base. He was then sent to the forward positions with his draft.

On Thursday 25th January the Wiltshires were preparing to attack Turkish positions near Abdul Hassan Bend on the river Tigris. At 9.42am under cover of intense British bombardment the Wiltshires attacked, their objective was to capture the Turkish first line, consolidate it and take a Turkish strong point. The war diary states:

"The enemy trench was strongly held but assisted by our artillery and all ranks working with great energy and determination, we successfully dislodged the enemy and firmly established ourselves under considerable enemy shellfire. Our bombing parties worked along their communication trench to P10 N driving the Turkish Bombers before them."

The Wiltshires took all their objectives and captured nearly 100 prisoners, 1 Austrian Machine Gun, practically new, two Trench Mortars, 1 Minenwerfer less breach block, many rifles, much S.A.A and stores. The Wiltshires casualties were 35 killed and 114 wounded.

George was seriously wounded in the left side and shoulder and died the following day in a field hospital. He was laid to rest in a village cemetery on the 30th January and the grave side service was conducted by the Chaplain in charge.

25th FEBRUARY 1917 – KUT EL AMARA IS REOCCUPIED BY THE BRITISH
11th MARCH 1917 – BAGHDAD IS CAPTURED BY THE BRITISH
15th MARCH 1917 – RUSSIAN TSAR NICHOLAS II ABDICATES
FOLLOWING THE START OF THE RUSSIAN REVOLUTION
18th MARCH 1917 – GERMANS RETIRE TO THE HINDENBURG LINE

Lieutenant Alfred Pocock Long   *Royal Flying Corps*

Service No.	N/A	Age:	29
Place of Birth:	Kellaways, Wiltshire	Home Country:	England
Date of Death:	23/03/1917	Cause of death:	Accident
Memorial:	Not Known		
War cemetery:	East Tytherton Moravian Burial Ground		
Theatre of war:	Home		
Next of Kin:	John William & Mary Ann Long		
Address:	71 Bloomfield Avenue, Bath, Somerset		

Alfred had originally joined the 7th Territorial Battalion Middlesex Regiment and rose to the rank of sergeant. With the expanding army and lack of officers the British were forced to look for soldiers with officer qualities serving in the rank and file. On 29th July 1915 Alfred received a commission, transferred to the Royal Flying Corps and was posted to the Central Flying School at Upavon, Wiltshire. By March 1917 he was a qualified pilot and was waiting for orders to proceed for the front.

On Friday 23rd March 1917 an instructor sent him up for practice with nineteen year old Second Lieutenant Philip Sellers. Alfred's instructions were to fly steadily up and down and present a good target for Lieutenant Sellers. Alfred was warned of the risk and told to keep a good look out for the attacking aeroplane.

Witnesses watching from the ground stated at about 3 o'clock, they saw the Scout aircraft flown by Sellers was slightly behind the two-seater aircraft flown by Alfred. The aircraft were flying at about 2500 feet. The scout dived in an attack but was not high enough to turn and collided with the tail of the two-seater. As the two machines fell the tail of the two-seater twisted round as it broke off.

Both pilots were killed suffering fractured sculls. At the inquest the Coroner stated;

"The accident was doubtless due to some mischance on the part of the lighter scout machine. It was obvious that a very slight error on the part of the uppermost machine (the scout) would be fatal to the occupant of the lower machine, who had only to remain passive and fly slowly up and down waiting to be attacked."

During the Great War parachutes were not issued to pilots because it was thought, by senior officers, it would lead them to jump from serviceable aircraft.

Right: The grave of Alfred Pocock Long in East Tytherton Moravian Burial Ground.

Below: A Vickers fighting Biplane.

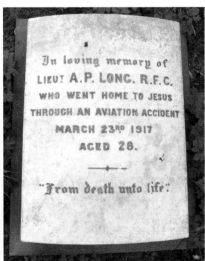

25th MARCH 1917 – THE BATTLE OF JEBEL HAMRIN
26th MARCH 1917 – THE FIRST BATTLE OF GAZA

Private Thomas Baker   *2nd Bn Wiltshire Regiment*

Service No.	8258	Age:	26
Place of Birth:	Langley Burrell, Wiltshire	Home Country:	England
Date of Death	26/03/1917	Cause of death:	Died
Memorial:	Bremhill - St Andrews Church Chippenham - Foxham - East Tytherton		
War cemetery:	Cologne Southern Cemetery		
Theatre of war:	Germany		
Next of Kin:	Thomas & Hannah Baker		
Address:	Stanley, Wiltshire		

Thomas was the sixth son of Thomas and Hannah Baker, he was a regular soldier and landed at Zeebrugge, Belgium on 7th October 1914. On Saturday 24th October the 2nd Battalion Wiltshire Regiment were in the trenches at Beselare, Belgium. At 5.30am, just before daybreak, the Germans attacked with a very superior force but were driven back with heavy losses. The Germans then attacked again and fighting carried on continuously for 2 hours. The Germans had hundreds of casualties killed and wounded, but eventually they broke through. With the exception of about 30 NCOs and men mostly from trenches on the right, the remainder of the Battalion were either killed or captured.

One of those taken prisoner was Thomas, he was transported to Germany and confined in Dulmen prison camp in Westphalia. He became sick most likely due to malnutrition and forced labour.

During the war prisoners of war in Germany were forced to work and the British naval blockade prevented not only war materials but food being transported to Germany. By 1917 food products were in short supply for the whole German population and the rations given to prisoners of war were very poor.

William died on Monday 26th March 1917 after two years and five months in captivity. He was buried in the Dulmen Prisoner of War Cemetery with ninety six other inmates. At the end of the Great War all the burials at Dulmes were exhumed and relocated to Cologne Southern Cemetery, which today contains the remains of over 2500 casualties of the Great War.

His family inserted the following memoriam in a local paper;

> *"A light from our household has gone*
> *A voice we loved is still*
> *A place is vacant in our home*
> *Which never can be filled".*

Private William John Cook   *5th Bn Wiltshire Regiment*

Service No.	22197	Age:	20
Place of Birth:	Devizes, Wiltshire	Home Country:	England
Date of Death:	29/03/1917	Cause of death:	Died of wounds
Memorial:	Compton Bassett		
War cemetery:	Basra Memorial		
Theatre of war:	Mesopotamia		
Next of Kin:	William & Mary Jane Cook		
Address:	59 Compton Bassett, Compton Bassett, Wiltshire		

Twenty year old William, a farm labourer, joined the 5th Service Battalion Wiltshire Regiment on Thursday 29th March 1915.

The Wiltshires were in attack at Palm Tree Post near the Nahrwan Canal and came under heavy Turkish shell and machine gun fire. They were finally held up about 1300 yards from the Turkish position.

The Wiltshires casualties were described as very heavy with 28 killed and 139 wounded. It is likely one of the wounded was William who succumbed to his wounds, he has no known grave.

William's brother Reginald Tom Raisley Cook was to be killed in Belgium in 1918.

Private Ernest George Dean		*5th Bn Wiltshire Regiment*	
Service No.	26316	Age:	37
Place of Birth:	Calne, Wiltshire	Home Country:	England
Date of Death:	30/03/1917	Cause of death:	Died of wounds
Memorial:	Calne		
War cemetery:	Basra Memorial		
Theatre of war:	Mesopotamia		
Next of Kin:	Bessie Dean (wife); George & Rebecca Dean (parents)		
Address:	14 Butlers Buildings; Cow Land, Calne, Wiltshire		

Ernest married Bessie Brewer at Calne in 1901, he was a Cater (cart driver) and at 37 with a young family would have thought twice about going off to war. It is likely that he either joined the army under the Derby scheme or was conscripted.

He died of wounds most likely in the action described for William John Cook at Palm Tree Post near the Nahrwan Canal in modern day Iraq. He has no known grave and is remembered on the Basra Memorial.

Members of the Wiltshire Regiment cheering as they head for the front.

7

ARRAS

The Nivelle Offensive started on Friday 9th April 1917, it was a joint action between the French and the British. The British attack took place around Arras.

Lance Corporal Herbert George Ealey
Service No.   26449
Place of Birth: Cherhill, Wiltshire
Date of Death: 04/04/1917
Memorial: Cherhill
War cemetery: Nouex Les Mines Communal Cemetery
Theatre of war: France
Next of Kin: Frederick & Mary Jane Ealey
Address: 49, Cherhill, Wiltshire

2nd Bn Ox & Bucks Light Infantry
Age: 22
Home Country: England
Cause of death: Killed in action

At the age of nineteen years Herbert had joined the 2nd Battalion Wiltshire Regiment and arrived in France on 11th November 1914. He was transferred to the 2nd Battalion Oxfordshire and Buckinghamshire Light Infantry. He died during the preparation for the British attacks at Arras in April 1917.

6th APRIL 1917 – THE UNITED STATES DECLARES WAR ON GERMANY

Private Alfred James Angell
Service No.   33216
Place of Birth: Calne, Wiltshire
Date of Death: 09/04/1917
Memorial: Calne
War cemetery: Arras Memorial
Theatre of war: France
Next of Kin: Isaac & Kate Angell
Address: 2 Victoria Terrace, Calne, Wiltshire

2nd Bn Wiltshire Regiment
Age: 20
Home Country: England
Cause of death: Killed in action

On Monday 9th April 1917 the 2nd Battalion Wiltshire Regiment were preparing to make attacks on the German Hindenburg line. Their first objective was a Mill on the Henin - Neuville Vitasse Road, south west of Arras, France. At 1.30am the Wiltshires attacked, but they met considerable resistance from the German defenders, which it was later found numbered about 120 men and two machine guns. The Wiltshires suffered 37 casualties and were forced to retire.

The main British attack started at 5.30am. Alfred and the 2nd Battalion Wiltshire Regiment attacked at 11.38am and were met by heavy shelling from the Germans, causing many casualties before the objective could be seen. When the Wiltshires arrived at the German wire it was found to be uncut and British troops took cover in shell holes in front of the German line, but were eventually forced to retire. All that was left of the 2nd Battalion was about 90 men. Total casualties for the second attack were 342. Alfred was killed in action on the battlefield at Arras and is remembered on the Arras memorial and has no known grave.

Sergeant Frederick George Drew   *2nd Bn Wiltshire Regiment*

Service No.	7986	Age:	28
Place of Birth:	Calne, Wiltshire	Home Country:	England
Date of Death:	09/04/1917	Cause of death:	Killed in action
Memorial:	Calne		
War cemetery:	Wancourt British Cemetery		
Theatre of war:	France		
Next of Kin:	Joseph & Harriet Drew		
Address:	13 Castle Street, Calne, Wiltshire		

Frederick had been a private when he arrived in France on 7th October 1914. He had been wounded in fighting during June 1915 and had returned to the 2nd Battalion Wiltshire Regiment. By April 1917 he had risen to the rank of sergeant.

Frederick was killed near Arras in the same action as Alfred Angell. It is likely he was originally buried in Henin North Cemetery at Henin-Sur-Cojeul about a mile north of Wancourt with 29 other British soldiers who fell on the 9th April 1917. He was later relocated to Wancourt British Cemetery where he lies today with over 1,000 soldiers who were killed during the Great War.

The Town Hall in Arras after various bombardments.

Private Frederick Willis   *2nd Bn Wiltshire Regiment*

Service No.	18160	Age:	30
Place of Birth:	Bremhill, Wiltshire	Home Country:	England
Date of Death:	09/04/1917	Cause of death:	Killed in action

Memorial: Chippenham
War cemetery: Arras Memorial
Theatre of war: France
Next of Kin: Beatrice Willis (wife) - George & Ellen Willis (parents)
Address: 30 London Road, Chippenham - Bremhill, Wiltshire

Frederick, a flour miller, had married his wife in Chippenham in the summer of 1908. He volunteered for the army leaving, behind a young family and arriving in France on the 8th December 1915. He was killed in the same action as Alfred Angel and Frederick Drew near Arras on Easter Monday 1917. He has no known grave.

Private Tom Weston   *75th Bn Central Ontario Regiment*

Service No.	681791	Age:	22
Place of Birth:	Calne, Wiltshire	Home Country:	Canada
Date of Death:	09/04/1917	Cause of death:	Killed in action

Memorial: Calne
War cemetery: Givenchy En Gohelle Canadian Cemetery Souchez
Theatre of war: France
Next of Kin: Tom & Sarah Weston
Address: 20 Curzon Street, Calne, Wiltshire.

On leaving Green School Calne, Tom was employed at Harris's in Calne. He left for Canada before the Great War with his friends William & Ernest Edwards. When they arrived in Canada they were employed at Harris's Abattoir in Toronto as butchers. On 1st May 1916 all three enlisted in the Canadian Army, arriving in England in November 1916 and were sent to Bramshot camp to complete their training. Just before Christmas they were sent to the firing line in France.

On Monday 9th April 1917 the Canadians attacked Vimy Ridge and all three took part in the attack. William was wounded in the back and legs and was also suffering from shell concussion (shell shock). He wrote to his uncle in Canada from his hospital bed in Sheffield;

"I got as far as the second line before I was hit, and then I was buried three times. I thought I could not get up believing my back was broken, but managed to crawl back through the lines to a dressing station and here I am in hospital."

Ernest also survived but he too was suffering from shell shock while Tom Weston was officially reported as missing. Later his body was found and he was reported killed in action on Easter Monday, 9th April 1917.

The village of Givenchy-en-Gohelle was taken by the Canadians on the 13th April 1917, where Tom lies in the Cemetery with 126 Soldiers of the Great War.

Private Francis William Gingell   *38th Bn Eastern Ontario Regiment*

Service No.	775872	Age:	25
Place of Birth:	Calne, Wiltshire	Home Country:	Canada
Date of Death:	10/04/1917	Cause of death:	Died of Wounds

Memorial: Calne - Derry Hill & Toronto Old City hall, Canada

War cemetery: Barlin Communal Cemetery Extension
Theatre of war: France
Next of Kin: Mary Gingell (wife); George & Elizabeth Gingell (parents)
Address: 210 Robert Street, Toronto, Ontario

The Great War had already started when Frank married Mary Naylor Bowman on 24th November 1914, he was employed by Toronto Railway Company as a Conductor. He enlisted on 24th February at Toronto, Canada. It is most likely he was wounded in the fighting on Vimy Ridge and died the following day at the 6th Casualty Clearing Station based at Barlin, France . He is buried at Barlin Communal Cemetery Extension where he lies with over 1,000 men killed during the Great War.

Private Albert Diccox   *2nd Bn Devonshire Regiment*
Service No.   22313   Age: 26
Place of Birth: Hilmarton, Wiltshire   Home Country: England
Date of Death: 14/04/1917   Cause of death: Killed in action
Memorial: Not known
War cemetery: Thiepval Memorial
Theatre of war: France
Next of Kin: John & Sarah Diccox
Address: Liddington, Wiltshire.

Albert was the youngest son of John and Sarah Diccox. He was killed in action on Saturday 14th April 1917 and is remembered on the Thiepval Memorial. He has no known grave.

Private Bernard Hepworth Brown   *20th Bn Royal Fusiliers*
Service No.   1308   Age: 31
Place of Birth: Penkridge, Herefordshire   Home Country: England
Date of Death: 16/04/1917   Cause of death: Killed in action
Memorial: Calne - Calstone & Blacklands
War cemetery: Heninel Croisilles Cemetery
Theatre of war: France
Next of Kin: Edward & Marianne G Brown
Address: Chalford, Gloucestershire

The 20th Service Battalion (3rd Public Schools) Royal Fusiliers was formed at Epsom on the 11th September 1914 by the Public Schools and University Men's Force. Bernard arrived in France on 14th November 1915. He was killed in action on Monday 16th April 1916, at the First Battle of the Scarpe when the 20th Royal Fusiliers attacked the Hindenburg line north of Fontaine-les-Croisilles, France. He is buried at the Heninel-Croisilles Cemetery with over 200 other soldiers who died in the Great War.

19th APRIL 1917 – SECOND BATTLE OF GAZA
20th APRIL 1917 – BRITISH FORCES OCCUPY SAMARRAH, 60 MILES NORTH OF BAGHDAD

Corporal Colin Garnett Fell   *4th Bn Worcestershire Regiment*
Service No.   31634   Age: 32
Place of Birth: Calne, Wiltshire   Home Country: England
Date of Death: 24/04/1917   Cause of death: Died of wounds
Memorial: Calne
War cemetery: Duisans British Cemetery Etrun
Theatre of war: France
Next of Kin: Elsie Elvina Fell (wife); Stephen & Emma Fell (parents)
Address: 76 The Mall, Swindon, Wiltshire – The Green, Calne

Colin was a schoolmaster and had trained under Mr Boden the headmaster of Green School. He had gone on to study at Culham College and after two years he obtained his certificate and was appointed to the staff of Clarence Street School, Swindon. Colin was the youngest son of Stephen and Emma Fell and at the close of the year in 1913 he married Elsie Elvina Wilcox.

In June 1916 he joined Worcester Regiment and was promoted to Corporal. In autumn 1916 he proceeded to France and took part in many engagements at the Somme. His scholarly attainments were recognized and he was transferred to the Casualty Record Office. In the discharge of his duties, he on 24th April accompanied by a comrade, went out into the battlefield to obtain a list of casualties. While they were returning Colin's companion was instantly killed by a shell and Colin was so seriously injured that he died the same afternoon. It is likely he died at one of the Casualty Clearing Stations based at Etrun, France, where he lies buried with over 3,000 men who were killed during the great war.

On the anniversary of his death in 1918 the following memoriam was inserted in a local paper by his family

"In loving memory, My country calls it is my duty to go - Thy will be done."

Private Arthur John Sumbler   *7th Bn Wiltshire Regiment*
Service No.   12390   Age: 17
Place of Birth: Calne, Wiltshire   Home Country: England
Date of Death: 24/04/1917   Cause of death: Killed in action
Memorial: Calne
War cemetery: Doiran Memorial
Theatre of war: Salonika
Next of Kin: Thomas William & Martha Sumbler
Address: Quemerford, Calne, Wiltshire

Seventeen year old Arthur was an underage soldier when he enlisted in 1915 as he was only just 16 years of age. In April 1917 the British forces in Salonika, Greece attacked Bulgarian lines near Lake Doiran.

Arthur was in A Company, 7th Battalion Wiltshire Regiment and during the night they attacked the Bulgarian trenches under cover of a British artillery barrage which had cut the first line of the enemy barbed wire. When they arrived at the second line of barbed wire and were held up due to it still being almost intact, the Bulgarian trenches were heavily manned, and the enemy made great use of bombs, (hand grenades), causing many injuries and forcing A Company to retire. The War diary for the day states:

"The Bulgars supports were seen coming down the CT (communication trenches), on left and the front line was very strongly manned. Our advance was held up and the company was

*forced to lie down in shell holes in front of the wire. The main party never got through the
wire. A few got into the enemy trenches but were not seen again."*

Arthur was listed as missing in the casualty return. Later he was officially reported killed in
action on Tuesday 24th April 1917. He is remembered on the Dorian Memorial, Greece and
has no known grave.

Private George Weston   7th Bn Wiltshire Regiment
Service No.   12408   Age: 38
Place of Birth: Chippenham, Wiltshire   Home Country: England
Date of Death: 24/04/1917   Cause of death: Died
Memorial: Chippenham & Derry Hill
War cemetery: Doiran Memorial
Theatre of war: Salonika
Next of Kin: Abraham & Sarah Weston
Address: Chippenham, Wiltshire

George, a masons labourer, had joined the 7th Service Battalion Wiltshire Regiment and
arrived in France with them on 21st September 1915. In November 1915 the 7th Wiltshires
were transferred to Salonika.
   George was serving with Arthur Sumbler as part of A company and was a casualty of the
Lake Doiran attack in April 1917. He was listed as missing and has no known grave.

Private William Henry Hyde   7th BnWiltshire Regiment
Service No.   12389   Age: 20
Place of Birth: Yatesbury, Wiltshire   Home Country: England
Date of Death: 24/04/1917   Cause of death: Killed in action
Memorial: Yatesbury
War cemetery: Doiran Military Cemetery
Theatre of war: Salonika
Next of Kin: Henry J & Emily Hyde
Address: 13, Yatesbury, Wiltshire

Twenty year old William had arrived in France on the 21st September 1915 with the 7th
Service Battalion Wiltshire Regiment. He was killed, in the same attack as Arthur Sumbler
and George Weston. He was a member of D company and it is likely he was killed close to
the British lines as his body was recovered. He is buried in Doiran Military Cemetery with
nearly 900 soldiers who died during the Great War.

Private Frederick William Cleverly   7th Bn Wiltshire Regiment
Service No.   12411   Age: 25
Place of Birth: Derry Hill, Wiltshire   Home Country: England
Date of Death: 25/04/1917   Cause of death: Died of wounds
Memorial: Derry Hill
War cemetery: Sarigol Military Cemetery Kriston
Theatre of war: Salonika
Next of Kin: William Frederick & Sarah Cleverly

Address: 40, Derry Hill, Wiltshire.

Frederick, a gamekeeper, arrived in France on 21st September 1915 with the 7th Service Battalion Wiltshire Regiment.

   He took part in the same action as Arthur Sumbler, in A company. He was wounded and died of his wounds the following day at the 35th Casualty Clearing Station at Sarigol, Greece. He is buried in Sarigol Military Cemetery, Kriston, with over 700 men who died during the Great War.

Bombardier Ernest Edward Carpenter   *63rd Bde Royal Field Artillery*

Service No.	94470	Age:	27
Place of Birth:	Derry Hill, Wiltshire	Home Country:	England
Date of Death:	27/04/1917	Cause of death:	Killed in action
Memorial:	Calne & Derry Hill		
War cemetery:	Feuchy Chapel British Cemetery Wancourt		
Theatre of war:	France		
Next of Kin:	Jesse & Harriett Carpenter		
Address:	Studley, Wiltshire		

Ernest was a house painter. He was killed in action on Friday 27th April 1914 probably due to counter battery fire during the preparations for the Battle of Arleux. The British objective was to capture Rouex, but owing to heavy enemy shellfire and machine guns firing from Roeux, the attack failed and the infantry fell back to its start point. Ernest is buried in Feuchy Chapel British Cemetery Wancourt, with over 500 men who were killed in the Great War.

Private Frederick Slade   *2nd Bn Royal Marine Light Infantry*

Service No.	CH/1825(S)	Age:	19
Place of Birth:	Calne, Wiltshire	Home Country:	England
Date of Death:	28/04/1917	Cause of death:	Killed in action
Memorial:	Calne		
War cemetery:	Arras Memorial		
Theatre of war:	France		
Next of Kin:	Albert H & Ellen Slade		
Address:	6 Victoria Terrace, Calne, Wiltshire		

Frederick, a milk sales man, enlisted in the Royal Marines on 31st October 1916 at the age of 18 years 7 months. He left for France in January 1917 and joined the 2nd Marine Battalion at the start of February 1917. At 4.25am on Saturday 28th April 1918 the 2nd Marines attacked German trenches north east of Gavrelle. The attack was held up by wire and the 2nd Marines had very heavy casualties due to the number of German machine guns. The casualties for the attack were 26 killed, 72 wounded and 395 missing.

   One of the missing was Frederick it was later assumed he had been killed in the attack. He is remembered on the Arras Memorial.

Private Arthur Edward Angell   *5th Bn Wiltshire Regiment*

Service No.	25806	Age:	30
Place of Birth:	Calne, Wiltshire	Home Country:	England
Date of Death:	30/04/1917	Cause of death:	Died
Memorial:	Calne		

War cemetery: Amara War Cemetery
Theatre of war: Mesopotamia
Next of Kin: Fredrick & Sarah A Angell
Address: 23c New Road, Calne, Wiltshire

Arthur was a brick layers labourer before the Great War. He died on Monday 30th April 1917 of dysentery at one of the medical units based at Amara, in modern day Iraq. He is buried in the war cemetery there with over 3500 soldiers who died of disease or from the fighting in Mesopotamia during the Great War. His Brother Percy was to die just two months later in Belgium in June 1917.

2nd Lieutenant Stephen Gilbert Haines   *75th Bde Royal Field Artillery*
Service No.   N/A   Age: 33
Place of Birth: Calne, Wiltshire   Home Country: England
Date of Death: 04/05/1917   Cause of death: Died of wounds
Memorial: Not known
War cemetery: Etaples Military Cemetery
Theatre of war: France
Next of Kin: John Haines & Mary Grace (Haines)
Address: Pen Craig Newbridge Hill, Bath, Somerset

Prior to the war Stephen had been a bank clerk. He died on Friday 4th May 1917 at one of the military hospitals based at Etaples, of wounds that were received on 22/04/1917. The Cemetery at Etaples contains the remains of nearly 11500 soldiers who died during the Great War.

Lance Corporal Charles Thomas Stanley Cox   *477th Field Coy Royal Engineers*
Service No.   494391   Age: 30
Place of Birth: Bristol, Gloucestershire   Home Country: England
Date of Death: 05/05/1917   Cause of death: Killed in action
Memorial: Calne
War cemetery: Villers Faucon Communal Cemetery
Theatre of war: France
Next of Kin: Gertrude Cox
Address: 7 Kingsbury Street, Calne

Charles was the grandson of Crimea war veteran Sargeant Major Thomas and prior to the war he was employed as an engineer at the brewers at Lansdowne Arms Hotel. In 1908 he married Gertrude Thomas in Calne and soon after the outbreak of war Charles joined the Royal Engineers. Charles arrived in France on the 6th June 1916 and was killed in action on Saturday 5th May 1917. His commanding officer Major Dring wrote to Gertrude;

"He was killed by a chance shell whilst working at night some distance from the firing line. He was buried in a military cemetery close by, and a cross made by his comrades marks the place where he lies. He was liked and respected by all of us, and we shall feel his absence for many a long day. Absolutely untiring in his duty, whatever it was, we shall find it hard to replace him, though our loss cannot be as great as yours. I am writing not only on my own behalf, but on behalf of the whole Company to tender you our deepest sympathy in your great loss."

Gertrude also received a letter from the Chaplain;

"The loss of any man is sad indeed, but somehow the loss of this man seems especially difficult to bear. All sections were present at the graveside. Be Confident in your trust that after work so well done and the greatest sacrifice so nobly offered he rests in the safe keeping of his Saviour."

He was buried in Villers Faucon Communal Cemetery where he lies with over 750 soldiers who died during the Great War.

Private Herbert John Sutton		*76th Machine Gun Corps*	
Service No.	57552	Age:	27
Place of Birth:	Calne, Wiltshire	Home Country:	England
Date of Death:	06/05/1917	Cause of death:	Killed in action
Memorial:	Calne		
War cemetery:	Arras Memorial		
Theatre of war:	France		
Next of Kin:	Joseph & Bessie Sutton		
Address:	Curzon Street, Calne, Wiltshire.		

Before the Great War, Herbert worked with his father, they were stone masons. He originally joined the Royal Field artillery but later transferred to the machine gun corps. The 76th Machine Gun corps were part of the 3rd Division which took part in the Third Battle of the Scarpe which was of the operations of the Arras offensive. He was killed in action on Sunday 6th May 1917, he has no known grave.

2nd Lieutenant Wilfred Arthur Douglas Carter		*Royal Flying Corps*	
Service No.	N/A	Age:	20
Place of Birth:	Kensington, London	Home Country:	England
Date of Death:	23/05/1917	Cause of death:	Accident
Memorial:	Not known		
War cemetery:	Yatesbury All Saints Churchyard		
Theatre of war:	Home		
Next of Kin:	Henry Wilfred & Elizabeth Napier Carter		
Address:	101 Palace Road, Tulse Hill, London.		

Wilfred enlisted as a private in the Royal Army Service Corps on 10th December 1914, he had previously been employed as a motor driver. On his enlistment papers he states his age as twenty years old, but he was only just eighteen. He arrived in France on the 18th December 1914 where his skill was in great demand because of the growing British army. In December 1915 he was commissioned as an officer and moved to the Dorset Regiment as a 2nd Lieutenant.

In 1917 Wilfred was attached to the Royal Flying Corps and sent to Yatesbury Aerodrome for training. At 8.30pm on 23rd May 1917 he was in flight with his instructor, William Britton, when something went wrong with the machine which made a dive and fell into some trees near the rectory. Both airmen were instantly killed, being thrown into the branches of the trees, from which they were lowered to the ground by means of ropes.

Captain K. M. Leak of the Royal Flying Corps witnessed the accident and stated;

"I was standing between the hangars of 59 squadron and the trees in the avenue at

Above: No. 2 Training camp at Yatesbury Aerodrome.

Right. The grave of Wilfred Carter, under the trees in Yatesbury All Saints Churchyard.

Yatesbury, when I saw a flying machine plane down. When it was about 400 feet above the ground it seemed to lose flying speed, and came down in a nose dive, which seemed unintentional on the part of the pilot. The machine came out of the nose dive and planed out, but it lost flying speed on the turn, the nose dived again within about 100 feet of the ground the pilot then, apparently, got control of the machine raising it about 40 feet, but it was too low to clear the trees, into which it crashed."

Another witness was Thomas Yorke a rigger/air mechanic who was first to the scene;

"Lieutenant Clarke and myself went up in the same machine in the morning, which came down with the deceased officers the same evening. The machine was flying alright when I was in it. The same day Lieutenant Britton went up in the machine with another officer and landed safely. I was in charge of the machine and I examined it before the deceased officers went up in it on that evening. About 7.45pm I was standing out by number 59 squadron hangar when I heard a machine approaching, and ran to where I saw it in the trees. I climbed up the tree and found both Britton and Carter dead; the switch was still on and the throttle was open."

Dr Walter Pidgeon of the Royal Army Medical Corps on seeing the machine come down ran immediately to the spot, where he found both the unfortunate men dead. Their heads were much injured and their necks were broken. He was of the opinion that death must have been instantaneous.

Wilfred was buried in the Yatesbury Churchyard. It is likely he was a Roman Catholic or a non conformist because he was buried in the corner of the Churchyard away from the other military graves. Today that corner of the churchyard is becoming overgrown, a very sad end for a young man who gave so much.

2nd Lieutenant William Kerr Magill Britton   *29th Sqdn Royal Flying Corps*

Service No.	N/A	Age:	25
Place of Birth:	Ireland	Home Country:	Ireland
Date of Death:	23/05/1917	Cause of death:	Accident
Memorial:	Trinity College Museum Building, Dublin		

Above: Officers Mess and Medical Reception Station at No.1 Camp Yatesbury aerodrome.

Right: William Britton killed in an accident with Wilfred Carter.

War cemetery:	Strabane Cemetery
Theatre of war:	Home
Next of Kin:	John & Margaret H Britton
Address:	Hazelwood, Strabane, County Tyrone

Twenty five year old William had graduated at the Engineering School in Dublin in 1912, he received a commission on 6th April 1916 with The Royal Munster Fusiliers and proceeded to France in September 1916. He was then attached to the Royal Flying Corps as an instructor. William was killed in the accident with Wilfred Carter at Yatesbury on Wednesday 23rd May 1917. His body was returned home to his parents and buried in Strabane Cemetery, County

Lance Coporal Edwin George Pottow   *2nd Bn Wiltshire Regiment*

Service No.	3/27	Age:	24
Place of Birth:	Cherhill, Wiltshire	Home Country:	England
Date of Death:	26/05/1917	Cause of death:	Died of wounds
Memorial:	Calne & Cherhill		
War cemetery:	Calne Holy Trinity Churchyard		
Theatre of war:	Home		
Next of Kin:	Albert & Fanny Pottow		
Address:	Quemerford Gate Farm, Calne, Wiltshire		

Edwin was a farm worker before the Great War. He volunteered for service in September 1914 and arrived in France on the 11th November 1914.

He was hit by a rifle bullet in his right elbow in France and because of the extent of his injuries he had to have his arm amputated. Following the operation he became seriously ill and died of acute pneumonia and mediastinitis exhaustion at Green Street Military Hospital, Stockport. His body was brought back to Calne. He is buried in Calne Holy Trinity Church-yard.

Edwin's brother Charles who also served during the war and his mother, Fanny Pottow, were to die from influenza on the same day, 2nd April 1919.

Above: the grave of Edwin Pottow in Calne Holy Trinity Churchyard.

Left: The Pottow Family, Edwin is standing second from the left, Charles is on his right.

Private Thomas Balfour Gornall		*4th Bn Worcestershire Regiment*	
Service No.	37510	Age:	29
Place of Birth:	Calne, Wiltshire	Home Country:	England
Date of Death:	01/06/1917	Cause of death:	Died of wounds
Memorial:	Not known		
War cemetery:	Duisans British Cemetery Etrun		
Theatre of war:	France		
Next of Kin:	Agnes Louisa Gornall (wife); Thomas and Annie Gornall (parents)		
Address:	Dean Bottom, Winsley, Wiltshire; Welclose Cottage, Bradford on Avon		

Thomas, a gardener, had married Agnes Louisa Pedley in 1910 at St Neots, Cambridgeshire. It is likely he joined the army under the Derby scheme or was conscripted. He was wounded during the Arras offensive and taken to one of the casualty clearing station at Duisans where he died of his wound on Friday 1st June 1917.

Private Harold Butcher		*15th Royal Warwickshire Regiment*	
Service No.	18595	Age:	27
Place of Birth:	Trowbridge, Wiltshire	Home Country:	England
Date of Death:	04/06/1917	Cause of death:	Died of wounds
Memorial:	Trowbridge		
War cemetery:	Etaples Military Cemetery		
Theatre of war:	France		
Next of Kin:	Daisey A. Butcher (wife); Benjamin W & Annie Butcher (parents)		
Address:	Nolans Cottage, Yatesbury, Wiltshire; Trowbridge		

Harold was employed as a carriage builder by Mr W Pike in Trowbridge. In 1915 he married Daisy Cook. Having enlisted in March 1916 either under the Derby scheme or conscripted, he was posted to the 15th Service Battalion Warwickshire Regiment and sent for training in the Isle of Wight. In the autumn of 1916 he went with his Regiment to France and took part in many engagements during the winter of 1916-17. He was severely wounded by shrapnel in the head in early May 1917 and died at the General Hospital in Etaples, France. His brother Fred had been drowned at the battle of Jutland in May 1916.

7th JUNE 1917 – THE BATTLE OF MESSINES, BELGIUM

Corporal Egbert Taylor		*1st Bn Wiltshire Regiment*	
Service No.	6754	Age:	31
Place of Birth:	Compton Bassett, Wiltshire	Home Country:	England
Date of Death:	07/06/1917	Cause of death:	Died of wounds
Memorial:	Trowbridge & Blacklands		
War cemetery:	Bailleul Communal Cemetery Extension Nord		
Theatre of war:	France		
Next of Kin:	Ethel F Taylor (wife); Thomas & Emily Taylor (parents)		
Address:	Steeple Ashton, Wiltshire; Cherhill, Wiltshire		

Egbert was employed as a farm labourer by Tom Tucker at Mill Farm, Steeple Ashton, where he took a keen intelligent interest in his work. In a ploughing competition organised by the Wiltshire Agricultural Education Committee at Keevil he won first prize and a special certificate. As a reservist, he was called to the colours on the outbreak of war and went over with the British Expeditionary Force. He was wounded in November 1915 by shrapnel in the chest and other parts of his body.

   He returned to France in the following June, but had only been with his regiment for a few weeks when he was again wounded and was treated at Chatham. On his recovery he was transferred to Weymouth, where after doing duty at the reinforcement camp, he again left for the fighting line in September 1916. After repeatedly refusing promotion, upon his return to France he was prevailed upon to accept the non commissioned officers stripes, and became a corporal. During the following eight months he saw much service with the Wiltshires and took part in every engagement, ultimately meeting his death on Thursday 7th June 1917, the date of his 31st birthday.

   The information was conveyed in a letter from Sister McPherson, in charge of a base hospital, who writing to Ethel Taylor said;

"I am extremely grieved to tell you that your husband, Corporal Taylor, was admitted to this hospital with multiple wounds of his body and hands. He was collapsed on admission, and

Right Egbert Taylor killed on his 31st Birthday.

Far right: George Peak-Garland memorial, killed at Messines Belgium.

IN SACRED AND LOVING MEMORY
— OF —
2nd. Lieut GEORGE PEAK-GARLAND
OF THE
11 BATT. ROYAL INNIS. FUSILIERS,
FORMERLY SERGT IN THE ROYAL WILTS YEOMANRY,
WHO WAS KILLED IN ACTION IN THE BATTLE OF MESSINES
ON JUNE 7TH 1917.
AND WAS LAID TO REST IN
LA LAITERIE MILITARY CEMETERY, KEMMEL.
AGE 30.
FOR GOD, RIGHT AND

although everything was done for him he never recovered, but passed peacefully away at 2.30pm the same day. He did not lave any message, as he was quite unconscious."

Lieutenant Swayne, Egbert's commanding officer also wrote to Ethel expressing his regret and sympathy and said;

"Corporal Taylor was appointed brigade orderly and put there especially so as to be safer,as we realized his worth and the gallant services he had rendered, and we were hoping to get him a months leave due to him as a time-expired soldier."

It is likely that Egbert was wounded during the preparation for an attack on Messines Ridge and evacuated to the hospital at Baileul, France
Egbert had three brothers in the army. One, who had also served in the army before the war had been captured in 1914 and was held in a German prisoner of war camp. Ethel had lost two brothers during the Great War Albert, who is remembered on Keevil war memorial and John who is remembered on Bulkington war memorial.

Lieutenant George Peak-Garland   *11th Bn Royal Inniskilling Fusiliers*

Service No.	N/A	Age:	30
Place of Birth:	Lewannick, Cornwall	Home Country:	England
Date of Death:	07/06/1917	Cause of death:	Killed in action
Memorial:	Winterbourne Monkton & Heddington		
War cemetery:	La Laiterie Military Cemetery		
Theatre of war:	Belgium		
Next of Kin:	James & Jane Peak-Garland		
Address:	Manor Farm, Avebury, Wiltshire		

Before the Great war George lived with his parents at Church Farm, Heddington where he worked with his father. He was a keen footballer and played for the village club and was well known in the area. He was also assistant secretary of the Calne Christmas Fat Stock Show.
Soon after the war broke out he joined the Wiltshire Yeomanry and went to France on the 5th May 1916. In December 1916 he received a commission and was transferred to the 11th Royal Inniskilling Fusiliers. His Battalion played a prominent part in the attacks at Messines, Belgium between the 7th and 9th of June 1917. He is remembered on a private memorial at Heddington St. Andrew Church.

Private William Frederick Godwin   *6th Bn Wiltshire Regiment*

Service No.	21325	Age:	21
Place of Birth:	Alderton, Wiltshire	Home Country:	England
Date of Death:	07/06/1917	Cause of death:	Killed in action
Memorial:	Not known		
War cemetery:	Ypres Menin Gate		
Theatre of war:	Belgium		
Next of Kin:	Frederick & Mary Jane Godwin		
Address:	Rodwell, Hilmarton, Wiltshire		

William, a volunteer, had arrived in France on Christmas Day 1916, he was part of a draft sent to the 6th Service Battalion Wiltshire Regiment. On Thursday 7th June 1917 he was waiting with his regiment to attack Messines – Wychaete Ridge - on the French / Belgium border. It is likely that at 3.10am, William would have witnessed 3 mines exploding and as the sound of the explosions faded the Wiltshires advanced. Their objective was the Hollande Salient which was successfully carried out and the Wiltshires captured 5 Machine guns, 3 Trench Mortars and 179 Prisoners with 80 of the enemy being killed during the advance.

During this advance William was one of nine of the 6th Wiltshires killed. He has no known grave.

2nd Lieutenant Frederick Cyril Hoey		*Royal Flying Corps*	
Service No.	N/A	Age:	18
Place of Birth:	Ireland	Home Country:	Ireland
Date of Death:	07/06/1917	Cause of death:	Accident
Memorial:	St. Mary's Catholic Church & Smith Memorial, Trinity College, Dublin		
War cemetery:	Yatesbury All Saints Churchyard		
Theatre of war:	Home		
Next of Kin:	Charles & Ida Hoey		
Address:	16 Shrewsbury Road, Ballsbridge, Dublin		

At the commencement of hostilities Frederick was studying at Trinity College, Dublin, but enlisted in the Royal Flying Corps and came to England.

At 6.40pm on Thursday 7th of June 1917 eighteen year old Frederick made his first solo flight. When he was about 3,000 feet up it was seen by onlookers that something went wrong. The Machine tilted and nose dived landing on the roof of the manor house. Frederick was thrown out of the machine and when taken from the roof he was found to be dead, having received terrible injuries, including a broken neck and a smashed thigh.

Second Lieutenant Mitchell witnessed the accident, he said;

"I was standing in No.1 Aerodrome at Yatesbury Camp when he saw an Avro aeroplane, flying at an altitude of 3,000 feet, stall, turn over on it's back, nose dive and nose dive again until it disappeared from view behind some trees."

Major Davey of the Royal Flying Corps in charge of 55th Squadron at Yatesbury said;

"This particular type of machine was used largely for training purposes, with excellent

Right: Smith Memorial, Trinity College, Dublin

Far Right: The grave of Frederick Hoey under the trees at Yatesbury All Saints Churchyard.

results being admirably adapted."

  The machine was examined and was found to be in very good order, however at the time another report stated the something evidently went wrong with the controllers, which caused Frederick to lose control of the machine.

  Frederick was buried in Yatesbury churchyard on Monday 11th June 1917, the service was conducted to the rites of the Roman Catholic Church. The burial was attended by Frederick's comrades and officers and men connected with the Aerodrome.

  Frederick received no medals for his time with the Royal Flying Corps; even though he gave his life he had not seen active service or been with the forces long enough to qualify. Being a Roman Catholic he was buried in the corner of the Churchyard away from the other military graves. Today that corner of the churchyard is becoming overgrown. A very sad end for a young man who volunteered and gave his life.

Private Percy Henry Angell   *6th Bn Wiltshire Regiment*
Service No.   13767   Age: 19
Place of Birth: Calne, Wiltshire   Home Country: England
Date of Death: 12/06/1917   Cause of death: Killed in action
Memorial: Calne
War cemetery: Ypres Menin Gate
Theatre of war: Belgium
Next of Kin: Frederick & Sarah Angell
Address: 23c New Road, Calne, Wiltshire

  Percy volunteered for service and arrived in France on 6th March 1915 with either the 1st or 2nd Battalion Wiltshire Regiment, it is likely he was wounded and when he recovered was sent to the 6th Battalion Wiltshire Regiment.

  On Tuesday 12th June 1917 the Wiltshires were at Oostterveane Wood, Belgium in trenches. During the afternoon the Germans shelled the Wiltshires continuously and the casualties were 3 killed and 2 wounded.

  One of those killed was Percy, he has no known grave. His brother Arthur died in Mesopotamia in April 1917.

2nd Lieutenant Albert Davies   *55th Sqdn Royal Flying Corps*
Service No.   N/A   Age: 24
Place of Birth: London   Home Country: England
Date of Death: 19/06/1917   Cause of death: Accident
Memorial: Not known
War cemetery: City of London Cemetery and Crematorium Manor Park
Theatre of war: Home
Next of Kin: J L Davies
Address: 10 Barkwell Road High Road, Lee, London

  Albert volunteered for service with the 20th London Regiment and arrived in France on 9th March 1915. He received a commission with the North Staffordshire Regiment on the 1st April 1916 and was later attached to the Royal Flying Corps.

  On the Morning of Tuesday 19th June 1917 Albert took off and having just left the Yatesbury aerodrome went up to about 70 feet. His machine suddenly fell to the earth and on impact the petrol tank burst setting the aeroplane on fire. Albert's body was dreadfully burnt before it could be recovered from the wreckage.

   Sergeant Boulton had examined the machine earlier that morning and found everything was in order. He witnessed the accident and said;

   "The deceased rose to a height of about 70 feet; then the machine swerved to the left as the deceased was about to make a circle of the aerodrome, and fell into a field. When I reached the scene of the accident the engine was still running."

Second Lieutenant Percy Robins who had been up in the same machine that day stated;

   "The rigging was alright but it was slightly inclined to the back. Some pilots preferred this. I had been up in the machine for three quarters of an hour and landed safely. I saw the accident, the machine banked a little and when it got to an angle of 45 degrees the rudder became an elevator and the machine nosed downwards."

Albert's parents requested that his remains were returned and he was buried in the City of London Cemetery.

Private William Rivers		*1st Bn Wiltshire Regiment*	
Service No.	19514	Age:	19
Place of Birth:	Swindon, Wiltshire	Home Country:	England
Date of Death:	20/06/1917	Cause of death:	Killed in action
Memorial:	Lyneham		
War cemetery:	Ypres Menin Gate		
Theatre of war:	Belgium		
Next of Kin:	John and Fanny Rivers		
Address:	Goatacre, Wiltshire		

From 16th to 20th June the 1st Battalion Wiltshire Regiment were tasked with supplying working parties of 350 other ranks to dig a communication trench from Messines Ridge, south east of Messines to the front line. The parties would work through the hours of darkness

Above: The dead mans penny issued to William Rivers parents at the end of the war.

Left : William Rivers.

from 8pm to 4am. During the day the men would rest, but still had inspections and a short parade in the afternoon.

During the night work the Wiltshires had to endure considerable hostile shelling and the war diary tells us;

"In spite of the shelling the work was carried to the entire satisfaction of the Royal Engineers."

Nineteen year old William was one of five men to be killed by the shellfire while digging the communication trench on Messines Ridge and has no known grave. His brother Walter Rivers was to die in October 1918.

Private William Howard Simpkins		*14th Bn Manitoba Regiment*	
Service No.	1000654	Age:	25
Place of Birth:	Derry Hill, Wiltshire	Home Country:	Canada
Date of Death:	26/06/1917	Cause of death:	Died
Memorial:	Derry Hill		
War cemetery:	Bramshott St Mary Churchyard		
Theatre of war:	Home		
Next of Kin:	David and Sarah Simpkins		
Address:	New Farm Cottages, Chiseldon, Wiltshire		

William enlisted in the Canadian army on Thursday 27th January 1916. He lived in Souris, Manitoba Canada and was an apprentice engineer.

During the First World War a Canadian Training Centre was placed in the open country on both sides of the Portsmouth road, between the turnings to Grayshott and to Bramshott; and the soldiers who died in No. 12 Canadian General Hospital, which served the camp, were buried in Branshott Churchyard.

William died most likely of illness on Tuesday 26th June 1917 and was buried at Bramshott

Lieutenant Edgar Kinsey Reynolds		*Royal Flying Corps*	.	
Service No.	N/A	Age:	27	
Place of Birth:	Alexandria, Egypt	Home Country:	Canada	
Date of Death:	27/06/1917	Cause of death:	Accident	
Memorial:	Not known			
War cemetery:	Hillington St Mary Churchyard			
Theatre of war:	Home			
Next of Kin:	Alfred & Emmil Kinsey Reynolds			
Address:	Deepdene, Glenair Avenue, Parkstone, Dorset			

Edgar was born on the 3rd July 1890 and before the Great War was a Line inspector in Calgary, Canada. He joined the Canadian Infantry on the 26th April 1917, and proceeded to England where he was attached to the Royal Flying Corps.

At 9.30pm on Wednesday 27th June 1917, Edgar took off from Yatesbury aerodrome with a passenger, Lieutenant Day. The machine was not very high when it developed a problem and crashed to earth. Both the occupants were seriously injured. Edgar succumbed to his injuries a short time after the accident. Lieutenant Day was taken to Chiseldon Hospital and recovering from his injuries, survived.

Edgar is buried in Hillingdon St. Mary Churchyard.

Lieutenant Arthur Sidney Dunne   *6th Dragoons*
Service No.   N/A.   Age: 25
Place of Birth: Bengal, India   Home Country: England
Date of Death: 02/07/1917   Cause of death: Killed in action
Memorial: Calne
War cemetery: Templux Le Guerard British Cemetery
Theatre of war: France
Next of Kin: Arthur Mountjoy Dunne KC
Address: Highlands, Calne, Wiltshire.

Arthur was educated at Eton and after deciding on a military career he went to Sandhurst, where he passed the usual course of military studies with credit. He was attached to the Inniskilling Dragoons, which he joined at Mhow, India, where he was stationed when the war broke out.

   The regiment was ordered home and arrived at Marseilles in December 1914, and was engaged in many battles. Arthur was killed on Monday 2nd July 1917 while leading a platoon on a trench raid. By his death this young officer had a promising career cut short. He was a good horseman and when at home on leave he hunted with the Beaufort Hounds. A Memorial service was held at the parish church on Tuesday 31st July 1917.

   Arthur's Father wrote the following letter to the Borough Tribunal:

   "My dear Mr Gough

   I thank the local Tribunal and Mr Clem Cole much for the kindness of your letter dated 14th July. My son died a soldiers death in the fulfilment of his simple duty, fighting to the end as so many around us have done, and are doing, and must sustain us all with a sense of pride. But the personal loss and sorrow remain, and for your touching words of sympathy which you convey to us, we are very grateful.—Believe me, yours very truly,

                              A.M.Dunne"

   Arthur is buried in Templux Le Guerard British Cemetery, France with nearly 600 other men who died in the Great War.

Private Ernest Charles Hunt   *1st Bn Royal Welsh Fusiliers*
Service No.   9185   Age: 29
Place of Birth: Heddington, Wiltshire   Home Country: Wales
Date of Death: 04/07/1917   Cause of death: Killed in action
Memorial: Not Known
War cemetery: Mory Abbey Military Cemetery
Theatre of war: France
Next of Kin: Mildred Adel Hunt (wife); Henry J. & Louisa Hunt (parents)
Address: 90 Cecil Street, Manselton, Swansea; Heddington

Ernest enlisted in the army in 1906 and at the outbreak of the war his Battalion were sent to France, arriving at Le Havre on 29th August 1914. In September 1914 he was transferred to the 2nd Battalion Royal Welsh Fusiliers and during the first winter of the war he suffered from bronchitis and influenza, but after spending some time in base hospitals he rejoined his unit. In December 1915 Ernest was granted 7 days leave to go to England and he married Mildred A. Ley in Swansea; he was back in France for Christmas 1915.

On the 17th July 1916, near Bazentin-le-petit, at the Somme, Ernest was injured with a gun shot wound to the right elbow. It was probably caused by German artillery, when the Royal Welsh Fusiliers had 5 killed and 21 wounded during a German barrage. After his recovery in England he returned to duty in France in September 1916. He was killed in action in July 1917 while serving with the 1st Royal Welsh Fusiliers.

Signalman Robert Wait   *HMS Vanguard Royal Navy*
Service No.   J/27168   Age: 19
Place of Birth: Cirecester, Gloucestershire   Home Country: England
Date of Death: 09/07/1917   Cause of death: Died
Memorial: Calne
War cemetery: Chatham Naval Memorial
Theatre of war: At Sea
Next of Kin: Ernest F & Ellen Wait
Address: The Marsh, Calne, Wiltshire

Nineteen year old Robert was a member of the crew of H.M.S. Vanguard, which on Monday 9th July 1917 was at anchor at Scappa Flow harbour.

Between 11pm and midnight there was a terrific explosion and the Vanguard blew up with the loss of 800 of her crew. One ammunition magazine had exploded without warning. The precise cause has never been identified but the Vanguard was one of many British ships to have blown up without reason during the Great War. Robert is remembered on the Chatham Naval Memorial.

Private Francis William Hornblow   *6th Bn Wiltshire Regiment*
Service No.   14288   Age: 24
Place of Birth: Calstone, Wiltshire   Home Country: England
Date of Death: 14/07/1917   Cause of death: Killed in action
Memorial: Seend
War cemetery: Oosttaverne Wood Cemetery
Theatre of war: Belgium
Next of Kin: Samuel & Emily Hornblow
Address: 12, Calstone, Wiltshire

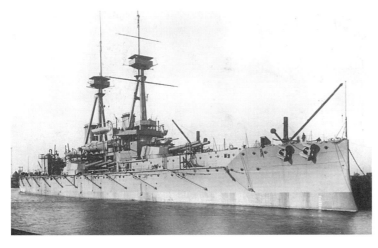

Left: H.M.S. Vanguard. Robert Wait was killed when the ship blew up at Scappa Flow.

Francis had joined the Wiltshire Regiment in December 1914 and in 1915 was sent to Salonika, where he arrived on the 12th July 1915, joining the 7th Service Battalion Wiltshire Regiment.

He was invalided home, most likely the result of illness, and on his recovery was transferred to the 6th Service Battalion Wiltshire Regiment.

On Saturday 14th July 1917 the 7th Battalion Wiltshire Regiment were in trenches at Wijtshate near Messines, Belgium. Francis was one of two men killed on that day most likely by German shell fire.

He is buried at Oosttaverne Wood Cemetery near where he died, with over one thousand men who were killed during the Great War.

Private Frederick Doble Smale		*253rd Siege Bty RASC*	
Service No.	M/304534	Age:	23
Place of Birth:	Kentisbeare, Devon	Home Country:	England
Date of Death:	20/07/1917	Cause of death:	Killed in action
Memorial:	Hilmarton		
War cemetery:	Lijssenthoek Military Cemetery		
Theatre of war:	Belgium		
Next of Kin:	Frederick & Mary A Smale		
Address:	Cowage, Hilmarton, Wiltshire		

In July 1916 Frederick was passed fit for General Service. He was his parents only son and his father appealed to the local Tribunal for the exemption of his son from Military Service. His father stated that twenty two year old Frederick was a shepherd and stockman at the farm at Cowage with 500 sheep and 145 grazing young cattle. All the staff consisted of two men in their 50's, another man medically unfit and Frederick. He found it impossible to get a shepherd to take his son's place, and three of his men had joined the Colours. Frederick's father was given until 1st October 1916 to find an ineligible man to replace his son.

At the end of September 1916 Frederick's father made a further appeal to the County Tribunal for the exemption of his son, he stated;

The private memorial to Frederick Doble Smale in Hilmarton St. Laurence Church.

Lijssenthoek Military Cemetery, Belgium.

"I will have to dispose of his flock if my son goes, he is my only son, and I bought the farm two years ago with the sole object of leaving it to my son."

Lord Bath chair of the County Tribunal stated;

"We will give further exemption till 14th November 1916 on the condition that there is no further appeal."

Frederick was conscripted into the army joining the Royal Army Service Corps. On the morning of Friday 20th July 1917 he was killed by a shell while serving near Poperinge, West of Ypres Salient. Frederick is buried in the Lijssenthoek Military Cemetery with over ten thousand other casualties of the Great War.

Private Adam Goddard		*Labour Corps*	
Service No.	144782	Age:	40
Place of Birth:	Shellingford, Berkshire	Home Country:	England
Date of Death:	22/07/1917	Cause of death:	Died
Memorial:	Not known		
War cemetery:	Shellingford St Faith Churchyard		
Theatre of war:	Home		
Next of Kin:	Annie Goddard		
Address:	Highfield, Foxley, Malmesbury, Wiltshire		

Adam was a cowman before the war. He had married Annie Lewis at Hilmarton in 1911 and they lived at Woodbine Cottage, Goatacre. He joined the army on the 31st May 1916 initially joining the Devonshire regiment and then transferring to the 3rd Labour Corps. Adam served all his time in the army in England, on the 15th July 1917 he was admitted to the 3rd S.G. Hospital, Oxford in a state of collapse. At 9.15am on Monday 22nd July after enduring a short painful illness Adam died. Tests showed that Tubercle Baccilli had been found in his urine and faeces and the cause of death was given as Tuberculosis. However Annie, Adams wife, refused to give permission for a post mortem.

Adam had been passed fit when he enlisted and it was accepted that his illness had been contracted while on military service and allowed his wife to obtain a pension.

The Commonwealth War Graves register and other lists state that Adam died on the 22nd July 1918, however Adam's military file has survived and gives the true date of 22nd July 1917. He is buried in Shellingford St Faith Churchyard where he was born.

Captain Percival Francis Crommelin D'Erf Wheeler   *Royal Flying Corps*

Service No.	N/A	Age:	23
Place of Birth:	Not known	Home Country:	England
Date of Death:	24/07/1917	Cause of death:	Accident
Memorial:	Worthing		
War cemetery:	Hammersmith Old Cemetery		
Theatre of war:	Home		
Next of Kin:	Percival D'Erf Wheeler		
Address:	Worthing, Sussex		

At the outbreak of war Percival was already an officer with the 3rd Battalion Dorset Regiment based at Dorchester in Dorset.

He arrived in France on 12th September 1914 probably as a replacement officer for one of the battalions. In 1917 he was attached to the Royal Flying Corps. On Tuesday 24th July 1917 the machine he was flying at Yatesbury crashed to the ground and he was killed instantly.

Percival's Body was returned to his parents and he was buried in Hammersmith Old Cemetery.

Gunner Frederick George Clifford   *168th Siege Bty RGA*

Service No	87052	Age:	30
Place of Birth:	Calstone, Wiltshire	Home Country:	England
Date of Death:	30/07/1917	Cause of death:	Killed in action
Memorial:	Poulshot & Keevil		
War cemetery:	Belgian Battery Corner Cemetery		
Theatre of war:	Belgium		
Next of Kin:	Amy Lilian Clifford (wife) - George H & Fanny J Clifford		
Address:	Mill Lane, Poulshot, Wiltshire		

At the end 1911 Frederick, a saw mill worker, married Amy Lilian Weston at Calne. He attested to join the Army on the 12th December 1915 at Devizes, probably under the Derby Scheme. Named after Lord Derby, the Scheme allowed men to register for the army and to be called up when the army needed them. Frederick was called up six months later and joined the Royal Garrison Artillery on 29th May 1916. After his short training he embarked from Southampton on 22nd September 1916 arriving at Le Harve the following day. During November 1916 he was attached to 2nd Army Signal School, for training as a signaler and then he returned to his unit.

Frederick was killed in action on Monday 30th July 1917, most likely by shelling during the battle of Messines, and is buried at Belgian Battery Corner Cemetery. The cemetery is at a road junction where three Belgium Artillery batteries were situated in 1915 and nearly all the 566 graves are from artillery units.

Frederick's personal possessions were returned to his wife Amy, and consisted of Letters, Photos, Religious Book, Penknife, 2 Cigarette Holders, Cards, Australian Cap, Badge, Medallions, Safety Razor, 9 Blades and a tin Cigarette Case.

2nd Lieutenant Arthur Measures Chatterton		*Royal Flying Corps*	
Service No,	N/A	Age:	23
Place of Birth:	Louth, Lincolnshire	Home Country:	England
Date of Death:	30/07/1917	Cause of death:	Accident
Memorial:	Not known		
War cemetery:	Yatesbury All Saints Churchyard		
Theatre of war:	Home		
Next of Kin:	William Chatterton		
Address:	Hallington, Louth, Lincolnshire		

Arthur qualified for his flying certificate on the 26th April 1917 at the London and Provincial School at Hendon. He qualified n one of the schools planes most likely a Maurice Farman biplane which was described as a pusher because the engine was behind the pilot and the propeller faced backwards.

He was killed in an accident on Monday 30th July 1917 at Yatesbury. He received no medal because he had not fulfilled the necessary service requirements.

Above left: Arthur Measures Chatterton.

Above Right: Arthur Measures Chatterton's broken grave marker under the trees at Yatesbury All Saints Churchyard.

8

PASSCHENDAELE

Private Leslie Edward J Lawrence   *2nd Bn Wiltshire Regiment*

Service No.	13956	Age:	19
Place of Birth:	Calne, Wiltshire	Home Country:	England
Date of Death:	31/07/1917	Cause of death:	Killed in action
Memorial:	Calne		
War cemetery:	Ypres Menin Gate		
Theatre of war:	Belgium		
Next of Kin:	Edward J & Florence B Lawrence		
Address:	36 Pippin Road, Calne, Wiltshire		

Seventeen year old Leslie had volunteered for service and joined the 2nd Battalion Wiltshire Regiment. It is likely he was under age when he arrived in France on the 18th May 1915.

The third Battle of Ypres commenced on Tuesday 31st July 1917 and it was better known as Passchendaele. To the British troops in the trenches it was none as Z day.

The first wave of men left the British trenches at 3.40am and were immediately met by a German artillery barrage and considerable machine gun fire. However, by 6.15am the Wiltshires had taken their objective and had captured and cleared the German Trenches taking 50 prisoners.

Leslie was killed during this attack and is remembered on the Ypres Menin Gate. He has no known grave.

Private Joseph Topp   *6th Bn Wiltshire Regiment*

Service No.	8735	Age:	23
Place of Birth:	Hilmarton, Wiltshire	Home Country:	England
Date of Death:	31/07/1917	Cause of death:	Killed in action
Memorial:	Calne		
War cemetery:	Somer Farm Cemetery		
Theatre of war:	Belgium		
Next of Kin:	Henry & Jane Topp		
Address:	Cowage Cottages, Hilmarton, Wiltshire		

Joseph volunteered and joined the 6th Service Battalion Wiltshire Regiment. He arrived in France on 19th July 1915.

Two years on the Wiltshires were in assembly positions for the third Battle of Ypres and were supporting the 56th Brigade near Wytschaete, (Wjtschate), Belgium. It was raining heavily and after the intense British barrage the Germans retaliated by shelling the British support areas.

The 6th Wiltshires suffered one casualty who was killed by the German shell fire while they waited in the support area at Estaminet Corner.

Joseph is buried in Somer Farm Cemetery, Belgium, with over 90 other men killed during the Great War.

Gunner Ephriam John Baker		*38th Bde Royal Field Artillery*	
Service No.	189167	Age:	33
Place of Birth:	Hilmarton, Wiltshire	Home Country:	England
Date of Death:	01/08/1917	Cause of death:	Killed in action
Memorial:	Not known		
War cemetery:	Railway Dugouts Burial Ground		
Theatre of war:	Belgium		
Next of Kin:	William Lewis & Sarah Baker		
Address:	Swindon, Wiltshire		

Ephriam was a carter and it is likely that he joined the army under the Derby scheme or was conscripted. He was probably put into the artillery because of his experience of dealing with horses and wagons and carts.

He was killed in action on Wednesday 1st August 1917 when his unit would have been supporting the British infantry in the Third Battle of Ypres.

It is likely Ephriam was killed by German counter battery shell fire. He is buried at Railway Dugouts Burial Ground east of the town of Ypres with over 2,00 other casualties of the Great War.

Private Frederick Albert Angell		*1st Bn Monmouthshire Regiment*	
Service No.	228257	Age:	26
Place of Birth:	Calne, Wiltshire	Home Country:	England
Date of Death:	03/08/1917	Cause of death:	Killed in action
Memorial:	Not known		
War cemetery:	Loos Memorial		
Theatre of war:	France		
Next of Kin:	Emily Frances Angell (wife); William & Agnes Angell (parents)		
Address:	Stock Elm, Compton Dundon, Somerset; 4, Patford Street, Calne		

Frederick was the manager of a grocers shop and one week before the declaration of war he married Emily Frances Curtis on 29th July 1914 at Compton Dundon parish church. He attested under the Derby scheme on 9th December and was called up on 20th of February 1917. Frederick joined the Monmouth regiment in France on 25th June 1917.

On Friday 3rd August 1917 Frederick was reported missing and was never seen again. On 12th April 1918 it was officially accepted that Frederick had died on the day he went missing.

Emily Angell received a pension of 22 shillings and 11 pence per week with effect from 8th April 1918, for herself and her two children.

Frederick is remembered on the Loos Memorial with over 20,000 casualties of the Great War.

Private Walter George Cole   *7th Bn Suffolk Regiment*

Service No.	50580	Age:	25
Place of Birth:	Derry Hill, Wiltshire	Home Country:	England
Date of Death:	09/08/1917	Cause of death:	Killed in action
Memorial:	Not known		
War cemetery:	Arras Memorial		
Theatre of war:	France		
Next of Kin:	John Cole		
Address:	Langley Burrell, Wiltshire		

George originally joined the Royal Army Service Corps and was later transferred to the 7th Service Battalion Suffolk Regimen. It is likely he joined under the Derby scheme or was conscripted. He was killed in action on Thursday 9th August 1917.

   George's Regiment was part of the 12th Eastern Division and between May and October 1917 held positions east of Monchy le Preux, near Arras, France. It is Likely he was killed in a raid or a small attack in this area; he has no known grave.

Gunner Thomas William Lawrence Flangham   *Royal Garrison Artillery*

Service No.	87577	Age:	33
Place of Birth:	Ramsgate, Kent	Home Country:	England
Date of Death:	10/08/1917	Cause of death:	Died of wounds
Memorial:	Not known		
War cemetery:	Brandhoek New Military Cemetery		
Theatre of war:	Belgium		
Next of Kin:	Isabel Flangham (wife); Harry Lawrence & Sarah Flangham (parents)		
Address:	Caslte Field Gardens, Curzon Street, Calne; Chipping Norton, Oxforshire		

Thomas was a gardner and had married Isabel Jolliffe on the 31st October 1908 at Cheshunt, Hertfordshire. He attested under the Derby Scheme on the 10th December 1915 and was called up on the 9th June 1916. After Training he was sent to France and the 1st Siege Battery in December 1916 and in February 1917 he spent 3 days sick in hospital and then returned to his unit.

British troops at Passchendaele.

On the 5th May 1917 Thomas was charged and awarded 3 days field punishment No2 for: *"hesitating to obey an order.."* He was wounded on 9th of August 1917, most likely by German shell fire while supporting the third battle of Ypres and died the following day at 32nd Casualty Clearing Station.

Isabel and her son Edward received a pension of 18 Shillings and nine pence per week and his personal possessions, which were sent home, consisted of Disc, letters, Photos, 2 Religious Books, purse, 2 Copper Coins, Photo Case, Styls Pen.

He is buried in Brandhoek New Military Cemetery, Belgium with over 500 other men who died in the Great War.

Lance Coporal Francis Sidney Williams   *1st Bn Wiltshire Regiment*
Service No.   32648   Age: 26
Place of Birth: Swindon, Wiltshire   Home Country: England
Date of Death: 12/08/1917   Cause of death: Died of wounds
Memorial: Calne
War cemetery: Brandhoek New Military Cemetery
Theatre of war: Belgium
Next of Kin: William S and Sarah A Williams
Address: Church Street, Calne, Wiltshire

In September 1917 news reached Calne of the death of Frank Williams, he had joined the 1st Battalion Wiltshire Regiment early in 1917, prior to which he assisted his father in the family business. He left for France in July and on the 12th of August, while engaged in action for Menin Road, he was struck by a shell splinter; he died the following day.

A comrade of Frank's, Lance Corporal Warwick, who was in the Red Cross Hospital at Exeter, wrote the following letter about the action;

"On Friday night, August 10th, we were ordered to take rations up to the front line, after which we were to go back for a good rest. We started from a dump in the Menin Road under shell fire. When we got near the front line our guide lost us, and we had to return with our burden to the place we had started, but that did not down hearten us. We received orders that the rations must be got up at all costs, and we succeeded in getting there and back without losing a man. No sooner had we returned when, 'pon my word, we had orders to go straight back again to the front line and hold it, but for how long we did not know. You can picture our thoughts and feelings to receive orders 3 times in succession to go to the front line trenches, but though foot sore and weary it was no good to grumble; we just had to do it.

We reached the line again much to our sorrow, as we were in a proper death trap. We arrived at 8am on August 11th, and I am deeply sorry to say that poor old Frank was hit by a piece of shell, commonly known as a "whiz-bang." The shell burst on top of the trench where he and several others of his comrades were digging in. Our serjeant-major and two men were killed by it, and Frank and another wounded. I saw him immediately after he was hit, and I understood him to say he was hit in the back and the right leg. We got him onto a stretcher and in less than half an hour he was on his way to the hospital. He told me to let his people know but I got wounded the next morning with a similar shell, and it is a miraculous how I escaped death. The strange thing about it is I must have been lying in the hospital bed where he died, but being badly wounded I did not realise where I was until I arrived at Hospital."

The Rev. Leonard T Pearson, C.F., writing from a casualty clearing station to Frank's mother, states;

"I am sorry to have to report the death of your dear son in this hospital, after being wounded in action. Everything possible was done for him, but without avail. I ministered to him before he died, and have buried him in the military cemetery."

In a subsequent letter the chaplain stated that Frank was wounded in the back by shell splinters which also penetrated his abdomen, he wrote;

"there is One in your home who can help you bear your sorrow, the Friend that sticketh closer than a brother, the Man of Sorrows acquainted with grief."

The following memoriam was inserted by Frank's parents in August 1918;

"In loving Memory of Frank youngest son
Far from his home he is laid to rest
And strangers tend his grave
But in the hearts that loved him best
Is dear the life he gave"

Frank was wounded on Westhoek Ridge east of the town of Ypres. He is buried in Brandhoek New Military Cemetery.

Lieutenant William Edward Tate			*Royal Flying Corps*	
Service No.	N/A		Age:	21
Place of Birth:	Eastham, Cheshire		Home Country:	England
Date of Death:	12/08/1917		Cause of death:	Accident
Memorial:	Not known			
War cemetery:	Yatesbury All Saints Churchyard			
Theatre of war:	Home			
Next of Kin:	Thomas & Mary E Tate			
Address:	4 Cleveland Terrace, Darlington, Durham			

Above: No. 2 Camp at Yatesbury aerodrome.

Left: The grave of William Edward Tate on the edge of Yatesbury All Saints Churchyard.

William had initially joined the Sherwood Foresters but had later transferred to the Royal Flying Corps. At 10am on Sunday 12th August 1917 William and Gilbert Pettigrew took off from Yatesbury after being sent up on duty. Gilbert Pettigrew was the pilot. There was a strong wind at the time, but no difficulty on that account was anticipated. They proceeded in the direction of Avebury, the machine rose to a height of 2,000 feet, when it was seen to nose dive. A motor ambulance was sent, but failed to find the airmen. An aeroplane went in search, and the aviator succeeded in locating the bodies, and flew around the spot, until the arrival of the ambulance. Both airmen were dead, and from the nature of their injuries there was no doubt that death in each case was instantaneous.

It is likely William was a Roman Catholic or a Nonconformist because he is buried on the edge of the cemetery at Yatesbury.

2nd Lt. Gilbert Thomas Richardson Pettigrew   *Royal Flying Corps*
Service No.   N/A   Age: 24
Place of Birth: Handsworth, Warwickshire   Home Country: England
Date of Death: 12/08/1917   Cause of death: Accident
Memorial: Not known
War cemetery: Warwick Cemetery
Theatre of war: Home
Next of Kin: William & Emma Pettigrew
Address: 17 Wharf Street, Emscote, Warwick, Warwickshire

Gilbert was Educated at Warwick School and became a journalist, afterwards leaving England for Canada to join the staff of the Winnipeg Telegram. He also served on the staff of the Montreal Daily Mail. Subsequently he was appointed private secretary to the Minister of public works for Manitoba.

At the commencement of hostilities he returned to England and enlisted in the Shropshire Light Infantry. He arrived on the continent on 22nd May 1915 and proceeded to the front. Having been seriously wounded at Hooge, Belgium, he was sent home and at the end of 1915 was offered a commission with the Herefordshire Regiment which he received on 6th January 1916. Shortly afterwards he transferred to the Royal Flying Corps and again went to the front. He returned home at the end of May 1916 after being found permanently unfit for war flying, and acted as an instructor in a training squadron at Yatesbury.

Gilbert was killed while flying with William Tate, his body was returned to his parents at Warwick where he was buried in the Cemetery.

Flight Lieutenant Alfred Stanley Hunt   *Royal Flying Corps*
Service No.   2875   Age: 22
Place of Birth: Nyngan, New South Wales   Home Country: Australia
Date of Death: 20/08/1917   Cause of death: Accident
Memorial: Not known
War cemetery: Yatesbury All Saints Churchyard
Theatre of war: Home
Next of Kin: Alfred Edgar & Sarah Ruth Hunt
Address: Robel, Rangers Avenue, Mosman, New South Wales

Alfred was a grazier, which is a rancher or farmer who keeps cattle or sheep on grazing land. He enlisted in the Australian Imperial Force on the 1st November 1915 at Holdsworthy, New South Wales. The following day he embarked from Sydney on the troopship Euripides and sailed for Alexandria in Egypt. He left Egypt on the 17th March 1916 and arrived at Marseilles, France six days later. He served in both France and Belgium and rose to the rank of Corporal being promoted in the field in November 1916. In March 1917 he was offered a commission in the Royal Flying corps and was discharged from the Australian Army, on his discharge form his character was described as very good. He was then sent to England and on to Yatesbury.

At 11.30 on Monday 20th August 1917 Alfred was flying in formation near the Lansdowne Monument, sergeant Charles Findlay was a passenger in his aircraft. Lieutenant Davey was watching the formation;

"I noticed the aeroplane piloted by Lieutenant Hunt when doing an S bend was getting very close to a machine piloted by Lieutenant Meggitt, who was on the left of the Lieutenant Hunt's machine. I heard a crack and realized there had been a collision. The aeroplane piloted by Lieutenant Hunt dived out of control and crashed to earth south of the Yatesbury aerodrome. I went to the spot where the machine fell and found Lieutenant Hunt and Sergeant Findlay dead. A portion of the wing of the damaged machine was found a few hundred yards away".

Lieutenant Meggit managed to land his machine safely near the aerodrome, even though his propeller had been smashed in the collision. The S bend was not a safe manoeuvre to carry out when flying in formation. The formation had a leader in front and the other machines behind. The aeroplanes should have been about 100 yards apart, but more often when pupils were flying it was customary to keep 200 Yards apart. When the collision occurred Lieutenant Meggit's machine was in the correct position. Lieutenant Meggitt reported;

"We had been flying in close formation for instructional purposes. Shortly after we got into formation, the leader turned, in the act of turning in order to keep my proper position on the left hand side of the formation, while at the same time watching the leader. The machine piloted by Lieutenant Hunt which was on my right and slightly above me, collided with me, my propeller making contact with Lieutenant Hunt's machine's wing."

Left: The grave of Alfred Stanley Hunt at Yatesbury All Saints Churchyard.

Above: The Hunt brothers remembered on the grave at Yatesbury.

Alfred is buried in Yatesbury churchyard and his brother George Bruce Fletcher Hunt, who died in France in 1916, is also remembered on his grave maker.

Sergeant Charles Findlay		*Royal Flying Corps*	
Service No.	7666	Age:	29
Place of Birth:	Scotland	Home Country:	Scotland
Date of Death:	20/08/1917	Cause of death:	Accident
Memorial:	Not known		
War cemetery:	Dalziel Airbles Cemetery		
Theatre of war:	Home		
Next of Kin:	Not known		

Charles was killed in the air accident with Alfred Hunt, it begs the question why was Sergeant Findlay flying with a trainee.

His body was returned home and buried at Dalziel Airbles Cemetery, Motherwell, Scotland.

2nd Lieutenant Thomas Thompson Pritchard		*General List Royal Flying Corp*	
Service No.	N/A	Age:	29
Place of Birth:	Knighton, Radnorshire	Home Country:	Wales
Date of Death:	30/08/1917	Cause of death:	Accident
Memorial:	Not known		
War cemetery:	Llanyre St Llyr Churchyard		
Theatre of war:	Home		
Next of Kin:	Edward J & Ann Pritchard		
Address:	Not known		

Thomas received a commission with the Royal Flying Corps in July 1917 and was sent to Yatesbury for training. He was killed instantly on Thursday 30th August 1917 when the machine he was flying nose dived into the ground. It was said at the time that he had been seen flying over Devizes earlier that day performing intricate feats.

Thomas's body was returned to his parents home town and he was buried in Llanyre St Llyr Churchyard. Because of the short time he was in the forces he received no medals.

Private Arthur Charles Smith		*1st Bn Dorsetshire Regiment*	
Service No.	18721	Age:	38
Place of Birth:	Calne, Wiltshire	Home Country:	England
Date of Death:	02/09/1917	Cause of death:	Killed in action
Memorial:	Calne & Calne Methodist Church Memorial		
War cemetery:	Coxyde Military Cemetery		
Theatre of war:	Belgium		
Next of Kin:	Martha Smith (wife); George & Emma Smith (parents)		
Address:	39 Pippin Road, Calne, Wiltshire		

Arthur had been employed as a mason at the Bowood Estate. In 1904 he married Martha Drewett at Calne and they had one child. It is likely that he joined the army under the Derby Scheme or was conscripted. For some years prior to his enlistment he was a teacher in the Primitive Methodist Sunday School, and was a founding member of the Male Voice Choir. In September 1917, Martha Smith received the following letter from the chaplain of the Regiment;

"It is with very great regret that I have to write to you about your husband, Private A. Smith. He was killed here in the line alas on the 1st; he met his end on duty doing his bit in the war, where a man should be. We all share in your loss and would send our sympathy to you. The awful toll of this war! It is hard to write to you, his wife; you must try to bear the dreadful blow with a courage and a brave heart worthy of those who bear so much every day. If we really believe our Lords words about faithful service, "Enter thou into the joy of thy lord," and if we really took Him at His word, how much our grief and feeling of loss would be lessened. Do not think of him as we say as "dead" but alive still, caring still, loving still, and only just passed on and before you into life. He will be so much missed; he has been so well spoken of. I have been in the line with the Regiment so another Chaplain officiated at the graveside some way back. I do not like leaving the Regiment to go away in times like those."

It is interesting to note that official records state he was killed on the 2nd September and the Chaplain states he died on 1st September. It is likely he was killed during the night.

A comrade, W. Cox, wrote to Martha on the 3rd of September and stated that he had just heard of her poor husbands death. The writer did not know what had happened as he was wounded at the time, but said he and all the rest of his mates were upset to hear of his death.

It is likely that Arthur was killed in the Lombartzyde sector of the front line in Belgium. He is buried in Coxyde Military Cemetery, Belgium with over 1500 soldiers who died in the Great War.

Private Clement John Strange   *2nd Bn Wiltshire Regiment*
Service No.   24146   Age: 22
Place of Birth: Calne, Wiltshire   Home Country: England
Date of Death: 03/09/1917   Cause of death: Killed in action
Memorial: Lydiard Millicent
War cemetery: Torreken Farm Cemetery No 1
Theatre of war: Belgium
Next of Kin: George & Lottie Matilda Strange
Address: Greatfield, Wiltshire

It is likely Clement joined the 2nd Battalion Wiltshire Regiment by registering for the Derby Scheme or was conscripted. He was killed in action on Monday 3rd September 1914 in the trenches near Wytschaete (now Wijtschate), Belgium. It is likely he was killed by shell fire because the artillery was described as very active. He is buried in Torreken Farm Cemetery No 1 with over 100 Casualties of the Great War.

His brother Zenas George Strange was killed in Gallipoli in 1915 while serving with the 5th Battalion Wiltshire regiment.

Sapper Henry George Panting   *227th Field Coy Royal Engineers*
Service No.   178172   Age: 23
Place of Birth: Chippenham, Wiltshire   Home Country: England
Date of Death: 04/09/1917   Cause of death: Died of wounds
Memorial: Calne
War cemetery: Reninghelst New Military Cemetery
Theatre of war: Belgium
Next of Kin: Edith E Panting (wife); Henry George & Rose Panting (parents)
Address: 25 High Street, Wooton Bassett; 2 Oxford Villas Pippin Road, Calne

Henry, known as Harry, was a cabinet maker and the only son of Henry and Rose Panting . In the summer of 1915 he married Edith Ayers in Swindon. It is likely he joined the Royal Engineers by registering for the Derby Scheme or was conscripted.

It is probable he was wounded somewhere around the Menin Road area of the front line. He died of wounds on Tuesday 4th September 1917 and was buried in Reninghelst New Military Cemetery which is where field ambulances were based at that time.

Pilot Cadet Alexander Vinogradoff   *66th Sqdn Royal Flying Corps*

Service No.	N/A	Age:	20
Place of Birth:	Petrograd, Russia	Home Country:	Russia
Date of Death:	06/09/1917	Cause of death:	Accident
Memorial:	Not known		
War cemetery:	Yatesbury All Saints Churchyard		
Theatre of war:	Home		
Next of Kin:	Not known		
Address:	House No. 67 Second Line, Petrograd, Russia.		

Pilot Cadet Alexander was attached to the Royal flying Corps from the Russian Army and qualified as a pilot at the Military School Oxford on the 15th August 1917 in a de Havilland Biplane.

On the evening of Thursday 6th September 1917 he was flying in the vicinity of Yatesbury when his machine nose dived and crashed to the ground. He received severe injuries to which he succumbed shortly after his admission to hospital.

Right: Alexander Vinogradoff.

Below: The Grave of Alexander Vinogradoff in Yatesbury All Saints Churchyard.

Above: The Nevsky Prospect, the chief street in Petrograd, now St. Petersburg, Alexander Vinogradoff's home.

Left: The grave of Albert Charles Dewey Drewett in the Huts Cemetery.

Gunner Francis Victor Sage		*19th Heavy Bty RGA*	
Service No.	109153	Age:	20
Place of Birth:	Calne, Wiltshire	Home Country:	England
Date of Death:	19/09/1917	Cause of death:	Killed in action
Memorial:	Calne		
War cemetery:	Canada Farm Cemetery		
Theatre of war:	Belgium		
Next of Kin:	Benjamin & Emily A Sage		
Address:	10 Alma Terrace, Calne, Wiltshire		

Francis, known as Vic, was the youngest son of Benjamin & Emily Sage and joined the Royal Garrison Artillery by registering for the Derby Scheme or was conscripted.

He was killed in action on Wednesday 19th September 1917 probably due to German shell fire. He is buried at Canada Farm Cemetery which was named after a farmhouse north west of Ypres which was used as a dressing station. The cemetery contains the graves of more than 900 casualties of the Great War.

Lance Coporal William John Fussell		*503rd Field Coy Royal Engineers*	
Service No.	504468	Age:	23
Place of Birth:	Bath, Somerset	Home Country:	England
Date of Death:	20/09/1917	Cause of death:	Killed in action
Memorial:	Calne		
War cemetery:	Buffs Road Cemetery		
Theatre of war:	Belgium		
Next of Kin:	Olive Edith Fussell		
Address:	1 Back Row, London Road, Calne, Wiltshire		

William, an electrical engineer, married Olive Drew at the beginning of 1916 in Bath, Somerset. He joined the Royal engineers by registering for the Derby Scheme or was conscripted.

He was killed in action on Thursday 20th September 1917 at The Battle of the Menin Road Ridge. He is buried in Buffs Road Cemetery near the hamlet of Wieltje, north east of the town of Ypres, Belgium.

Private Herbert Henry Rumming   *6th Bn Wiltshire Regiment*
Service No.   18391   Age: 23
Place of Birth: Bremhill, Wiltshire   Home Country: England
Date of Death: 20/09/1917   Cause of death: Killed in action
Memorial: Bremhill - Foxham - East Tytherton Morovian Church
War cemetery: Bedford House Cemetery
Theatre of war: Belgium
Next of Kin: Frederick & Sarah Rumming
Address: East Tytherton, Wiltshire

Herbert volunteered for service with the 6th Battalion Wiltshire regiment and arrived in France on 1st June 1915. On Thursday 20th September 1917 the Wiltshires were at Opaque Wood, Belgium and formed the right flank of an attack to be made by the 2nd and 5th Armies on the Menin Road. At 5.40am the Wiltshires advanced behind a creeping barrage of the British artillery. The companies on the left (the Wiltshires), after a little opposition and taking 19 prisoners, succeeded in taking all their objectives after about thirty five minutes. As the Wiltshires began to consolidate the position they had several casualties from German snipers; the ground was very wet and waterlogged and in places the fire steps were formed by sandbags. The companies on the right had all their officers killed as they reached their objectives. They spent the night consolidating their positions.

Herbert was killed during this attack. He is buried at Bedford House Cemetery which was the name given to Chateau Rosendal, a country house in a small wooded park with moats, near Zillebeke village. The cemetery now contains over 2000 casualties of the Great War and many of the graves had been relocated from smaller cemeteries at the end of the Great War.

Gunner Albert Charles Dewey Drewett   *132nd Heavy Bty RGA*
Service No.   116706   Age: 19
Place of Birth: Calne, Wiltshire   Home Country: England
Date of Death: 21/09/1917   Cause of death: Killed in action
Memorial: Calne
War cemetery: The Huts Cemetery
Theatre of war: Belgium
Next of Kin: Albert & Emma Drewett
Address: 15 North Street, Calne, Wiltshire

Albert was the oldest son of Albert & Emma Drewett and he was educated at Marden School, Calne. On leaving school he was apprenticed as a grocer at the Co-operative Stores, where he served four years and then removed to the Co-operative stores in Trowbridge were he remained for nearly a year. During his youth he was a member of the Castle Street chapel and he was described as a steady lad, giving evidence of a high Christian character. For many years he was a teacher at Castle Street Sunday School, a work which he delighted in up to the time he enlisted.

Albert attested on the 23rd of May 1916 and was called up in September 1916 joining the Royal Garrison Artillery. He then spent some time at the Signaling School at Southampton. He left for France in January 1917 and joined the 132nd Heavy Battery. The intimation of Albert's death was conveyed in a letter to his parents received at the start of October:

"Dear Mr Drewett. It is my sad task to inform you that your son, Gunner A.C.D. Drewett was killed in action on September 21st. He was on duty at the time as an aeroplane look out in a battery position and was killed instantly by a fragment of a bomb dropped by an enemy

aeroplane. It will be some comfort to you and your family to know that he died doing his duty and did not suffer any pain. The funeral took place yesterday behind the lines in a little cemetery and I will arrange to have his resting place permanently marked. Your son always did his work cheerfully and well and was respected and loved by all ranks in the battery. His death is a great blow to us all. May God comfort you in your great loss. With deepest sympathy. Yours faithfully, J.Williams, Major, R.G.A."

The small cemetery referred to was the Huts Cemetery, named after a row of huts that were at Dickebusch (now Dikkebus), Belgium. It contains the graves of over 1000 casualties of the Great War.

Corporal George Herbert Moody		*10th Bn West Riding Regiment*	
Service No.	235444	Age:	29
Place of Birth:	Romsey, Hampshire	Home Country:	England
Date of Death:	21/09/1917	Cause of death:	Killed in action
Memorial:	Calne		
War cemetery:	Tyne Cot Memorial		
Theatre of war:	Belgium		
Next of Kin:	Clara Moody (wife); Thomas & Mary Moody (parents)		
Address:	Curzon Street, Calne; 25 Narrow Lane, Romsey, Hampshire		

George had only been on the Continent three weeks when he was killed in action in Belgium. He had joined the West Riding Regiment by registering for the Derby Scheme or was conscripted. Before he joined up he had been engaged as a scout in connection with the Automobile club in the Calne district.

He was killed when his Regiment was engaged in the fighting at the Menin Road. News was received on Clara, his wife on Sunday 30th September, she was left with four young children.

He is remembered on the Tyne Cot Memorial with the names of nearly 35,000 men who were casualties of the Great War; he has no known grave.

Major Sidney Miles Toppin MC		*151st Heavy Bty RGA*	
Service No.	N/A	Age:	39
Place of Birth:	Cloumel, Ireland	Home Country:	England
Date of Death:	27/09/1917	Cause of death:	Died of wounds
Memorial:	Memorial Blacklands Church, Sandown, I.O.W. & Branksome Dorset		
War cemetery:	Lijssenthoek Military Cemetery		
Theatre of war:	Belgium		
Next of Kin:	Viva Toppin (wife); James Morris Toppin & Mrs. J. Toppin (parents)		
Address:	Rose Bank, Sandown, Isle of Wight; Blacklands Park, Calne		

Sidney was the younger son of Major-General J. M. Toppin. He was educated at Clifton College and Gonville and Cains College, Cambridge. While studying for a medical degree he was offered a commission in the Royal Artillery and was gazzetted in May 1900. He was then posted to India and after learning Hindustani, was given charge of a mountain battery on the Afghan frontier at Chitra. After two years he was transferred to Burma. He was then appointed company commander and transferred to Egypt and then returned to England in 1914. On 17th of August 1914, ten days after war had been declared, he married Jessie Viva Coleman. He was initially sent to Ireland where he formed an artillery battery and then on to France.

He was mentioned in dispatches for his services at the Battle of Loos and was awarded the Military Cross. He was wounded near Ypres and taken to the Military Hospital at Lijssenthoek, where he died of his wounds on Thursday 27th September 1917, leaving a widow and infant child. His elder brother Harry Toppin was killed during the Battle of the Aisne in 1914.

Captain Lewis Scott White MC   *Royal Flying Corps*
Service No.   N/A   Age: 21
Place of Birth: Bath, Somerset   Home Country: England
Date of Death: 29/09/1917   Cause of death: Accident
Memorial: Not known
War cemetery: Bath Locksbrook Cemetery
Theatre of war: Home
Next of Kin: Dr Edward & Fanny White
Address: 2 Green Park, Bath, Somerset

Twenty one year old Lewis was the youngest son of,Mr Edmund J. White, M.B & Fanny; he was educated at Victoria College, Grosvenor. He always took a keen interest in aviation, and was a prominent member of the Bath Aerial Club. He joined the Royal Flying Corps as a mechanic in October 1914, received a commission and was gazetted Captain on May 5th 1916. While a 2nd Lieutenant and serving on the continent he was awarded the Military Cross and the citation reads;

"When acting as observer he cooperated in an infantry raid by flying over the enemy's trenches at a height of only 1,500 feet for more than an hour and a half in very adverse weather conditions. He attacked the enemy in the trenches with machine-gun fire, and located 16 active enemy batteries during this flight."

He was transferred to England and was promoted to Flight-Commander of a training squadron at Yatesbury Aerodrome. On the 19th September 1917 Lewis attended an Investiture at Buckingham Palace and was decorated by the King with the M.C. He was due to return to the front in the next few weeks.

On Saturday 29th September 1917 Lewis left his home in Bath at 7.30am and proceeded to Yatesbury on his motorcycle. During the day Lewis was scheduled to fly to Bath where he

The result of an air crash.

would take part in a demonstration at 2pm and another at 4pm. Lewis then flew back to Yatesbury where he learned that the pilot of a new machine which was being sent to the aerodrome had had to descend near Wantage, Berkshire, through engine trouble. Lewis then went to the place where the aviator had come down and went up in the machine himself. Soon afterwards, however the aeroplane nose dived and crashed to earth. Lewis died almost immediately after being extricated from the wreckage.

Private Henry James Reeves   *8th Bn Somerset Light Infantry*
Service No.   27781   Age: 37
Place of Birth: Lyneham, Wiltshire   Home Country: England
Date of Death: 04/10/1917   Cause of death: Killed in action
Memorial: Hilmarton
War cemetery: Tyne Cot Memorial
Theatre of war: Belgium
Next of Kin: Lydia Reeves (wife); Geoge & Sarah Reeves (parents)
Address: Snow Hill, Hilmarton; 21 Hilmarton

Prior to the Great War Henry was the village postman. He had married Lydia Thorpe in the spring of 1903 and they had four children. He was also a member of the Foresters Friendly Society and one of four brothers serving in the forces. He joined the 8th Battalion Somersets by registering for the Derby Scheme or was conscripted. On Thursday 4th October 1918 the 8th Somersets were south of the Menin Road near the Village of Gheluvelt. They were to attack two German strong points. At this point in the third battle of Ypres the landscape around this area was a mass of shell holes and there was an absence of landmarks. Even the Menin Road had been obliterated. Communication with the front line was only possible during the hours of darkness; during the day even individual runners were shot at as soon as they left headquarters. The Somersets reached their assembly points without incident. Due to the hurried preparations and the state of the ground the assembly trenches were limited and over crowded for the attack.

   At 6am the British barrage began but it was at once noticed that the veil of fire appeared very thin. As the Somersets advanced the barrage was already beyond the first objective and there was no chance of getting close to it; the enemy was holding a number of posts north and south of the strong point. As soon as the Somersets reached the ridge line they came under heavy machine gun and rifle fire. With a series of sectional rushes the Somersets reached their objective and attempted to consolidate the position, but again came under heavy fire from four German machine gun positioned to the right. It had been hoped that these guns would have been put out of action by the British Barrage. The Germans now counterattacked; each of their bombers advanced carrying no equipment and each threw two stick bombs simultaneously. Two of the Somersets' companies tried to overcome the German machine guns but were almost annihilated in the process. Another attack was tried by Lieutenant Smith of the Somersets, unfortunately the brave lieutenant was killed before the attack had gone far and none of the thirty men who made the attack were able to reach the strong point. At the end of the day the Somersets were back in there original positions. The Casualties were 30 killed, 77 wounded and 12 missing. The action was part of the Battle of Broodseide. Official dispatches stated;

   "The success of this operation marked a definite step in the development of our advance. Our line had now been established along the main ridge line, 9,000 yards starting from Mount Sorrel. From the farthest point reached the well marked Gravenstafel Spur offered a defensible feature which our line could be bent back from the ridge."

Henry was described as always cheerful and obliging. The following memoriam appeared in the local paper;

We think we can see his smiling face
As he bade us his last Goodbye
And left his home for ever
In a foreign land to die
But the bitterest blow is yet to come
When the warriors all return
And we miss among the cheering crowd
The face of our dear son
He little thought when he left us
He never would return
His heart was good, his spirit brave
He is now resting in a soldier's grave

Henry was killed by one of the German machine guns on the ridge near the Menin Road, he has no known grave.

Private William Henry Fry Vines		*3/4th Bn Royal West Surrey Regiment*	
Service No.	205792	Age:	31
Place of Birth:	Christian Malford, Wiltshire	Home Country:	England
Date of Death:	06/10/1917	Cause of death:	Died of wounds
Memorial:	Not known		
War cemetery:	Godewaersvelde British Cemetery		
Theatre of war:	France		
Next of Kin:	Joseph Daniel & Jane Vines		
Address:	Calstone, Wiltshire		

William, a grocers assistant, was the youngest son of Joseph Daniel & Jane Vines. He joined the 3/4th Royal West Surrey Regiment by registering for the Derby Scheme or was conscripted.

He was wounded in the Battle of Broodseide on the ridge near the Menin Road, Belgium on 4th October 1917. He was then taken to one of the casualty clearing stations that were based at Godewaersvelde, France where he died of his wound on Saturday 6th October 1917, where he is buried in the cemetery.

Private William Edward Corderoy		*1/4th Bn TF York & Lans Regiment*	
Service No.	33334	Age:	42
Place of Birth:	Brixton, London	Home Country:	England
Date of Death:	09/10/1917	Cause of death:	Killed in action
Memorial:	Calne		
War cemetery:	Tyne Cot Memorial		
Theatre of war:	Belgium		
Next of Kin:	Charlotte A Corderoy (wife); Clement & Lucy Corderoy (parents)		
Address:	The Chantry, Calne, Wiltshire; Dulwich London		

William came to Calne in 1899 as a works Manager for Harris & Co. At the end of four years he relinquished that position and in the summer of 1904 he married Charlotte Anabal Coleman in London and went to South America, where he remained for a time. He left America to accept an appointment as a tourist conductor in the East for Cook and Son. He received a commission in the Royal Army Service Corps in August 1915 and was promoted to full lieutenant in December 1915.

In 1916 William was attached to the Guards in London and was in charge of forage supply. On the 5th January 1917 Dorothy Lindsell-Stewart, known as Meum, went to William's commanding officer, Major Cleve, and accused William of threatening her. Meum had been a secretary in the office where William worked but had left to take up a post at a Canadian Hospital in London. She produced a letter that was allegedly written by William which stated;

"Meum Stewart, You must resign your present post immediately. You are no longer a fit or proper person either to associate with decent girls or to hold any appointment in any department of His Majesty's Government. If you let me have the M.O.'s (medical officer) acceptance of your resignation before 10am on Saturday 6th inst. I shall place before him proofs that what I say is true, before lunch that day."

In a statement Meum stated that William had threatened to murder her if she did not go and live with him at his flat. Stating also that on 3rd January 1917 he called at her home at 11 o'clock, was very violent and told her that he would fix her because he would not have anything to do with her.

On Thursday 4th January Meum stated that William had handed in a most libellous statement concerning her to an orderly at her place of employment with instructions to; *"pass it all round the office."* She again stated she was in great fear that he would do her some violence as he carried a fully loaded revolver and a large knife about 8 inches long.

On 6th January Meum again wrote to Major Cleeve and attached a letter addressed to her husband that had been received by Jacob Epstien, Meum said the letter was from William, though it was not signed, she stated she recognized the hand writing. Meum described the contents of the letter as fabrication but since it was addressed to her husband, she was worried what her husband would do. The letter stated:

"To 2nd Lieutenant Lindsell- Stewart,Sir,
The following facts may interest you. Your wife Meum, against the advice of her friends has left Sally, lost her government job and is in all probability, since she admits it, the Mistress of the sculptor Jacob Epstein who lives at 23 Guildford Street, Russell Square. Epstein's Wife is agreeable to the arrangement, presumably to encourage his art. Your wife posses for him in the nude. In case you have not made suitable arrangement for your pension re your next of kin, should you be unlucky, lose no time in doing so. She is in with a very fast crowd at the Café Royal and booked for hell, also worthy of no mans sympathy."

Major Cleeve made a decision to hand all the information to the Provost Marshall and a Captain Trevor took up the case. Captain Trevor went to William's lodgings, William was not in but he managed to gain entrance and conducted a search. Captain Trevor found a loaded automatic pistol and a long pointed knife. He took possession of these items along with some letters and other things. The following day Captain Trevor returned to William's lodgings and having again gained entrance found William in pyjamas and an old pair of flannel trousers. According to Captain Trevor's statement:

"Corderoy said he thought I (Captain Trevor) was Mr Epstien and having turned sideways to conceal his intentions then suddenly swung round and produced a fully loaded revolver which he pointed at my head".

Captain Trevor disarmed William after a struggle and took him in his own car to Millbank Hospital, where he handed William over to the Provost Marshall and he was placed in a cell. At the time of these events William had been on sick leave from the army and it was assumed by the Provost Marshall William had had a nervous breakdown.

Meum, wrote to one of the officers involved in the case stating:

"Dear Billy, Write and tell me what has happened about W.E.C. I am very anxious to know – not so much out of curiosity, as I am placed in a rather awkward position with regard to the letter he sent to my husband. If Tony takes it seriously I am let in for a divorce, which I want very much to avoid. But if as I strongly suspect, W.E.C. has gone a trifle insane, and would be likely to be put under supervision, I can make it alright with my husband since I can write to put the facts before him.

Send me a few lines addressed here, Miss D. Stewart, C/o A/D.D.M.S. Canadians, 86 Strand, W.C.

I will be awfully obliged to you, Billy, if you will. I am rather worried, although Major Cleeve has been such a brick over the matter. Yours, Meum"

Meum typed the letter on official note paper from the department where she worked, after she hand wrote;

"you may rely that I would regard anything you might tell me as confidential in haste."

On the 14th February 1917 William was Court Martial ed at the Guild hall, Westminster. He was charged with;

"Offering violence to his superior officer being in execution of his office, in that he at No. 7 Crown Office Row, Temple, London, E.C., on the 6th January 1917 pointed a loaded revolver at Captain Keith Trevor, MC., Assistant Provost Martial, London District, who was at the time about to put him under arrest."

William was found guilty and sentenced to be dismissed from His Majesty's Service. However, William was still liable for service under the Military Service Act and the director of Recruiting, Major Sinclair, insisted he was called up at once. On the 10th March 1917 William was conscripted into the Royal Army Service Corps as a private soldier and at the end of Mach 1917 he was compulsorily transferred to the infantry joining the 1/4th York & Lancaster Regiment on the continent in July 1917.

William's commanding officer wrote to Charlotte Corderoy on the 16th October 1917;

"Dear Mrs Corderoy, - I take this first opportunity of sending my deepest sympathy on the death of your husband. He was killed instantly by a bullet through the heart on the 9th October 1917, during a British attack. Though he had been with us a short time he had endeared himself to all around by his gentle manners and indomitable courage. He had been offered posts that would keep him out of the front line, but he refused as he wanted to get at the enemy, and even the short periods of rest behind the lines seemed irksome to him. He went over the top with his Battalion at 5.20am on the 9th and his conduct throughout was heroic. He was killed by a sniper soon after the capture of the enemy position. I only rejoined the battalion myself on the 1st September after being wounded, but at once I realized your husband was a man of unusual ability. I had many talks with him and we were friends, and knowing him as I did I can more deeply realize your terrible loss. Assuring you of my deepest sympathy, in which the whole platoon and officers of A Company Join me. - I am your sincerely William Ryan O.C."

In May 1918 Charlotte Corderoy received William's personal possessions, photos, disc, metal mirror, notebook, diary and letters, and a pension of 20 shillings and 5 pence per week. William was killed at the Battle of Poelcapelle, which prepared the way for the attack on Passchendaele, he has no known grave.

It is interesting that at Williams Court Martial no mention was made of Meum, or the fact that Captain Trevor gained entry to Williams lodging's, without permission, on two occasions. There was also the question of why did he remove personal letters and other things, and what were the other things? It is now known that Meum was Jacob Epstein's mistress and the mother of his first child. Meum modelled for Epstein who sketched her and made four busts between 1916 and 1918.

Sergeant Harry Lucas Hillier Perrett   *3rd Bn Coldstream Guards*

Service No.	5279	Age:	35
Place of Birth:	Rowde, Wiltshire	Home Country:	England
Date of Death:	09/10/1917	Cause of death:	Killed in action
Memorial:	Calne		
War cemetery:	Artillery Wood Cemetery		
Theatre of war:	Belgium		
Next of Kin:	Rhoda Perrett		
Address:	Marsh Lane, Rowde, Wiltshire		

On 11th November 1917 a memorial service was held for Harry at the parish church at Rowde. As a boy Harry had been a member of the Choir for a good many years and was generally entrusted with the solos. He Joined the Coldstream Guards, was a first class shot and had won many prizes with his regiment in various competition. At the outbreak of the war Harry was living with his grandmother in Rowde and as a reservist he was called to his Regiment arriving in France on 12th August 1914. Harry was probably on leave when he married Rhoda Brewer at Calne in the summer of 1915; he then returned to the front. In January 1917 Harry was granted a months leave in England which must have been a welcome relief from the front line and it is likely it was the first time he had seen his daughter who had been born in the summer of 1916. Toward the end of October 1917 unofficial news was received from another man from Rowde in the Coldstream Guards, that Harry had been killed. The soldier had been in the habit of spending time with Harry when the battalions were stationed near each other as it was good to meet someone from the old village and talk of those at home. The soldier enclosed some photos found on Harry by a Stretcher bearer.

The news was confirmed in early November that Harry had been killed at the Battle of Poelcapelle, he left a widow and little daughter.

He is buried today in Artillery Wood Cemetery with over 1300 men, casualties of the Great War.

Private Frederick Charles Smith   *7th Bn Royal West Kent Regiment*

Service No.	241254	Age:	24
Place of Birth:	Calne, Wiltshire	Home Country:	England
Date of Death:	12/10/1917	Cause of death:	Killed in action
Memorial:	Calne		
War cemetery:	Cement House Cemetery		
Theatre of war:	Belgium		
Next of Kin:	James & Annie Smith		
Address:	35 London Road, Calne, Wiltshire.		

Frederick Joined the Royal West Kent Regiment by registering for the Derby Scheme or was conscripted. He was killed in action on Friday 12th October 1917 at the first battle of Passchendaele.

He is buried in Cement House Cemetery, named after a fortified farm building on the Langemark to Boesinghe road; within its walls are buried over 1000 casualties of the great war.

Airman 1st Class John Herbert Whiston   *Royal Flying Corps*
Service No.   28622   Age: 21
Place of Birth: Leicester, Leicestershire   Home Country: England
Date of Death: 14/10/1917   Cause of death: Accident
Memorial: Not known
War cemetery: Leicester Gilroes Cemetery
Theatre of war: Home
Next of Kin: Herbert & Mary Whiston
Address: Leicester, Leicestershire

On the evening of Saturday 14th October twenty one year old John, and Charles Haggart, left Yatesbury; they were road testing a motor cycle that had proved troublesome on a previous journey.

John was in the side car and Charles riding the vehicle; they descended the hill toward Cherill at a speed of 18 to 20 miles per hour and Charles put the machine into neutral. It was a very dark evening and at the bottom of the hill they were on the right hand side and occupying about half the road. In front of them was a lorry which was stationary. The headlight on the lorry was bright and for a moment or two Charles was blinded by the glare and sounded the horn loudly. He pulled to the left as he passed the lorry which was heading for London and before he could regain his seeing power, he found as he passed the lorry the side car struck an object, which proved to be another airman who had been walking to Calne.

The motorcycle went out of control hit a bank and overturned. John was thrown from the side car. An ambulance was sent for and John was taken to the hospital at Yatesbury, on admission John was unconscious and was suffering from a fractured scull. He succumbed to his injuries about an hour later.

2nd Lieutenant Thomas Herald   *Royal Flying Corps*
Service No.   N/A   Age: 31
Place of Birth: Glasgow, Lanarkshire   Home Country: Scotland
Date of Death: 20/10/1917   Cause of death: Accident
Memorial: Not known
War cemetery: Yatesbury All Saints Churchyard
Theatre of war: Home
Next of Kin: Thomas & Elizabeth Margaret Herald
Address: 19 Leslie Street, Pollock Shields, Glasgow, Lanarkshire

Thomas received his commission in July 1917. He was killed in an accident on Saturday 20th October 1917 and was subsequently buried at Yatesbury. Because of Military regulations he received no medals.

Far left: the grave of Thomas Herald in Yatesbury All Saints Churchyard.

Left: Australian , Stanley Pilkington died in an accident at Beckhampton.

Private Victor Arthur Bull   *12th Bn Middlesex Regiment*

Service No.	TF235005	Age:	22
Place of Birth:	Walcot, Somerset	Home Country:	England
Date of Death:	23/10/1917	Cause of death:	Killed in action
Memorial:	Calne		
War cemetery:	Tyne Cot Memorial		
Theatre of war:	Belgium		
Next of Kin:	Arthur W Bull & Alice Bull		
Address:	1 Bennetts Cottages, Walcot, Somerset		

Victor volunteered for service with the Somerset Light Infantry but was transferred to the 12th Battalion Middlesex Regiment. He arrived in France with them on the 24th July 1915. He was killed in action on Tuesday 23rd October 1917 at Passchendaele and is remembered on the Tyne Cot Memorial. He has no known grave.

2nd Lieutenant Stanley Howard Pilkington   *2nd Sqdn Australian Flying Corps*

Service No..	N/A	Age:	28
Place of Birth:	Avondale, New Zealand	Home Country:	New Zealand
Date of Death:	24/10/1917	Cause of death:	Accident
Memorial:	Not known		
War cemetery:	Brookwood Military Cemetery		
Theatre of war:	Home		
Next of Kin:	Edmund & Jane Pilkington		
Address:	Avondale, Auckland		

Before the Great War Stanley was employed as a fitter turner. He Joined the Australian Flying Corps as an Air Mechanic on 11th October 1916 at the Show Ground Camp, New South Wales. On 22nd December 1916 he left Melbourne on the Troopship Persic, arriving at Devonport on 3rd March 1917 and was then sent to the Australian Flying Corps Depot at Perham Downs, between Tidworth & Ludgershall. In July 1917 he became a cadet and started his flying training. He graduated as a flying officer and was promoted to the rank of 2nd Lieutenant on 18th October 1917 and was posted to Yatesbury.

On Wednesday 24th October 1917 Stanley took off from Yatesbury Aerodrome, flying towards Avebury. Ploughman Arthur Pearce, in a field near Beckhampton, witnessed the accident;

"About 11 o'clock on the 24th October 1917 I saw a flying machine, about 20 feet high over a field where we were ploughing,, with the engine shut off. The machine suddenly put it's nose down and crashed. I went to the machine and found the pilot quite dead. When the machine fell its nose went straight down into the ground."

A court of inquiry was held and the verdict was Stanley had been flying when his machine nose dived into the ground and he suffered a broken neck, caused by the accident. However, another pilot had flown the same aircraft earlier that day and complained of vibration in the rigging. When the pilot gave his account his last statement said the plane's engine was satisfactory. Other witness's said the aircraft was in good order and no mention was made of the vibration.

The crashed aircraft was examined but was found to be too badly damaged to discover what caused the accident. The engine however was found to be in good order.

Stanley was buried in the Brookwood Military Cemetery in Surrey with full military honours.

Lance Corporal Albert Thomas Taylor		*1st Bn Wiltshire Regiment*	
Service No.	11041	Age:	22
Place of Birth:	Hilmarton, Wiltshire	Home Country:	England
Date of Death:	25/10/1917	Cause of death:	Died of wounds
Memorial:	Hilmarton		
War cemetery:	Bethune Town Cemetery		
Theatre of war:	France		
Next of Kin:	James and Elizabeth Taylor		
Address:	Rose Cottage, Goatacre, Wiltshire		

Albert, known as Tom, had volunteered for service with the 1st Battalion Wiltshire Regiment and arrived in France on 7th April 1915. During 1916 he was wounded and came home to Hilmarton on leave in November 1916. At the beginning of November 1917 Tom's parents received the news that their youngest son had been severely wounded, the information was followed by a letter from a Nursing Sister at a Casualty Clearing Station to which Tom was taken saying he had died of his wounds. Tom's mother then received the following letters from the Officers of Toms section; the Captains letter states;

"Dear Mrs Taylor – I am very sorry to tell you that your son Lance Corporal Taylor died of wounds on the 25th October. He, with four of his friends was wounded on the 23rd October by a shell in the front line. At first I thought that your son was the least badly wounded. He was not in nearly so much pain, and seemed so cheerful through it all. I am afraid there must have been some internal bleeding which we could not see. Of your son, of course, no one could speak too highly. He was a Lance Corporal in charge of a Lewis gun; the shell fell right in the middle of the gun team, wounding all but two. I don't believe there was a man in the company who was more popular with all. His loss to us can never be replaced."

The 2nd Lieutenant wrote;

"I am afraid it is small comfort to you to know that your son did his work well to the last, and even when hit seemed bright and cheerful. He was extremely popular with every one and we shall miss him very much indeed."

A friend who was there when Tom was wounded, writes saying how cheery he was, and that he could, even in his wounded condition, think of others for he promised to send one of his chums some cigarettes from "Blighty."

The Wiltshire at the time were in trenches near Gorre, France and the war diary states;

"23rd. Wounded, 5 other ranks : one of these died on 25th."

The following memoriam appeared in a local paper in November 1918

"In ever loving memory of our dear son

Who was killed in action
Interred in Bethune Town Cemetery

Fondly we loved him he is dear to us still
But in grief we must bend to God's Holy Will
Our Sorrow is Great Our Loss Hard to Bear
But Angels will guard our dear loved one with care

Ever remembered by his sorrowing Mother and Sisters"

Toms brother, John Taylor, died of wounds in India that he had received in Mesopotamia in May 1916.

Tom is buried in Bethune Town Cemetery with over 3,000 casualties of the Great War.

Above: Stretcher bearers in action.

Left: Tom Taylor died of wounds.

Private Frederick George Wheeler   *5th Bn Wiltshire Regiment*

Service No.	7021	Age:	Not known
Place of Birth:	Calne, Wiltshire	Home Country:	England
Date of Death:	26/10/1917	Cause of death:	Died
Memorial:	Calne		
War cemetery:	Amara War Cemetery		
Theatre of war:	Mesopotamia		
Next of Kin:	Annie Wheeler		
Address:	Shelbourne, Calne, Wiltshire		

It is likely Frederick was serving with the Wiltshire Regiment prior to the Great War and he arrived in France on 14th August 1914. It is probable he was wounded during the early part of the war and transferred to the 5th Battalion Wiltshire Regiment.

   He died most likely of illness at one of the Military hospitals at Amara, Iraq and is buried in the cemetery at the same place.

Private Maurice Heath   *2nd Bn RN Div RM Light Infantry*

Service No.	PO/17776	Age:	20
Place of Birth:	Chippenham, Wiltshire	Home Country:	England
Date of Death:	26/10/1917	Cause of death:	Killed in action
Memorial:	East Tytherton Morovian Church		
War cemetery:	Tyne Cot Cemetery		
Theatre of war:	Belgium		
Next of Kin:	Sidney & Kate Heath		
Address:	West Tytherton, Wiltshire		

At the age of seventeen years, seven months and twenty eight days Maurice, a farm labourer, volunteered for service with his brother Fred on the 9th September 1914 at Bristol, arriving in France on 19th May 1917.

   On Friday 26th October 1917 Maurice was in the front line and at 5.40am his battalion attacked a German position directly to the front, all the objectives were gained and consolidated. The 2nd Battalion Royal Marines suffered 308 casualties.

   Maurice was one of those listed as missing and as his parents prepared for Christmas 1917 they received the news that their 5th son had been killed in action at Passchendaele. He has no known grave and is remembered on the Tyne Cot Memorial.

   His brother Fred was to die in November 1918 when H.M.S. Britania was torpedoed by a German Submarine.

Private Reginald Alfred Freegard   *2nd Bn Devonshire Regiment*

Service No.	30939	Age:	19
Place of Birth:	Sutton Benger, Wiltshire	Home Country:	England
Date of Death:	27/10/1917	Cause of death:	Killed in action
Memorial:	Bremhill - Foxham - East Tytherton Morovian Church		
War cemetery:	Lancashire Cottage Cemetery		
Theatre of war:	Belgium		
Next of Kin:	William & Sophia Freegard		
Address:,	Foxham, Wiltshire		

Reginald was a rural postman and was well known in the Foxham area. It is likely he was conscripted into the army in late 1916 and sent to Exmouth, Devon for training. He was sent to France in July 1917 and was killed in action on Saturday 27th October 1917.

The Chaplain, who buried Reginald beside two of his comrades who were killed at the same time by the same shell, wrote the following to Reginald's mother;

"The men were in a Lewis gun position and the shell burst in the middle of them, killing all three on the spot. One consolation is he did not suffer for an instant. Another consolation is that he died doing his duty, and doing it well, and has gone to join the noble army of men who have given their lives for the good of humanity."

The Corporal of the platoon wrote to Reginald's sister;

"Your brother was killed by the concussion of the shell as he had only a slight wound on his leg. He had been in my section of bombers all the time until last week, he was taken from me and put in the machine gun section, so as one of my old boys I knew him well. I always considered him one of the best in my section and for digging a bit of trench he was the master piece. You should be quite proud of Reg; he was a brave lad. He and four others were with me in a tight corner, but came through safe, so I knew his worth. He was quiet, reliable, and fond of you and home, also his girl."

Miss Hillier, Reginald's fiancée, received two letters, one from the Company Sergeant Major and the other from a private, one of Reginald's pals. The former stated that;

"Reginald was well liked by the company and was admired by all the officers and N.C.O's. for his great coolness under fire. He would have done well if he had pulled through this terrible war."

His comrade also wrote to Miss Hillier;

"Bare your loss bravely and remember that he died fighting for you and he will be sadly missed by us all in the company, but much more so you and his dear mother."

In October 1918 the following memoriam was inserted in the local paper;

"In loving memory of Reg
A few more struggles here
A few more partings o'er
A few more tolls a few more tears
And we shall weep no more
Father, Mother, Sisters and Brother at Foxham"

31st OCTOBER 1917 – BRITISH OCCUPY BEERSHEBA, PALESTINE

Chief Petty Off. Geoffrey Charlton Paine Rumming   Royal Navel Air Service

Service No.	F/813	Age:	29
Place of Birth:	Purton, Wiltshire	Home Country:	England
Date of Death:	04/11/1917	Cause of death:	Died of wounds
Memorial:	Calne - Calne Methodist Chapel - Calstone & Blacklands		
War cemetery:	Calne Curzon Street Cemetery		
Theatre of war:	Home		
Next of Kin:	William T P & Mary N Rumming		
Address:	Capenor, Portishead, Somerset		

Above: Armoured cars in crude garages to hide them from the Turks.

Top: A depiction of armoured cars in Gallipoli.

Right: Geoff Rumming proudly displays his CGM.

Geoff was educated at the Calne Secondary School and upon leaving he was employed as a miller. He was the only son of William & Mary Rumming of Quemerford Mill, where he worked for his father for four years and later held a position at Holbeach, Lincolnshire. On the 27th October 1914 Geoff enlisted as an air mechanic with the Royal Naval Air Service. He transferred to the Royal Navel Motor Armed Car Section, was promoted to Petty Officer and embarked from Devonport in March 1915.

During the landings at Gallipoli in 1915 Geoff, who was a member of No 3 Armoured Car Squadron, was detached with some other men of the squadron, they were to provide cover for the landing forces leaving the SS River Clyde. They had removed the Maxim guns from the armoured cars and had built barricades on the decks of the SS River Clyde to act as cover.

When the River Clyde was beached at V beach near Helles point, Gallipoli, on 24th April 1915 the landing forces were met with devastating fire. Geoff and the men of the Royal Naval Air Service were beginning to expend their ammunition. Sub Lieutenant Tisdall, who was Geoff's commanding officer, heard wounded men on the beach calling for assistance. After jumping in the water Tisdall pushed a boat in front of himself to the beach. He managed to ferry many wounded back to the SS River Clyde with the help of Geoff and three seamen. Another four or five trips were made.

Writing to his parents from Gallipoli on 30th April 1915 Geoff states;

"You will be glad to know that the commander has recommended me for the VC for bringing away a few wounded under fire."

Sub Lieutenant Tisdall was killed in May at Gallipoli, in 1916. He was posthumously awarded the Victoria Cross and Geoff and two of the seaman were awarded the Conspicuous

Gallantry Medal. Geoff was also promoted to Chief Petty Officer and received his medal in August 1915.

While in action with the first attack on Gallipoli made by armoured cars at Krithia on 4th June 1915, Geoff was shot in the head. In the same action Frederick Curtis, one of those who had taken part in the rescue on the day of the landings, was listed as missing in action. Geoff was severely wounded and evacuated to the Royal Navel Hospital, Chatham. He made a rapid recovery but a few months later Geoff again had problems with his wound and he returned to Chatham for a further operation. His Surgeon, the eminent Sir Watson Cheyne, performed the operation and again Geoff made a quick recovery. However, he was now suffering from epilepsy and was ultimately discharged from the Royal Navy on 3rd October 1915, being unfit for further service.

The Navy's Armoured Car Sections were disbanded in 1916 and Geoff decided to apply for a commission in the Machine Gun Corps. Being accepted he he was sent to an officers training camp at Gailes, Scotland. He was there for only one month when his condition once more developed and he became a patient in the Stobhill Hospital, Glasgow. While he was there Major Pringle performed a very skilful operation and Geoff was discharged from hospital in January 1917, and returned to Quemerford. After a while however Geoff's condition began to deteriorate and a further medical examination became necessary. He returned to Stobhill, where it was found medical skill could do no more than it had done to prolong his life, and the end came on Sunday 4th November 1917.

Geoff's body was returned to his parents and a service was held at the Primitive Methodist Chapel. He was buried in Curzon Street Cemetery which was the nonconformist cemetery in Calne. The coffin was covered with a number of wreaths of white flowers, and several wounded soldiers from the Calne Red Cross Hospital followed the coffin, along with many tradesmen and friends.

In 1918 Geoff posthumously received the Medaille Militaire, presented by the French republic for his bravery in Gallipoli.

Geoff Rummings grave displaying his conspicuous Gallantry Medal in Curzon Street Cemetery.

6th NOVEMBER 1917 – PASSCHENDAELE WAS CAPTURED, BRINGING TO AN END THE THIRD BATTLE OF YPRES, BELGIUM

Private Frederick Henley   *12th Somerset Light Infantry*

Service No.	36518	Age:	26
Place of Birth:	Calne, Wiltshire	Home Country:	England
Date of Death:	06/11/1917	Cause of death:	Killed in action
Memorial:	Calne		
War cemetery:	Beersheba War Cemetery		
Theatre of war:	Palestine		
Next of Kin:	Henry & Kate Henley		
Address:	11 North Street, Calne, Wiltshire		

Frederick, a baker, joined the 12th Battalion Somerset Light Infantry by registering for the Derby Scheme or was conscripted. He was killed in action on Tuesday 6th November 1917 during an attack east of the railway and south of the town of Tel es Sheria in modern day Israel while fighting Turkish forces.

He is buried in the Beersheba War Cemetery, in modern day Israel, with over 1,100 casualties of the Great War.

Private Percival John Hacker   *1st Bn Devonshire Regiment*

Service No.	205147	Age:	23
Place of Birth:	Hilmarton, Wiltshire	Home Country:	England
Date of Death:	06/11/1917	Cause of death:	Killed in action
Memorial:	Nettleton		
War cemetery:	Hooge Crater Cemetery		
Theatre of war:	Belgium		
Next of Kin:	Eli & Elizabeth Hacker		
Address:	Keeper's Cottage, West Kington, Wiltshire		

Percy was a cowman and carter employed at Fosse Farm. He was conscripted in late 1916 and originally joined the Dorset Regiment before being transferred to the Wiltshire Regiment and then to the 1st Battalion Devonshire Regiment. He was killed in action on Tuesday 6th November during the 2nd Battle of Passchendaele; the same day the Canadians captured the Passchendaele village. Thirty one member of the 1st Battalion Devonshire Regiment were killed on the same day.

He is buried in Hooge Crater Cemetery with nearly 6000 casualties of the Great War; his brother Ernest had been killed at the Somme in October 1916.

7th NOVEMBER 1917 - BRITISH CAPTURE GAZA

Gunner Fred Cleverley Robbins   *123rd Siege Bty RGA*

Service No.	63186	Age:	27
Place of Birth:	Bremhill, Wiltshire	Home Country:	England
Date of Death:	12/11/1917	Cause of death:	Died of wounds
Memorial:	Bremhill - Foxham - East Tytherton Morovian Church		
War cemetery:	Level Crossing Cemetery Fampoux		
Theatre of war:	France		
Next of Kin:	Albert Esau Cleverly Robbins & Mary Ann Robbins		
Address:	East Tytherton, Wiltshire		

Fred was a grocers assistant and joined the Royal Garrison Artillery by registering for the Derby Scheme or was conscripted. He died of wounds on Monday 12th November 1917, most likely as a result of German shellfire when his battery was based in the area of Fampoux east of Arras, France.

He is buried in the Level Crossing Cemetery, Fampoux, with over 400 casualties of the Great War.

17th NOVEMBER 1917 - BRITISH CAPTURE JAFFA

Sergeant John Alfred Gingell		*1/4th Bn TF Wiltshire Regiment*	
Service No.	200353	Age:	31
Place of Birth:	Calne, Wiltshire	Home Country:	England
Date of Death:	22/11/1917	Cause of death:	Killed in action
Memorial:	Calne		
War cemetery:	Jerusalem War Cemetery		
Theatre of war:	Egypt		
Next of Kin:	Emma Gingell (wife); John & Emma Gingell (parents)		
Address:	1 Back Row, London Road, Calne; 93 London Road, Calne		

John, a woodcutter, was the only son of John & Emma Gingell. He married Emma Dennis in the winter of 1910 and was a territorial soldier belonging to the Wiltshire Regiment at the outbreak of war. Territorial units had been created to be a home defence force and most were initially used for garrison duties in 1914, but as the war progressed a lack of fighting units meant they were used as regular fighting troops.

The 1/4th Battalion sailed from Southampton for garrison duties in India arriving at Bombay on 9th November 1914, where they remained for 3 years. In September 1917 they were moved to Egypt for front line duties against the Turkish forces.

At the end of January 1918 Emma Gingell, Johns wife, received the following letter from the Chaplain of the 12th Bn Somerset Light Infantry who were serving with the Wiltshires:

"On November 22nd the Somersets, assisted by a company of the Wilts Regiment attacked a precipitous hill about 3,000 yards due north of the village of Beit Izza north west of Jerusalem. The Natural difficulties in climbing such a hill were great in themselves, quite apart from shell and machine gun fire. Nevertheless our boys advanced and almost reached the summit when they were held up in a depression quite near the top by deadly accuracy of the fire of the enemy sharp shooters. Our men had to remain under cover until the evening. Your dear husband was shot by an enemy marksman. At dark we recovered their bodies and buried them a few hundred feet below on the hill they had so gallantly held. He lies in truly holy ground almost within sight of Jerusalem. He died as he lived, a brave and true man who worthily led men under his command."

Captain Pye Smith, John's company officer, having been in hospital at Giza, Cairo only heard of his death on the report of another sergeant from the front, some day's after it happened. He wrote to Emma Gingell expressing his sympathy and said;

"I had the privilege and pleasure of serving with your husband, and latterly commanding him, sometime before we left India. I had known him ever since the regiment was in Plymouth at the outbreak of the war, and I always respected him as a man of great and true worth and

an example to all about him and we feel his loss deeply."

John left a wife and two children. He is now buried in Jerusalem War Cemetery, his grave being relocated after the war, with nearly 2,500 other casualties of the Great War.

Chaplain 4th Class Oswald Addenbrooke Holden CF 60th Infantry Bde

Service No.	N/A	Age:	43
Place of Birth:	Kingwinford, Worcestershire	Home Country:	England
Date of Death:	01/12/1917	Cause of death:	Killed in action
Memorial:	Blacklands - Calstone & St. Bartholomew's Church Penn.		
War cemetery:	Fifteen Ravine British Cemetery Villiers Plouich		
Theatre of war:	France		
Next of Kin:	Ella Mary Holden (wife); Oswald Mangin & Henrietta Holden (parents)		
Address:	Penn Cot, Cooden Drive, Bexhill on Sea, Sussex; Gailey Vicarage, Staffs		

Oswald was the rector of Calstone Williangton with Blacklands from 1902 to 1907. He was the son of Oswald Mangin Holden who was the Vicar of Steeple Langford and later of Weston Super Mare. He was born in 1874 in Kingswinford, where his father was beneficed; he was educated at Rossall and Exeter College, Oxford, where he took honours in Classics, Moderstions and Theology. At the turn of the century 1900 Oswald married Ella Mary Beresford who received a letter from the senior chaplain. There had been terrific fighting on the front where he was serving, he said;

"On Saturday morning Mr Holden set off with a Nonconformist padre in his brigade to get up to his men and look after the wounded. As they were wending their way along a shell pitched right into the trench and they were both killed instantaneously, without suffering. They were buried together at once by an officer at the spot and later a colleague went up and took a funeral service."

The Bishop of Litchfield, speaking at Oswald's memorial service, testified to the devotion of Mr Holden to his many-sided work in the parish and to the esteem and affection in which he was held. Even in the farthest confines of the parish, he said;

"He was known for his self sacrifice and zeal."

The Rev. F R Barry D.S.O and the Senior Chaplain in the division paid tribute to Oswald stating;

"Both in his ministry at home and on active service Mr Holden won the love and admiration of all who knew him, and his genuineness, humility and devotion influenced all who came in touch with him. He was a remarkably fine preacher, and his sermons made deep impressions on his brigade, by who he was greatly loved and revered. All through his time at the front he had been regardless of danger and discomfort, always living with his battalion when in the line, welcomed in every kind of circumstances: though rather older than most chaplains at the front he always refused to consider himself at all and set the most splendid example to his men as well as his brother chaplains. He was a tower of strength, with a gentleness of real power. Wherever he went one felt the presence of his Master."

Oswald left a widow and two little boys, one four and one of two. He is buried in Fifteen Ravine British Cemetery Villiers Plouich with over 500 casualties of the Great War.

Rifleman Walter John Cook Brittain   *16th Bn Kings Royal Rifle Corps*

Service No.	C/1591	Age:	20
Place of Birth:	Foxham, Wiltshire	Home Country:	England
Date of Death:	02/12/1917	Cause of death:	Killed in action
Memorial:	Bremhill - Foxham - East Tytherton Morovian Church		
War cemetery:	Passchendaele New Cemetery		
Theatre of war:	Belgium		
Next of Kin:	William & Emma Brittain		
Address:	Foxham, Wiltshire		

Twenty year old Walter joined the 16th Battalion Kings Royal Rifle Corps by registering for the Derby Scheme or was conscripted. He was the youngest son of William and Emma Brittain of Foxham. William was wounded in the leg and foot at the Somme in August 1916 and after spending some time in the 3rd Western General Hospital at Cardiff once he had recovered he returned to action.

   He was killed in action near Passchendaele village on Sunday 2nd December 1915 and is buried in Passchendaele New Cemetery with over 500 casualties of the Great War.

Private Walter Angell   *5th Bn Wiltshire Regiment*

Service No.	25866	Age:	32
Place of Birth:	Calne, Wiltshire	Home Country:	England
Date of Death:	05/12/1917	Cause of death:	Killed in action
Memorial:	Calne		
War cemetery:	Basra Memorial		
Theatre of war:	Mesopotamia		
Next of Kin:	Lily Angel(wife); Harry & Mary Angell (parents)		
Address:	Mile Elm, Calne, Wiltshire; 15 Victoria Terrace, Calne		

Walter was a bacon curers labourer at Harris & Co in Calne. He was the second son of Harry & Mary Angell and in 1912 he married Lily Butler. He joined the 5th Battalion Wiltshire Regiment by registering for the Derby Scheme or was conscripted.

   At 6.45am on Wednesday 5th December 1917 the Wiltshires were to attack Turkish Positions at Kara Tepe in Mesopotamia. They advanced in Artillery formation through the foothills under constant Turkish shrapnel fire. They captured and occupied the ridges taking 9 prisoners. The Wiltshires casualties were 24 wounded and 4 killed. One of those killed in action was Walter. Walter's wife and parents inserted the following memoriam:

> *Alas a bullet laid him low*
> *While fighting for his native land*
> *And thus the one we loved so well*
> *Lies buried in that far off Land*
> *So far from home but loved so well*
> *How much we miss him none can tell*
> *But god in love has thought it best*
> *To take our loved one home to rest*

Walter is remembered on the Basra Memorial and has no known grave.

9th DECEMBER 1917 - JERUSALEM SURRENDERS TO BRITISH FORCES

9
1918

Guardsman Reginald Herbert George Jones

Service No.	28589
Place of Birth:	Derry Hill, Wiltshire
Date of Death:	01/01/1918
Memorial:	Derry Hill
War cemetery:	Etretat Churchyard Extension
Theatre of war:	France
Next of Kin:	George & Sarah Annie Jones
Address:	New Road, Studley, Wiltshire

2nd Bn Grenadier Guards

Age:	23
Home Country:	England
Cause of death:	Died of wounds

Reginald joined the 2nd Battalion Grenadier Guards by registering for the Derby Scheme or was conscripted. He was wounded in the fighting of late 1917 and evacuated to No.2 Presbyterian USA, Base Hospital Unit, Etretat, North of Le Harve, where he died on new years day 1918. He is buried in Etretat Churchyard Extension with nearly 300 casualties from the Great War.

Captain Arthur Raymond Marshall

Service No:	N/A
Place of Birth:	Mussooree, India
Date of Death:	02/02/1918
Memorial:	Yatesbury
War cemetery:	St Sever Cemetery Extension Rouen
Theatre of war:	France
Next of Kin:	Charles & Lucy Marshall
Address:	Yatesbury

34th Bde Royal Garrison Artillery

Age:	27
Home Country:	England
Cause of death:	Died of wounds

Arthur volunteered and enlisted with the Deal Battalion Royal Marines on the 21st September 1914 where he attained the rank of Corporal with the divisional engineers. He served at Gallipoli from the day of the landings until December 1915 when he was evacuated sick with a fever.

He returned to the Marines on 26th January 1916. He was offered a commission and in September 1916 he returned to England, transferred to the Royal Engineers and became a 2nd Lieutenant on 19th December 1916. On the 8th January 1917 he joined the Royal Garrison Artillery and was promoted to the Rank of Captain, Arthur was attached to 34th Brigade.

He was mortally wounded during a reconnaissance on December 8th 1917 and succumbed to his wounds on Saturday 2nd February 1918 at one of the Military hospitals at Rouen.

Driver Edwin Minty   *20th Bde Royal Horse Artillery*
Service No.   206585   Age: 27
Place of Birth: Lacock, Wiltshire   Home Country: England
Date of Death: 05/02/1918   Cause of death: Died
Memorial: Bremhill - Foxham - East Tytherton Morovian Church
War cemetery: Deir El Belah War Cemetery
Theatre of war: Egypt
Next of Kin: Myra Grace Minty (wife); John Francis & Mary Jane Minty (parents)
Address: The Bakery, Bremhill, Wiltshire; Hare Street Farm, East Tytherton

It is likely Edwin, known as Ted, was conscripted into the Royal Horse Artillery. He married Myra Fry at Calne in 1917, just prior to leaving for Egypt. He died most likely due to disease at the 69th General Hospital at the town of Deir el Belah on the Egypt Israel border, which was the site of a large British camp. He is buried in the cemetery that bears the same name as the town, with over 700 casualties of the Great War.

Lieutenant John Thomas Gibson   *Royal Flying Corps*
Service No: N/A   Age: 28
Place of Birth: Marysville, Canada   Home Country: Canada
Date of Death: 10/02/1918   Cause of death: Accident
Memorial: Not known
War cemetery: Yatesbury All Saints Churchyard
Theatre of war: Home
Next of Kin: Alexander & Charlotte J. Gibson
Address: Fredericton, New Brunswick

John was educated in Marysville School and Fredericton High School in Canada. He then studied Civil Engineering at the University of New Brunswick and, after he graduated in 1910, accepted a position with Dominion Public Works Department, St. John. He joined the 71st regiment in 1906, and when he enlisted in the regular army in 1916 he was offered a commission and promoted to lieutenant. In September 1916 he was appointed recruiting officer for the counties of Kings and Sunbury, which position he filled until January 1917. In

Left: John Gibson.

Far left: John Gibson's grave in Yatesbury All Saints Churchyard.

June of that year he was granted a cadetship in the Royal Flying Corps. He sailed for England on the 1st September, with a detachment of the Canadian Air Force, passed all the tests successfully and was posted to Yatesbury.

On Sunday 10th February 1918, John was making a "solo" flight in the vicinity of Yatesbury Aerodrome when he made a bad landing. He took to the air again, and rose properly, but whilst doing a sharp turn to the left he lost flying speed and crashed to earth. He was found to be unconscious and was taken to the camp hospital where he died soon afterwards, having suffered a fractured skull. He was buried with full military honours at Yatesbury All Saints churchyard.

2nd Lieutenant Walter Sondheim		*16th Sqdn Royal Flying Corps*	
Service No.	N/A	Age:	20
Place of Birth:	South Africa	Home Country:	South Africa
Date of Death:	04/03/1918	Cause of death:	Accident
Memorial:	King Edward VII School & Ferreira Deep Ltd Memorial Johannesburg		
War cemetery:	Yatesbury All Saints Churchyard		
Theatre of war:	Home		
Next of Kin:	S & Ada Sondheim		
Address:	17 West Park Flats, Westcliffe, Johannesburg, Transvaal		

Walter was educated at King Edward VII School, Johannesburg and on leaving was employed by Ferreira Deep Ltd, a mining company based in Johannesburg. He traveled to England and on 10th October 1917 received a commission with the Royal Flying Corps.

During the afternoon of Monday 4th March 1918 Walter had taken off from Yatesbury aerodrome, and was flying in the surroundings of Stanton St.Bernard. At about three O'clock some workers on Mr W. J. Read's farm saw Walter's machine come down rapidly in a field. It was obvious that something was wrong and the people hurried to the spot with the view of rendering assistance. Upon their arrival they found that the machine was enveloped in flames and the pilot was so pinned beneath the machine that it was impossible to get at him. It was obvious he was dead and it was subsequently found that the body was considerably injured by fire. The machine was upside down when it fell, which probably caused the petrol to ignite, and the plane was completely destroyed. A party of airmen arrived from Upavon, and Walters remains were taken to the Central Flying school. Walter is buried at Yatesbury All Saints Churchyard.

Right: The Ferreira memorial in Johannesburg.

Far Right: Walter Sondheim's grave at Yatesbury All Saints Churchyard.

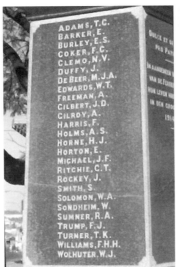

Corporal Roland George Manners		*13th Bn Kings Royal Rifle Corps*	
Service No.	R/1770	Age:	23
Place of Birth:	Calne, Wiltshire	Home Country:	England
Date of Death:	09/03/1918	Cause of death:	Killed in action
Memorial:	Calne		
War cemetery:	Tyne Cot Memorial		
Theatre of war:	Belgium		
Next of Kin:	Fred & Emma Manners		
Address:	Curzon Street, Calne, Wiltshire		

Roland was a grocer. He volunteered for service with the 13th Service Battalion Kings Royal Rifle Corps and arrived in France on 21st July 1915. He was killed in action along with 2 other men from his battalion on Saturday 9th March 1918 while on duty on the Ypres front line, most likely near Polderhoek Chateau. He is remembered on the Tyne Cot Memorial.

Gunner Charles William Gingell		*15th Bde Royal Horse Artillery*	
Service No.	212624	Age:	29
Place of Birth:	Goatacre, Wiltshire	Home Country:	England
Date of Death:	16/03/1918	Cause of death:	Killed in action
Memorial:	Hilmarton		
War cemetery:	Ypres Reservoir Cemetery		
Theatre of war:	Belgium		
Next of Kin:	Emily Gingell (wife); Arthur & Eliza Gingell (parents)		
Address:	Beacon Hill, Goatacre, Wiltshire		

Above: Charles William Gingells grave in 1938.

Right: Charles William Gingell.

Charles had lived in Goatacre all his life. In the years of his youth he was a scholar at the Goatacre Primitive Methodist Sunday School and later he was a teacher; he was also an active member of the congregation. In the spring of 1913 Charles married Emily King at Calne. He was drafted to the Warwickshire Royal Horse Artillery and after a period of training he was to go to the continent. In April 1918 news reached Goatacre of the death of Charles in Belgium. Emily received a letter from Charles's Commanding officer, who wrote;

"I am writing to offer you the heartfelt sympathy of all the officers and men of the battery. Your husband is a great loss to us all, particularly to my section and myself, to which he belonged. He was equally good up at the gun line or with the horses at the wagon line. It was at the latter that I particularly appreciated him. It made no difference whether they were his own horses or somebody else's: he did them equally well".

She also received a letter from the Battery Quarter Master Sergeant, who wrote:

"Your husband was killed during a heavy bombardment whilst standing at the look-out to see if the infantry were in need of help. A shell passed through the sandbag wall and burst straight behind, killing him instantly. The boys brought his body down, and he was buried by the Chaplain in the presence of his Commanding Officer and comrades. Your husband was always cheerful and was a wonderful man to work with, and we all grieve very much at his loss, and sympathise with you in your bereavement".

Charles left a widow and two children. He is buried at Ypres Reservoir Cemetery with over 1500 casualties of the Great War.

21st MARCH 1918 – THE GERMANS LAUNCH THEIR SPRING OFFENSIVE CODE NAMED KAISERSCHLACT

Private Frederick Joseph Park

Service No.	29454
Place of Birth:	Calne, Wiltshire
Date of Death:	21/03/1918
Memorial:	Calne
War cemetery:	Pozieres Memorial
Theatre of war:	France
Next of Kin:	William Henry & Eliza Park
Address:	57 London Road, Calne

6th Bn Somerset Light Infantry

Age:	19
Home Country:	England
Cause of death:	Killed in action

It is likely nineteen year old Frederick was conscripted into the 6th Service Battalion Somerset Light Infantry.

On Thursday 21st March 1918 the Germans launched a spring offensive called Kaiserschlacht. The offensive became possible with the removal of Russia from the war and this enabled the Germans to redeploy 40 Divisions from the Eastern to Western Front. The Somersets were part of the 14th Light division and were one of the British units to feel the brunt of the attack. Between 21st March and the 4th April 1918 the 14th Light Division suffered nearly 6,00 casualties and were withdrawn from the line on the 6th April, most likely fighting at the Battle of St Quentin.

Frederick was one of 60 men of the 6th Somersets killed on that day. He is remembered on the Pozieres Memorial France.

CSM Walter John Morley   *2nd Bn Royal Dublin Fusiliers*
Service No.   10700   Age: 26
Place of Birth: Calne, Wiltshire   Home Country: England
Date of Death: 21/03/1918   Cause of death: Killed in action
Memorial: Not Known
War cemetery: Pozieres Memorial
Theatre of war: France
Next of Kin: Charles Morley (uncle)
Address: Calne, Wiltshire

Walter was a professional regular soldier. He arrived in France on 3rd May 1915 and would have taken part in many major battles. By 1918 he had risen through the ranks and was a Company Sergeant Major. He was killed on Thursday 21st March 1918 during the Battle of St. Quentin during the German offensive. The 2nd Battalion Royal Dublin Fusiliers were part of the 16th Irish Division which sustained over 7,000 casualties during this period.

   Walter was one of over 100 members of the 2nd Battalion Royal Dublin Fusiliers to be killed on this day, and has no known grave.

Private Frederick Watson Carpenter   *7th Bn Somerset Light Infantry*
Service No.   39577   Age: 24
Place of Birth: Calne, Wiltshire   Home Country: England
Date of Death: 22/03/1918   Cause of death: Killed in action
Memorial: Calne
War cemetery: Pozieres Memorial
Theatre of war: France
Next of Kin: Josphn & Sarah E Carpenter
Address: Calne, Wiltshire

Frederick had been a drapery assistant working at Wigston Magna, Leicestershire. He enlisted in 1914, most likely in the 1/4th Battalion Wiltshire Regiment and served in India. He was then transferred to the 7th Service Battalion Somerset Light Infantry.

   He was killed in action on Friday 22nd March 1918 at the Battle of St. Quentin during the German offensive. Frederick was one of 22 members of the 7th Somersets to be killed on this day, and has no known grave.

Private Herbert William Hillier   *1st Bn Wiltshire Regiment*
Service No.   13972   Age: 20
Place of Birth: Calne, Wiltshire   Home Country: England
Date of Death: 22/03/1918   Cause of death: Killed in action
Memorial: Calne
War cemetery: Arras Memorial
Theatre of war: France
Next of Kin: George & Elizabeth Kate Hillier
Address: 4 Victoria Terrace, Calne

Twenty year old Herbert was probably conscripted into the 1st Battalion Wiltshire Regiment. On Friday 22nd March 1918 the Wiltshires were at east of Fremicourt near Arras, France. The weather was fine but cold at night. The Wiltshires were waiting to come into contact with the German advance. Herbert was one of seven victims of German shelling and he has no known grave.

Above: Albert Vinson.

Left : Albert Vinson ready for flying at Yatesbury aerodrome.

Captain Albert Higgs Vinson		*13th Sqdn Royal Flying Corps*	
Service No.	N/A	Age:	21
Place of Birth:	Belvedere, Kent	Home Country:	England
Date of Death:	22/03/1918	Cause of death:	Accident
Memorial:	Mill Hill School Gate of Honour		
War cemetery:	Erith Brook Street Cemetery		
Theatre of war:	Home		
Next of Kin:	Nora E Vinson (wife); Albert Vinson & Mrs. A. M. Vinson (parents)		
Address:	Sheepcote Farm, St Mary Cray, Kent		

Albert was the eldest son of Albert Vinson, J.P educated at Mill Hill School, London and was a member of Burton Bank House. He was a Senior Monitor and in the 1stXV and 1st XI for Hockey. While at school he joined the Officer Training School. He Left Mill Hill in 1915 and in March 1916 obtained a lieutenancy in the Royal Flying Corps. He qualified as a pilot on the 22nd May 1916 in a Maurice Farman biplane at the Military School at Catterick Bridge. He arrived in France on 12th July 1917, was promoted to Lieutenant and then Captain. While on the continent he was mentioned in dispatches.

Albert was attached to 13th Training Squadron at Yatesbury and in February 1918 he married Nora E Williams at Calne. On Friday 22nd March 1918 he was flying as an instructor with Edward Leadbetter-Gray, they ascended to about 200 feet over the aerodrome, when something went wrong. The machine nose dived and crashed to earth, instructor and student were killed instantaneously. It is thought he was killed when the pupil fell across the controls. An extract from a letter from Captain Hyne of the Royal Flying Corps Yatesbury states;

"If ever a chap was loved by everyone who knew him that Boy was . . . . , in all my service, I never saw the like of it. He has left an irreplaceable gap in the squadron."

He had only been married six weeks before his death and is buried in Erith Brook Street Cemetery.

2nd Lieutenant Edward Leadbetter-Gray		*13th Sqdn Royal Flying Corps*	
Service No.	N.A	Age:	21
Place of Birth:	Not known	Home Country:	England
Date of Death:	22/03/1918	Cause of death:	Accident
Memorial:	Not known		
War cemetery:	Mordington Burial Ground		
Theatre of war:	Home		
Next of Kin:	Edward & Annabella Gray		
Address:	Edrington Castle, Berwick on Tweed, Northumberland		

Edward was commissioned in January 1918 as a 2nd Lieutenant and was killed in training while flying as a student with Albert Vinson. His body was returned to his parents and he is buried in Mordington Burial Ground. Because of his length of service in the army he received no medals.

Lieutenant Walter Earl Carter		*Royal Flying Corps*	
Service No.	N/A	Age:	25
Place of Birth:	Edmonton, Alberta	Home Country:	Canada
Date of Death:	22/03/1918	Cause of death:	Accident
Memorial:	Not known		
War cemetery:	Yatesbury All Saints Churchyard		
Theatre of war:	Home		
Next of Kin:	Charles & Matilda Carter		
Address:	1033 France -15th Street, Edmonton, Alberta		

Walter, a bank clerk, volunteered for service on the 25 September 1914 with the Canadian Expeditionary Force. He Transferred to the Royal Flying in Corps and was sent to Yatesbury. He died on Friday 22 March 1918, while flying over Yatesbury aerodrome. His machine fell to earth and he was killed instantly.

Above: A British aircraft.

Right: The grave of Walter Carter in Yatesbury All Saints Churchyard.

Sergeant Carol James Pocock   *6th Bn Wiltshire Regiment*

Service No.	203177	Age:	23
Place of Birth:	Heddington, Wiltshire	Home Country:	England
Date of Death:	23/03/1918	Cause of death:	Killed in action
Memorial:	Heddington		
War cemetery:	Arras Memorial		
Theatre of war:	France		
Next of Kin:	Harry James L & Bertha Anne Pocock		
Address:	Stockley, Wiltshire		

Carol worked for his father at Lower Farm, Heddington. He volunteered for service and arrived in France on 7th December 1917 with the Wiltshire Yeomanry. On 20th September 1917 the Wiltshire Yeomanry was amalgamated with the 6th Service Battalion Wiltshire Regiment, which became the 6th Royal Wiltshire Yeomanry Battalion.

On Saturday 23rd March 1918 the Wiltshires were facing the German advance in trenches near Morchies, north east of Baupaume, France. The war diary states;

"The stand made by the Battalion at MORCHIES from 4p.m on the 22nd March to 5p.m on the 23rd and all that it meant, is a glorious episode in the history of the Wiltshire Regiment. It is a heroic record of self sacrifice stemming the victorious rush of a superior enemy and a model lesson of a rearguard fight. The subsequent retirement from FREMICOURT through BAPAUME to GREVILLERS and thence to BAYENCOURT was only one endless and stubborn fight. Suffice it to say that only one Officer, 1 Sergeant, and 18 Other Ranks came out the struggle, and that officer had also been wounded."

At 4pm on 22nd March 1918 the Germans attacked from the North East, British troops were holding the line between Morchies and Crucifix. The weight of the German attack then forced these British troops to fall back on the Wiltshires positions. The Germans continued to advance and the Wiltshires fired on them at 1200 yards forcing the enemy to take cover in lower ground. At 5pm British tanks counter attacked forcing the Germans to withdraw and at 8pm an advance post near Morchies, occupied by the Wiltshires was raided by a German patrol from the village. This was subsequently repulsed leaving one German dead. The remainder of the night was quiet.

On the 23rd March patrols were sent out and they reported that the Germans were occupying the former British line between Morchies and Crucifix.

At 8am the Germans continued to advance and the British Artillery began a bombardment but unfortunately they also shelled the Wiltshires Head Quarters. German shell fire now increased on the Wiltshires position and German machine gun fire swept the line making movement difficult.

At 2pm the Germans attacked the Wiltshires position and orders were received at 2.15pm for the Wiltshires to withdraw. Because the Wiltshires were engaged in battle with the Germans a withdraw was considered to be impossible and it was decided to hold on until nightfall and keep the enemy in check until a further line of resistance was organized.

At 4pm the Germans began to get around the flanks of the Wiltshires but they held on for another 30minutes inflicting heavy casualties on the German attackers. But it became necessary for the Wiltshires to withdraw under heavy shell fire and crossfire by German machine guns.

Carol was killed during this action and is remembered on the Arras Memorial. He has no known grave.

Private George Stone   *6th Bn Wiltshire Regiment*

Service No.	204428	Age:	23
Place of Birth:	Calstone, Wiltshire	Home Country:	England
Date of Death:	23/03/1918	Cause of death:	Killed in action
Memorial:	Calne - Calstone & Blacklands		
War cemetery:	Beaumetz Les Cambrai Military Cemetery No 1		
Theatre of war:	France		
Next of Kin:	James & Adelaide Stone		
Address:	Calstone, Wiltshire		

George was a farm labourer. He volunteered for service and arrived in France on 4th December 1917 with the Wiltshire Yeomanry. On 20th September 1917 the Wiltshire Yeomanry was amalgamated with the 6th Service Battalion Wiltshire Regiment, which became the 6th Royal Wiltshire Yeomanry Battalion.

   He was killed in action on Saturday 23rd March 1918, in the same action as Carol Pocock and is buried very near where he fell in Beaumetz Les Cambrai Military Cemetery No 1.

Private Clement James Eatwell   *1st Bn Wiltshire Regiment*

Service No.	33261	Age:	26
Place of Birth:	Bremhill Wick, Wiltshire	Home Country:	England
Date of Death:	24/03/1918	Cause of death:	Killed in action
Memorial:	Bremhill - Foxham - East Tytherton Morovian Church		
War cemetery:	Arras Memorial		
Theatre of war:	France		
Next of Kin:	David & Dinah Eatwell		
Address:	Wick Farm, Bremhill Wick, Wiltshire		

Clement worked for his father on Wick Farm and it is likely he was conscripted into the army joining the 1st Battalion Wiltshire Regiment. On Sunday 24th March 1918 the Wiltshires were East of Fremicourt, which is near Baupaume, France. During the morning the German aeroplanes directed shelling across the whole of the British trench system. The British artillery retaliated but unfortunately a considerable amount of shells fell into the Wiltshires trenches causing many casualties. In the afternoon there was an intense bombardment by the Germans followed by an enemy assault. The German attack failed on the Wiltshires front but an order was received for the Wiltshires to retire. The British battalions on the flanks broke and though they attempted to fall back as ordered they were practically exterminated by German machine gun fire. What was left of the Wiltshires reassembled at Achiet-Le-Petit and consisted of 3 officers and 54 other ranks. The casualties suffered in the fighting up to that date amounted to 413.

   Clement is remembered on the Arras Memorial and has no known grave.

Private Arthur Francis Ponting   *14th Coy Machine Gun Corps*

Service No.	70219	Age:	22
Place of Birth:	Bremhill, Wiltshire	Home Country:	England
Date of Death:	28/03/1918	Cause of death:	Died of wounds
Memorial:	Bremhill - Foxham - East Tytherton Morovian Church		
War cemetery:	Doullens Communal Cemetery Extension No 1		
Theatre of war:	France		
Next of Kin:	Lewis & Annie Maria Ponting		
Address:	Bremhill, Wiltshire		

Arthur, a farm labourer, volunteered for service in 1914 with the Wiltshire Regiment and arrived in France on 7th April 1915. He was wounded in 1915 and again in 1916 and had to undergo a serious operation in the same year on account of a severe strain and he was then badly gassed in 1917.

At some point he transferred to the Machine Gun Corps and was wounded in the German offensive which commenced on the 21st March. He died of wounds on Thursday 28th March 1918 most likely at the Canadian Stationary Hospital at Doullens, France. He is buried in the Doullens Communal Cemetery Extension No 1 with over thirteen hundred casualties of the Great War.

His brother Tom Pointing was to die in September 1918 at Salonika.

Private Percy James Matthews		*8th Hussars*	
Service No.	29767	Age:	27
Place of Birth:	Foxham, Wiltshire	Home Country:	England
Date of Death:	31/03/1918	Cause of death:	Killed in action
Memorial:	Bremhill - Foxham - East Tytherton Morovian Church		
War cemetery:	Pozieres Memorial		
Theatre of war:	France		
Next of Kin:	Fanny Matthews (wife); John and Emily Matthews (parents)		
Address:	East Tytherton, Wiltshire - Wick Hill, Wilts		

Percy was a farm labourer and in the summer of 1916 he married Fanny Haddrell, and it is likely he was conscripted into the Army joining the 8th Hussars.

He was killed in action on Sunday 31st March 1916 during the German Offensive, he is remembered on the Pozieres Memorial and has no known grave.

9th APRIL 1918 – THE GERMANS LAUNCH THEIR SECOND SPRING OFFENSIVE CODE NAMED GEORGETTE

Walter Weston from Calne survived the war serving with the Warwickshire Regiment, he was 18 years old when he saw his first action, Below is a transcript from him:

"About an hour before dawn the German barrage came down on our line. I hugged the wall of the trenches the high explosives rocked the ground like an earthquake, showers of earth and sand bags fell on us, we clawed at the earth with our bare hand to release two lads who were buried. The din was terrific, the blast flashes from the shells and choking cordite fumes made it difficult to breathe. I thought, my god will this never end, at this moment I new the meaning of fear. The barrage continued until it was almost light, and then it ceased suddenly.

Immediately I heard our Sergeant Wilkins shout, Jerry's coming, we scrambled to what was left of our position, I took one look, and could see in the distance men advancing, - what to do next - it was then I noticed Mason my pal - good old Mason - he was calmly placing clips of ammo in a little hollow in front of him, he gestured me to do the same.

Now the shelling had stopped I felt better, and settled down with those who were left in our bay. It is difficult to describe one's feelings as you see Germans advancing for the first time. Officers Shouted "Hold your Fire", but they seemed awfully close, - at last, - when they were some 150 yards away, came the order "Rapid Fire".

One group were making their way to a big gap torn in the wire by the barrage, as Lewis guns and rifles opened up, they began to fall, but others took their place, and soon they stormed through. Everything seemed to happen at once, in the confusion that followed a big Jerry Officer, firing his pistol, was right on our parapet. Sergeant Wilkins shot him through the head at point blank range, he fell over us into the trench, quivered and lay still. I stopped one as he drew back his arm to throw a stick bomb. Mason drove his bayonet into another as he tried to jump into the trench, another lunged forward and pierced the collar bone of a boy named Clayton, standing next to me, as Clayton fell backwards, the Jerry overbalanced into the trench, Sergeant Patterson promptly smashed his face in with the butt of his rifle, other Jerries tried to force through, but were mown down by machine gun fire. We seemed to be holding them on our immediate front, but our left flank was being overrun. Someone must have had the situation in hand, as in the slight lull on our position, we saw our support company drive forward with fixed bayonets, and force the enemy out.

At this turn of events the Germans withdrew, but not for long. He started another attack, as he did so our artillery opened up with shrapnel over the enemy line, preventing a second wave following the first, this made our task easier, we were able to prevent them making headway, in fact a number surrendered and came towards our line with hands raised. The attack petered out, and we were able to get a little respite.

About twenty Germans came in having had enough. They were soon put to work taking our wounded to the dressing station. I did what I could for Clayton, he had lost a lot of blood. I made a pad from his field dressing, but the bayonet had gone right through, and he needed more attention, so was packed off down the line.

Now began the work of making our position habitable - what a mess. First, the dead Jerries were tossed over the back of the trench, and those that were able began to restore the parapet, taking care not to expose ourselves too much. Our section were lucky, only three wounded, the bay to our right had two killed, four wounded, Sergeant Gayton had a nasty bayonet thrust right through his thigh. The bay on our left had not taken part in the fighting, they had taken a direct hit during the bombardment. The bay was a shambles, of the ten men in there, two lay shattered, with flesh ripped from there bones. Half lying,, half sitting on the fire step was another, his intestines were hanging down where the shell had ripped, the others had disappeared except for an odd arm or leg. All this was too much for a young stomach, I was violently sick. I was given a shot of rum, and gradually began to shake off the feeling. As a kid, I always wanted to be a soldier and used to read about charging the enemy, the glory and all that stuff, but somehow, just now it didn't seem so glorious."

Lance Coporal Godfrey Lawes Godfrey   *1/4th Bn TF Wiltshire Regiment*

Service No.	203676	Age:	30
Place of Birth:	Calne, Wiltshire	Home Country:	England
Date of Death:	10/04/1918	Cause of death:	Killed in action
Memorial:	Calne		
War cemetery:	Ramleh War Cemetery		
Theatre of war:	Egypt		
Next of Kin:	John & Mary Elizabeth Godfrey		
Address:	Quemerford House, Calne, Wiltshire		

Godfrey was the third son of John & Mary Godfrey. He was an assistant to his father who was the surveyor to Calne Rural District Council. He volunteered for service at the outbreak of war and was attached to the 2nd Royal Wilts Yeomanry. In August 1917 he was sent to the 1/4th Battalion Wiltshire Regiment.

At 6am on Wednesday 10th April the 1/4th Battalion Wiltshire Regiment were attacking Turkish positions on the Sheik Subih ridge in Palestine. As they advanced they were met by a Turkish Artillery barrage and machine guns firing from the side. The war diary states;

"To advance under such conditions meant very heavy losses before the attack could be launched against our objective, and the Battalion halted, taking what cover it could."

In the same afternoon the Wiltshires were ordered to support an attack by the Gurkhas and as they moved into position they suffered more casualties. The Gurkhas managed to reach the top of the ridge but were then driven off by Turkish shell fire.

Twenty four members of the 1/4th Wiltshires were killed during the attack. One of these was Godfrey, he is buried in the Ramleh War Cemetery with over 3000 casualties of the Great War.

Lance Bombardier Walter Alfred Soley		*10th Heavy Bty RGA*	
Service No.	293408	Age:	29
Place of Birth:	Calne, Wiltshire	Home Country:	England
Date of Death:	12/04/1918	Cause of death:	Died of wounds
Memorial:	Calne		
War cemetery:	Locre Hospice Cemetery		
Theatre of war:	Belgium		
Next of Kin:	William & Louisa Soley		
Address:	116 London Road, Calne, Wiltshire		

On Sunday 21st April 1918 William & Louisa Soley received the news that their fourth son, Walter, had been mortally wounded in action on Friday 12th April. They received a letter from Walter's Commanding Officer in which he wrote:

"We had been heavily engaged all day, and at about 6pm it was decided to move the guns. I called for volunteers to load up ammunition limbers on the road where the enemy were shelling, and Bombardier Soley and three men were the first to come forward. Whilst we were at work an unlucky round fell amongst us, and we were all wounded, Bombardier Soley very seriously. He never regained consciousness and died in the dressing station the same night. We are terribly upset about his death, as he was a prime favourite with all, officers and men, a thorough sportsman and the best gun layer in the battery. All the men in his sub-section wish me to forward their deepest sympathy to your family."

It is likely Walter was conscripted into the army, was then sent to the Royal Garrison Artillery and after training was sent to the continent. He was wounded near the Belgium town of Poperinghe and then taken to one of the field ambulances based at Locre where he died.

In April 1919 Walter's parents inserted the following memoriam in a local paper;

"If we could have raised his dying head
Or heard his last farewell
His memory would not be so hard
For us who loved him well
No one knows the heartache
Only those can tell
Who have lost their loved and best
Without saying Farewell
From his sorrowing Mother Father Brothers and Sisters
In proud and loving memory of our dear brother."

Walter is buried in Locre Hospice Cemetery with almost two hundred and fifty casualties of the Great War.

2nd Lieutenant Eric Charles Terry		*11th Sqdn Royal Air Force*	
Service No.	N/A	Age:	19
Place of Birth:	Islington, London	Home Country:	England
Date of Death:	12/04/1918	Cause of death:	Accident
Memorial:	Not known		
War cemetery:	Yatesbury All Saints Churchyard		
Theatre of war:	Home		
Next of Kin:	Charles E & Minnie M Terry		
Address:	1 Suffolk House, Dartmouth Park Hill, London		

On 1st April 1918 the Royal Flying Corps and the Royal Naval Air Service were merged with the formation of the Royal Air Force. Eric had received a commission in the Royal Field Artillery and then transferred to the new Air Force. On Friday 12th April he was flying near Yatesbury aerodrome when his machine plunged to earth and he was killed instantly. He was the first member of the newly formed Royal Air Force to be killed at Yatesbury.

Driver Leopold Arthur Walker		*104th Bde Royal Field Artillery*	
Service No.	936226	Age:	21
Place of Birth:	Heddington, Wiltshire	Home Country:	England
Date of Death:	21/04/1918	Cause of death:	Died
Memorial:	Heddington		
War cemetery:	Wimereux Communal Cemetery		
Theatre of war:	France		
Next of Kin:	William & Sarah Walker		
Address:	Heddington, Wiltshire		

It is likely Leopold was conscripted into the army and he died of illness or disease. He is buried in Wimereux Communal Cemetery.

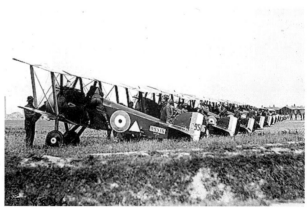

Left: The grave of Eric Charles Terry in Yatesbury All Saints Churchyard

Below: British aircraft.

Above: William Fitzroy, Viscount Ipswich.

Left : The grave of William Fitzroy at Euston St. Genevieve Churchyard.

Lieutenant William Henry Alfred Fitzroy   *Royal Air Force*

Service No.	N/A	Age:	33
Place of Birth:	London, Middlesex	Home Country:	England
Date of Death:	23/04/1918	Cause of death:	Accident
Memorial:	Potterspury, Northamptonshire & Wye Agricultural College & Village		
War cemetery:	Euston St. Genevieve Churchyard		
Theatre of war:	Home		
Next of Kin:	Auriol, Viscountess Ipswich (wife); Alfred William, 8th Duke of Grafton		
Address:	Whittlbury, Northamptonshire		

Viscount Ipswich, William Henry Alfred Fitzroy, served in the Great War under the alias William Henry Alfred Ipswich, but he was known as Tim. He was the son of the Earl of Euston and grandson of the Duke of Grafton. He inherited his title when his Grandfather the Duke of Euston died in 1912. The family seat (Duke of Grafton) was at Euston Park and Euston Hall which is about 10 miles north east of Bury St Edmunds in Suffolk.

  He was educated at Harrow and Trinity College, Cambridge and went from Cambridge to Wye Agricultural College. He obtained his diploma in July 1907 and from 1913-14 was a member of staff at the college. In June 1905 he had a serious accident on the Wye Bridge whilst riding a bicycle. A heavily laden wagon drawn by a steam tractor crushed him. He recovered and took up an appointment at the Egyptian Estates Company in Alexandria. In 1913 he married Auriol Margaretta, only child of Major Brougham, of Potterapury House, Northamptonshire. They lived at The Firs, Wye where in his student days he had stayed whilst attending the college. They had three children.

  At the outbreak of war he acted for some time as a Remount Officer and then enlisted in the 5th territorial battalion, the East Kent Regiment as an enlisted soldier. On the 24th August 1914 he was given a commission with the Coldstream Guards following family intervention.

  He embarked for France in November 1914 and saw considerable service on the continent. In the spring of 1915 he was invalided home with shell-shock, and did not return to France until the summer of 1916.

In the autumn of 1917 he returned to England to train as an observer in the Royal Flying Corps. and obtained his wings in February 1918. Although considerably above the recognised age-limit he passed on to a pilot's course and was attached to No. 17 Training Squadron.

On Tuesday 23rd April 1918, he was flying a machine near Yatesbury aerodrome when it was noticed that his machine was seen to be gliding down as if the aviator intended to land. The aeroplane suddenly stalled and then appeared to lose flying power, with the result that it crashed to earth and the pilot was killed instantly, suffering from a fractured scull.

He was buried with full military honours at Euston St. Genevieve Churchyard.

2nd Lieutenant John Boyd Chamberlin		*13th Trg. Sqdn Royal Air Force*	
Service No.	N/A	Age:	19
Place of Birth:	Mylor, Cornwall	Home Country:	England
Date of Death:	23/04/1918	Cause of death:	Accident
Memorial:	Mylor		
War cemetery:	Mylor St. Mylor Churchyard		
Theatre of war:	Home		
Next of Kin:	Hugh Whitmore & Aileen Chamberlin		
Address:	Restronguet, Penryn, Cornwall		

Nineteen year old John was the second son of Hugh Whitmore and Aileen Chamberlin, He joined the Royal Flying Corps and received a commission on 26th March 1918 and on 1st April 1918 he was transferred to the Royal Air force.

On the evening of Tuesday 12th April John was engaged in aerial firing to a ground target near Avebury. He had circled twice firing at the target and was preparing to fire a third time when the top wing of the aircraft was seen to fall back and the machine dived to earth. John was killed instantly.

His body was returned to his parents and he was buried in Mylor St. Mylor Churchyard.

Gunner Albert Edward Tom Gunning		*291st Bde Royal Field Artillery*	
Service No.	141673	Age:	21
Place of Birth:	Calne, Wiltshire	Home Country:	England
Date of Death:	24/04/1918	Cause of death:	Killed in action
Memorial:	Not known		
War cemetery:	Pozieres Memorial		
Theatre of war:	France		
Next of Kin:	Ernest & Agnes Gunning		
Address:	Church Street, Calne, Wiltshire		

Albert was the eldest son of Ernest and Agnes Gunning and it is likely he was conscripted into the Army and was sent to Royal Field Artillery.

It is likely he was killed by German shell fire on Wednesday 24th April 1918, three days into the third German spring offensive. He is remembered on the Pozieres Memorial and has no known grave.

2nd Lieutenant James Horace Farnham		*17th Trg. Sqdn Royal Air Force*	
Service No.	N/A	Age:	26
Place of Birth:	Nova Scotia, Canada	Home Country:	USA
Date of Death:	25/04/1918	Cause of death:	Accident

Above: Regimental Institute (Canteen) at No.1 camp Yatesbury aerodrome.

Right: The grave of James Farnham in Yatesbury All Saints Churchyard.

Memorial:	Not known
War cemetery:	Yatesbury All Saints Churchyard
Theatre of war:	Home
Next of Kin:	Thomas H & Mary Farnham
Address:	Boston, Massachusetts

James was a Book keeper and cashier for C. P. Rockwell in Boston, U.S.A., and was drafted into the American army on 5th June 1917. In March 1918 he transferred to the British Army receiving a commission and then transferring in April to the Royal Air Force. On Thursday 25th April 1918 James was flying at Yatesbury aerodrome when it was seen that the machine made a decent as if the aviator intended to effect a landing. However the machine crashed to earth and the occupant was found to have been killed due to a fractured scull. James is buried in Yatesbury All Saints Churchyard.

Gunner Reginald James Victor Clifford		*85th Siege Bty RGA*	
Service No.	171002	Age:	27
Place of Birth:	Cherhill, Wiltshire	Home Country:	England
Date of Death:	27/04/1918	Cause of death:	Killed in action
Memorial:	Calne – Lacock Church & Keevil		
War cemetery:	Ploegsteert Memorial		
Theatre of war:	Belgium		
Next of Kin:	Emily Jane Clifford (wife); George Hyde & Anne Jane Clifford (parents)		
Address:	Lacock; 1 Freeth, Compton Bassett, Wiltshire		

Reginald, known as Victor, was a farm labourer and in 1915 married Emily Jane Walker. It is likely that he was conscripted into the army and then sent to the Royal Garrison Artillery, probably because he was used to working with horses. In May 1918 Emily received a notice informing her that Victor had been missing since 23rd April, when he was last seen transporting munitions to the firing line. It was later found that he had been killed in action on Saturday 27th April 1918. He is remembered on the Ploegsteert Memorial with over 11,000 casualties of the Great War. He has no known grave.

Pioneer Gilbert Allen Ponting   *62nd Signal Coy. Royal Engineers*

Service No.	165760	Age:	19
Place of Birth:	Calne, Wiltshire	Home Country:	England
Date of Death:	05/05/1918	Cause of death:	Died
Memorial:	Calne		
War cemetery:	Etaples Military Cemetery		
Theatre of war:	France		
Next of Kin:	John Gilbert Ponting		
Address:	16 Castle Street, Calne, Wiltshire		

It is likely nineteen year old Gilbert was conscripted into the army and then sent to the Royal Engineers. He was then attached to the 186th Infantry Brigade and died of illness or disease at one of the base hospitals at Etaples where he is buried in the Military Cemetery.

Lieutenant Charles Leonard Price   *Royal Air Force*

Service No.	N/A	Age:	18
Place of Birth:	Ramsgate, Kent	Home Country:	England
Date of Death:	11/05/1918	Cause of death:	Accident
Memorial:	Not known		
War cemetery:	Ramsgate and St Lawrence Cemetery		
Theatre of war:	Home		
Next of Kin:	Charles & Lilian Price		
Address:	Ramsgate, Kent		

On Saturday 11th May 1918, eighteen year old Charles was flying at a height of 600 feet near Yatesbury aerodrome. He made a sharp turn to the left and his machine suddenly nose dived to earth causing instantaneous death.

His body was returned to his parents and buried in Ramsgate and St Lawrence Cemetery.

Above: The Broken grave marker and over grown grave of Charles Price in Ramsgate and St Lawrence Cemetery, killed at Yatesbury aerodrome.

Right: the grave of William Haddrell in Hilmarton St. Laurence Churchyard.

Private Francis William Haddrell   *Reserve Coldstream Guards*

Service No.	21212	Age:	20
Place of Birth:	Goatarce, Wiltshire	Home Country:	England
Date of Death:	13/05/1918	Cause of death:	Died
Memorial:	Calne & Hilmarton		
War cemetery:	Hilmarton St Laurence Churchyard		
Theatre of war:	Home		
Next of Kin:	William & Sarah Haddrell		
Address:	Goatarce, Wiltshire		

Francis was conscripted into the Army in 1917 and sent to The Coldstrem Guards. While undergoing military training he developed pneumonia so seriously that he was admitted to Bath hospital for six months. He was then transferred to Calne Red Cross Hospital where he died on Monday 13th May 1918. He was interred at Hilmarton with full military honours.

Lieutenant Charles Gerald Valentine Smith   *66th Training Sqdn Royal Air Force*

Service No.	N/A	Age:	19
Place of Birth:	British Columbia, Canada	Home Country:	Canada
Date of Death:	21/05/1918	Cause of death:	Accident
Memorial:	Not known		
War cemetery:	Yatesbury All Saints Churchyard		
Theatre of war:	Home		
Next of Kin:	Henry Valentine & Kathleen Smith		
Address:	Vancouver, British Columbia		

Nineteen year old Charles was an Instructor at Yatesbury aerodrome and on Tuesday 21st May 1918 he was flying with a student George Howard. They had made their ascent at 5am and were practicing making landings near the aerodrome. At about 5.15am the machine they were flying was seen on fire by a vehicle and both student and instructor were found to be dead, the cause of death being fractured sculls. Charles is buried in Yatesbury All Saints Churchyard.

Above Y.M.C.A. hut at Yatesbury aerodrome, this building was re-erected in Cherhill amd used as the village hall.

Left : The grave of Charles Gerald Valentine Smith in Yatesbury All Saints Churchyard.

2nd Lieutenant George Stanley Howard   *Royal Air Force*

Service No.   N/A   Age: 18
Place of Birth: Leeds, Yorkshire   Home Country: England
Date of Death: 21/05/1918   Cause of death: Accident
Memorial: Not known
War cemetery: Leeds Beeston Cemetery
Theatre of war: Home
Next of Kin: Herbert S & Jane H Howard
Address: 68 Cross Flatts Grove Beeston, Leeds, Yorkshire

Eighteen year old George received his commission in March 1918. He was killed in a flying accident with his instructor Charles Smith on Tuesday 21st May 1918. His Body was returned to his parents and he is buried in Leeds Beeston Cemetery.

Private Maurice Gough   *2nd Bn Hampshire Regiment*

Service No.   33151   Age: 30
Place of Birth: Calne, Wiltshire   Home Country: England
Date of Death: 23/05/1918   Cause of death: Killed in action
Memorial: Calne
War cemetery: Nieppe Bois (Rue Du Bois) British Cemetery Vieux B
Theatre of war: France
Next of Kin: Louis & Ellen Gough
Address: Calne, Wiltshire

Maurice was a builder and it is likely he was conscripted into the army joining the 2nd Battalion Hampshire Regiment. He was killed in action on Thursday 22nd May 1918 during fighting in the Nieppe Forest near Hazebrouck. He is buried in Nieppe Bois (Rue Du Bois) British Cemetery with 70 casualties of the Great War.

27th MAY 1918 - THE THIRD GERMAN SPRING OFFENSIVE CODE NAMED BLUCHER

Private Reginald George Coombs   *1st Bn Wiltshire Regiment*

Service No.   37491   Age: 19
Place of Birth: Cherhill, Wiltshire   Home Country: England
Date of Death: 27/05/1918   Cause of death: Killed in action
Memorial: Cherhill
War cemetery: Soissons Memorial
Theatre of war: France
Next of Kin: George & Annie Coombs
Address: 38, Cherhill, Wiltshire

On Monday 27th May 1918 the Germans launched their third spring offensive operation "Blucher" against the British. The 1st Battalion Wiltshire Regiment were the support lines near Guyencourt, north east of Rheims, France. At 1am the German advance commenced with a heavy gas bombardment which lasted 4 hours, then the British front line was attacked.
  At 7.30am the Wiltshires were ordered to go forward to cover the retirement of the front line troops and a further advance was made at 10.15am to a line in front of Bouffignereux . They

were subjected to heavy German shelling and machine gun fire. At 5.30pm the Germans attacked in vastly superior number and the Wiltshires were compelled to retire, fighting rearguard actions, splitting into two small parties as they retreated. Nineteen year old Reginald was missing. In January 1919 the following notice was inserted into a local paper by his parents:

*"**Information Wanted**, Mrs Coombs, of 38 Cherhill, would be very grateful if any returning prisoner of war could give any tidings of her son No. 37491 Pte. R. G. Coombs, 1st Wilts, D Company, reported missing on May 27th, 1918."*

Reginald was never seen again and was eventually listed as killed in action on Monday 27th May 1918 at Bouffignereux, France. He is remembered on the Soissons Memorial with nearly 4,000 Casualties of the Great War.

Private Jacob Andrews   *14th Royal Warwickshire Regiment*
Service No.   34503   Age: 20
Place of Birth: Calne, Wiltshire   Home Country: England
Date of Death: 29/05/1918   Cause of death: Killed in action
Memorial: Calne
War cemetery: Thiennes British Cemetery
Theatre of war: France
Next of Kin: Henry & Emily Andrews
Address: Hungerford Row Curzon Street, Calne, Wiltshire

Jacob, known as Jake, was conscripted into the army and had expected to join the Wiltshire Regiment but was sent to the 14th Battalion Royal Warwickshire Regiment. He was killed in action while holding the line on Wednesday 29th May 1918. He is buried in Thiennes British Cemetery.

Private Herbert Thomas James Fortune   *2nd Bn Devonshire Regiment*
Service No.   290779   Age: 20
Place of Birth: Calne, Wiltshire   Home Country: England
Date of Death: 31/05/1918   Cause of death: Killed in action
Memorial: Chippenham – St. Andrews Church, Chippenham - Derry Hill
War cemetery: Soissons Memorial
Theatre of war: France
Next of Kin: Thomas & Mary Jane Fortune
Address: Fair View, Sheldon Road, Chippenham, Wiltshire

Herbert worked for his father who was a market gardener and it is likely he was conscripted into the army joining the 2nd Battalion Devonshire Regiment. He was reported missing during the German advance toward the river Marne on Friday 31st May 1918. Later he was listed as killed in action on that day. He is remembered on the Soissons Memorial and has no known grave.

Lieutenant Stanley Burnet   *17th Trg Sqdn Royal Air Force*
Service No.   N/A   Age: 19
Place of Birth: Luton, Bedfordshire   Home Country: England
Date of Death: 31/05/1918   Cause of death: Accident

Above left: Stanley Burnet killed at Yatesbury aerodrome.

Above right; Comrades in arms, all three joined the Wiltshire Regiment but were transferred to the Royal Warwickshire Regiment. Back: Walter Weston , Survived the war, front left: Percy Dolman killed in action August 1918, front right: Jacob Andrews killed in action May 1918.

Memorial:	Not known
War cemetery:	Luton General Cemetery
Theatre of war:	Home
Next of Kin:	Arthur & Gertrude Burnet
Address:	18 Conway Road, Luton, Bedfordshire

Stanley was originally commissioned into the Bedfordshire regiment and transferred to the Royal Flying Corps and then the Royal Air Force. He had qualified as a pilot on 4th March 1918 at Ruffy-Baumann School, Acton in a Caudron biplane.

At 9pm on Friday 31st May Stanley was flying in the vicinity of Yatesbury aerodrome when he collided with a machine piloted by Ernest Tracey, with the result that both machines crashed to earth with Stanley's machine catching fire. Ernest Tracey was killed instantly. Stanley was removed to hospital where he died about two hours later, the cause being shock from the burns that were inflicted on him. His remains were returned to his parents and he was buried in Luton General Cemetery.

Flight Cadet Ernest Osborne Tracey		*13th Sqdn Royal Air Force*	
Service No.	100438	Age:	18
Place of Birth:	Dartmouth, Devon	Home Country:	England
Date of Death:	31/05/1918	Cause of death:	Accident

Memorial: Blundells College,Memorial Devon.
War cemetery: Townstall St Clement Churchyard
Theatre of war: Home
Next of Kin: Rev. Harry Frank & Alice Rose Tracey
Address: Montagu, Dartmouth, Devon

Ernest was educated at Blundell's College Devon where he received shooting colours and the Coles Science Prize. He passed the exam for Woolwich and enlisted as a cadet in the Royal Air Force. He was killed at Yatesbury aerodrome at 9pm on Friday 31st May in a collision with Stanley Burnet.

Private 2nd Class Harold Edwin Goodwin   *1st Training Sqdn Royal Air Force*
Service No.   186809   Age: 22
Place of Birth: Worcestor, Worcestershire   Home Country: England
Date of Death: 06/06/1918   Cause of death: Died
Memorial: Not known
War cemetery: Yatesbury All Saints Churchyard
Theatre of war: Home
Next of Kin: George Edwin & Catherine Goodwin
Address: Worcestor, Worcestershire

On the afternoon Thursday 6th June 1918 Harold was in his hut at Yatesbury aerodrome writing letters when Arthur Withers, a hut mate of Harold, entered the room and found him lying on the floor pen in hand in a collapsed and dying condition. Doctor Pigeon was called and tried artificial respiration but Harold died almost immediately. After a post mortem Dr. Pigeon gave the cause of death as being due to fatty degeneration of the heart.

Rifleman William Ebden Wilkinson   *2nd Bn Kings Royal Rifle Corps*
Service No.   R/34448   Age: 36
Place of Birth: Peterborough, Northamptonshire Home Country: England
Date of Death: 07/06/1918   Cause of death: Killed in action
Memorial: Derry Hill & Castor and Alsworth
War cemetery: Cambrin Military Cemetery
Theatre of war: France
Next of Kin: William & Caroline Wilkinson
Address: Castor, Peterborough, Northamptonshire

For several years William was a forester on the Fitzwilliam estate, and was also a member of the Castor Church choir and Brass Band. After leaving the Milton Estate he was appointed second forester to Lord Lansdowne at Bowood House, Wiltshire. He volunteered for service and arrived in France on 22nd July 1915. In June 1916 he was wounded at Ypres and after his recovery returned to his Regiment in December 1917. He was also in the Battle of the Dunes, in Belgium, when he had to swim the river to save himself. He was killed by a shell, which fell at his feet, whilst standing at the door of his dug-out on Friday 7th June 1918, and was buried the following day.
     At Castor churchyard there is a memorial stone with the following inscription:

"In loving memory of William Ebden Wilkinson. Who was killed in action at Cambrin June 7th 1918. Aged 36 years. Gone but not forgotten."

2nd Lieutenant Ruby Harold Morton MM   *66th Training Sqdn Royal Air Force*

Service No.	106408	Age:	33
Place of Birth:	Crewkerne, Somerset	Home Country:	Canada
Date of Death:	03/07/1918	Cause of death:	Accident
Memorial:	Not known		
War cemetery:	New Southgate Cemetery		
Theatre of war:	Home		
Next of Kin:	William Wilce Morton & Sarah Ann Morton		
Address:	102 Tollington Road, Holloway London		

Ruby, short for Ruben, emigrated to Canada prior to the Great War and was a telegrapher. He enlisted in the Canadian Army on 30th December 1914 and arrived in France on 22nd September 1915. He was promoted to Corporal and in July 1916 probably at the Somme, received the Military Medal whilst serving with the Canadian Engineers. He received a commission in 1918 on transferring to the Royal Air Force.

   He was killed during training while flying at Yatesbury on Wednesday 3rd July 1918 and his body was returned to his parents. He is buried at New Southgate Cemetery, London.

2nd Lieutenant John Leslie Colbourne   *16th Training Sqdn Royal Air Force*

Service No.	N/A	Age:	18
Place of Birth:	Lancing, Sussex	Home Country:	England
Date of Death:	04/07/1918	Cause of death:	Accident
Memorial:	Worthing, Sussex		
War cemetery:	Heene St Botolph Chruchyard Extension		
Theatre of war:	Home		
Next of Kin:	Charles E & Ethel M Colbourne		
Address:	5 Broadway, Worthing, Sussex		

Eighteen year old John ascended in his machine from Yatesbury aerodrome and while flying in the vicinity of Marlborough on Thursday 4th July 1917 something went wrong and his machine crashed to earth. John was killed instantly and his body was returned to his parents in Sussex.

British aircraft on the ground.

Above : Early Aircraft Carrier.

Right: Henry Adam , whose father was well known in Calne.

Lieutenant Henry William Adam		*Royal Air Force*	
Service No.	N/a	Age:	22
Place of Birth:	Chirton, Wiltshire	Home Country:	England
Date of Death:	04/07/1918	Cause of death:	Accident
Memorial:	Not Known		
War cemetery:	Lytham St Cuthbert Churchyard		
Theatre of war:	Home		
Next of Kin:	Rev H T & Emily Adam		
Address:	14 Stanley Rd, Lytham, Lancashire		

Henry was the second son of the Rev. Henry T Adam, who from 1879 to 1892 was the curate of Calne and from 1892 to 1899 was Vicar of Chirton, for five years of that time he was also vicar of Marden. Henry junior was educated at St. Bees College, Cumberland, where he was in the officers training corps, and Queens College Cambridge. He was intended to follow his father into the ministry but the Great War changed these plans and he entered the Royal Naval Air Service and later transferred to the Royal Air Force. He qualified as a pilot on the 20th November 1916 at Royal Naval Air Station at Vendome, France in a Caudron biplane. Henry junior lived in Chirton and was well known in the Calne area due to his father's relationship with the area.

On Thursday 4th July 1918, Henry was serving on H.M.S. Glorious, a light battle cruiser with flying off platforms on the 15" main gun turrets. While flying his seaplane it fell into the sea; the plane was very badly damaged and Henry was seriously injured. His observer Lieutenant Russell, managed to keep him afloat until a rescue boat arrived but Henry died shortly after being taken to a hospital ship. The captain of the Glorious wrote to Henry's parents and said their son was deeply mourned on board. His body was landed at Thurso and taken to Lytham for burial. Henry had seen considerable service not only in the northern waters where he met his death but also on the coast off France and Belgium.

2nd Lieutenant Stanley Arthur Burree		*16th Training Sqdn Royal Air Force*	
Service No.	24171	Age:	25
Place of Birth:	Richmond, Surrey	Home Country:	England
Date of Death:	05/07/1918	Cause of death:	Accident
Memorial:	Croydon Surrey		
War cemetery:	Croydon Mitcham Road Cemetery		

Theatre of war: Home
Next of Kin: Lillian Ruth Burree
Address: Heath Villa, Beulah Road East Thornton Heath, Croydon, Surrey

Before he left for France on the 29th September 1916 Stanley married Lillian Ruth Woode at Richmond, Surrey. He joined the Grenadier Guards and on 8th March 1918 he received a commission in the Royal Flying Corps and was then transferred to the Royal Air Force. On Friday 5th July while flying at Yatesbury aerodrome Stanley was killed in an accident. His body was returned to his home and he was buried in Croydon Mitcham Road Cemetery.

Corporal Reginald Watson Lewis   *21st Coy Machine Gun Corps*
Service No.   12526   Age: 37
Place of Birth: Derry Hill, Wiltshire   Home Country: England
Date of Death: 10/07/1918   Cause of death: Died
Memorial: Not known
War cemetery: Sissonne British Cemetery
Theatre of war: France
Next of Kin: Thomas Walton & Harriett Anne Lewis

Reginald was classed as an old soldier. He had been in the army before the Great War and had landed in France on 13th August 1914 with the 2nd Battalion Welsh Regiment, surviving many of the initial battles of the War. On 1st July 1916 he transferred to the Machine Gun Corps.

He was killed during fighting in the region of Aisne on Wednesday 10th July 1918. At the end of the war his remains were relocated to Sissonne British Cemetery were he lies with over 160 casualties of the Great War.

18th JULY 1918 - ALLIES MOUNT A MASSIVE COUNTERATTACK

Sergeant Alfred James Davis   *116th Bn Chinese Labour Corps*
Service No.   100317   Age: 37
Place of Birth: Enford, Wiltshire   Home Country: England
Date of Death: 19/07/1918   Cause of death: Died
Memorial: Holt
War cemetery: St Sever Cemetery Extension Rouen
Theatre of war: France
Next of Kin: Maud Eliza Davis (wife); Henry Davis (parent)
Address: Mill Cottages, Great Chalfield, Wiltshire

Alfred had served in the Boer war with the Wiltshire Regiment and after he finished his engagement with the army he became a water bailiff in the Employment of Major Robert Fuller. On 13th April 1907 he married Maud Eliza Church at Hilmarton Church. He volunteered for service on 15th March 1915 and was made a sergeant in December 1915. With his experience in the army he was used to train new recruits for the Wiltshire Regiment at Bovington in Dorset and at Devizes. On 13th of February 1917 he was transferred to the Devon Regiment and went to France with a Labour Battalion.

Labour battalions were used predominantly for manual tasks such as digging trenches, gun pits, repairing roads or unloading trains and ships. In January 1918 he was given leave to England and afterwards returned to France. In July 1918 Maud, Alfred's wife, received a telegram stating that her husband was seriously ill with pneumonia at No.12 General Hospital, Rouen. Later came a letter from the hospital stating that he had died on Friday 19th July 1917.

Captin L Moore of the Labour Company wrote the following to Maud;

"Your husband proved himself one of my best and most efficient non-commissioned officers. He was always bright and cheerful and a willing worker, and his loss is keenly felt."

In July 1919 the following memoriam was inserted in a local paper;

"Time may heal the broken heart
And make the wound less sore
But it cannot stop the longing
For the loved one gone before

Sadly missed by his loving Wife and Children"

Alfred left a widow and two children, Mary and Francis, he is buried at St. Sever Cemetery Extension, Rouen.

2nd Lieutenant Reuben John Davidson   *36th Trg Depot Royal Air Force*

Service No.	H/73268	Age:	21
Place of Birth:	Not known	Home Country:	Ireland
Date of Death:	27/07/1918	Cause of death:	Accident
Memorial:	Not known		
War cemetery:	Yatesbury All Saints Churchyard		
Theatre of war:	Home		
Next of Kin:	Rev J E Davidson		
Address:	24 Clifton Park Avenue, Belfast		

Reuben originally joined the Southern Irish Horse, a cavalry regiment raised in Ireland, and later transferred to the Royal Air force. The afternoon of Saturday 27th July 1918 was an ideal day for flying, the wind was of moderate velocity and the weather was generally clear. The Squadron Commander Captain F Kettle, who was an instructor, had been ordered to take up a formation of four machines and reports what happened;

"I left the ground at 2.35pm in a dual machine, I had a pupil in the front seat. I told Lieutenant Gorman to fly on my right, with Lieutenant Davidson in the rear and another officer on the left, making what we call a   diamond formation. I instructed them to join me at 2,000 feet over the aerodrome (Yatesbury). I circled over the aerodrome at 2,000 feet and waited until they had got in position. We then flew off in the direction of Devizes. When we reached a point near Devizes, I went to the left to turn in the direction of Marlborough. As I did so I looked round over the tail of my machine to see that the others had turned alright.. I then saw Lieutenant Davidson lose height on his turn and disappeared behind the right hand machine which Lieutenant Gorman was flying. The next thing I saw was the two machines breaking to pieces and spinning toward the earth pinned together."

The formation was flying over Stert, near Urchfont, when the collision occurred and the fall of the machines was witnessed by a number of people, who, it being the popular half holiday, were spending the afternoon in their allotments and gardens. They witnessed the two aircraft come perilously close to each other and one crashed into the other and the spectators were

Far left: The grave of Robert Gorman and left: the grave of Reuben Davidson, both are in Yatesbury All Saints Churchyard.

horrified to see the machines heading straight for the earth. When the onlookers arrived at the scene of the crash they found a mass of tangled wood and wire and they removed the bodies of the aviators from the wreckage. The machines were smashed, the spot at which they fell was wet and marshy being not far from a pond. The force of the fall had driven the engines into the earth and they had to be dug out by a party of soldiers.

Captain Kettle returned to Yatesbury to raise the Alarm and a motor ambulance was sent to the scene to remove the bodies to the mortuary. Reuben is buried in Yatesbury aerodrome.

2nd Lieutenant Robert Emmett Gorman   *36th Trg Depot Royal Air Force*

Service No.	N/A
Place of Birth:	Mattawa Nippising, Ontario
Date of Death:	27/07/1918
Memorial:	Not known
War cemetery:	Yatesbury All Saints Churchyard
Theatre of war:	Home
Next of Kin:	Norine Gorman (wife); Robert & Marguerite Gorman
Address:	San Galbriel California, USA; Ontario, Canada

Age:	31
Home Country:	Canada
Cause of death:	Accident

Robert, an advertising manager, was married and living with his wife in California when he enlisted in the Canadian army at Ottawa on 22nd February 1916. He later received a commission and was transferred to the Royal Air Force. He was killed in the collision with Reuben Davidson on Saturday 27th July 1918. Robert is buried near Reuben in Yatesbury Churchyard.

Private Ernie George Blackford   *6th Bn Wiltshire Regiment*

Service No.	22594
Place of Birth:	Calne, Wiltshire
Date of Death:	01/08/1918
Memorial:	Calne
War cemetery:	Cologne Southern Cemetery
Theatre of war:	Germany
Next of Kin:	Mark & Emily Blackford

Age:	22
Home Country:	England
Cause of death:	Died

Address: 1 Zion Lane, Calne, Wiltshire

As the war ended in November 1918 Emily Blackford received the news of the death of the third son she had lost in the conflict. Ernie was a Wiltshire Territorial and had served with the 1/4th Wiltshire Regiment in India.

When his term of service had ended he returned to England and in December 1915 he joined the 6th Battalion Wiltshire Regiment. He was taken prisoner at Morchies, north east of Baupaume, France, while resisting the German onslaught in March 1918.

Ernie died from influenza while a prisoner of war and was buried at Friedhofe, Friemersheim a Nieedershiem Cemetery in Germany. After the war his remains were relocated to Cologne Southern Cemetery. A German Pastor wrote to Ernie's mother and said her son's friends had accompanied the coffin to the grave and laid a wreath on it, he stated;

"I held the service from the common prayer book. May God comfort you in your sorrow."

Ernie was to die 19 days before his brother Sydney Blackford, Lewin Blackford had been killed in action at the Somme in 1916.

Sergeant Frank Bernard Brown   *6 Trg Depot Sqdn Royal Air Force*
Service No.   44921   Age: 19
Place of Birth: Hove, Sussex   Home Country: England
Date of Death: 03/08/1918   Cause of death: Accident
Memorial: Hove
War cemetery: Hove Old Cemetery
Theatre of war: Home
Next of Kin: Frederick Edward & Alice Adeline Brown
Address: 177 Westbourne Street, Hove, Sussex

Early on the morning of Saturday 3rd August 1918 nineteen year old Frank made an ascent from Yatesbury aerodrome. He did so without orders, and before an air test had been made by an instructor officer.

He was lost sight of in the air owing to the fog, and when he did not return a search was made. It was found that the machine in which he was flying had crashed to earth and the occupant was found to be dead. Frank's body was returned to his parents and he is buried in Hove Old Cemetery, Sussex.

2nd Lieutenant Edward McEvoy   *36th Trg Depot Sqdn Royal Air Force*
Service No.   N/A   Age: 27
Place of Birth: Bradford, Yorkshire   Home Country: England
Date of Death: 04/08/1918   Cause of death: Accident
Memorial: Not known
War cemetery: Bradford Bowling Cemetery
Theatre of war: Home
Next of Kin: Mary McEvoy (wife); David and Mary Agnes McEvoy (parents)
Address: 96 Kensington Street, Bradford, Yorkshire

In 1915 Edward married Mary Mullany at Bradford and three years later he was a 2nd Lieutenant in the Royal Air Force training at Yatesbury aerodrome.

On Saturday 3rd August 1918 Edward was flying in the vicinity of Yatesbury aerodrome when the machine he was flying crashed to earth. He was extracted from the wreckage of his aircraft and was found to be severely injured. He was taken to the camp hospital where he subsequently succumbed to his injuries the following day.

His body was returned to his parents and he was buried in Bradford Bowling Cemetery.

Private Reginald Thomas Bull		*1st Duke of Cornwalls Light Infantry*	
Service No.	38935	Age:	19
Place of Birth:	Calne, Wiltshire	Home Country:	England
Date of Death:	06/08/1918	Cause of death:	Died of wounds
Memorial:	Calne		
War cemetery:	Calne Holy Trinity Churchyard		
Theatre of war:	Home		
Next of Kin:	John & Alice Bull		
Address:	18 New Road, Calne, Wiltshire.		

Nineteen year old Reginald was conscripted into the army and sent to the Training Reserve. Prior to 1916 regiments recruited men locally and trained them at their depots. After 1916, and the introduction of conscription, the regimental system could not cope with the numbers of men so a new system was introduced where men were recruited into the reserve and posted to whichever regiment needed replacements.

Reginald was sent to the 1st Battalion Duke of Cornwall's Light Infantry and it is likely he was wounded while serving in France. He died of wounds on Tuesday 6th August 1918 at Dover. His body was returned to Calne, where he is buried in Calne Holy Trinity Churchyard.

Above: War graves on the continent.

Left: The grave of Reginald Bull in Calne Holy Trinity Churchyard.

10

A BLACK DAY FOR THE GERMAN ARMY

Private Harry Parsons   *2nd Bn Wiltshire Regiment*

Service No.	9649	Age:	24
Place of Birth:	Calne, Wiltshire	Home Country:	England
Date of Death:	08/08/1918	Cause of death:	Killed in action
Memorial:	Sutton Benger		
War cemetery:	Loos Memorial		
Theatre of war:	France		
Next of Kin:	Henry & Sarah Parsons		
Address:	Sutton Benger, Wiltshire		

Harry was a farm labourer. He volunteered for service and joined the 2nd Battalion Wiltshire Regiment arriving in France on 19th July 1915.

On Thursday 8th August 1918 the British and French launched a massive attack against the Germans which was known as the Second Battle of Amiens. The 2nd Battalion Wiltshire Regiment were patrolling near Bethune and trying to find out where the Germans were. During the morning the Wiltshires were heavily shelled by the Germans and were forced to hold their position near a place called Vertbois Farm. It is likely Harry was killed by the German shelling.

He is remembered on the Loos Memorial with over 2000 casualties of the Great War who have no known grave.

Private Rowland Charles Lane   *10th Bn Essex Regiment*

Service No.	46118	Age:	19
Place of Birth:	Sandy Lane, Wiltshire	Home Country:	England
Date of Death:	08/08/1918	Cause of death:	Killed in action
Memorial:	Not known		
War cemetery:	Dive Copse British Cemetery Sailly Le Sec		
Theatre of war:	France		
Next of Kin:	Stafford James & Mary Anne Lane		
Address:	Calne, Wiltshire		

Nineteen year old Rowland was conscripted into the Army and sent to the 10th Service Battalion Essex Regiment. He was killed in action on Thursday 8th August 1918 during the advance of the Second Battle of Amiens.

The Cemetery where he is buried is called Dive Copse British Cemetery Sailly Le Sec. Dive Copse was a small wood close by, under the Bray-Corbie road, and is named after the officer commanding a dressing station that was based there in 1916. It was the area captured in the spring of 1918 in the German Offensives and it is likely that Rowland was killed very near to this during the British advance.

Lieutenant Gerald Henry Perrett   *10th Hussars*

Service No.	N/A	Age:	23
Place of Birth:	Heddington, Wiltshire	Home Country:	England
Date of Death:	08/08/1918	Cause of death:	Killed in action
Memorial:	Heddington		
War cemetery:	Caix British Cemetery		
Theatre of war:	France		
Next of Kin:	Henry J & Edith M Perrett		
Address:	Manor Farm, Heddington, Wiltshire		

Gerald worked with his father who was a farmer at Manor Farm, Heddington. At the out break of war he joined the Wiltshire Yeomanry and attained the rank of Sergeant. On 1st January 1917 he received a commission and was posted to 10th Hussars. He met his death by a shell behind the lines on the 8th August 1918. One of his colleagues, an officer, wrote the following to Gerald's parents.

"While I know anything I can say is of little avail, I must write and offer you my real sincere sympathy in the loss of your son. We had been holding a small piece of the line all night, and the next morning he had gone down to take charge of the horses behind, and it was there he was killed by a shell".

The chaplain wrote;

"I went out with an ambulance and brought him back, and buried him at Cayeux. I sympathise with you greatly. Your son was a splendid fellow. His men loved him and would go anywhere with him."

The private memorial in Heddington St. Andrew church to Gerald Henry Perrett.

His commanding officer also wrote;

"I always looked on him as 'one of the best,' and we shall suffer from his absence among us. He was a good soldier indeed, and one with a strong influence which was appreciated by everyone. I send my utmost sympathy."

Private Maurice Herbert Lawrence   *7th Bn London Regiment*

Service No.	368119	Age:	18
Place of Birth:	Calne, Wiltshire	Home Country:	England
Date of Death:	09/08/1918	Cause of death:	Died of wounds
Memorial:	Calne		
War cemetery:	Querrieu British Cemetery		
Theatre of war:	France		
Next of Kin:	Frank & Emily Lawrence		
Address:	24 New Road, Calne, Wiltshire		

Prior to the Great War eighteen year old Maurice was a messenger for the post office. He was conscripted into the army and sent to the 8th London Regiment and then transferred to the 7th Battalion London Regiment.

During 1918 after the German offensives there was an increased need for recruits especially when the British offensives needed extra manpower. To answer this the age for new recruits serving overseas was dropped to eighteen and a half. This led to the British army of 1918 being called the 19 and 18 army, because it was made up of so many eighteen and nineteen year old soldiers.

Maurice died of wounds received on Friday 9th August 1918, during the British advance, it is likely he was wounded near Querrieu north east of Amiens, France. He is buried in the Querrieu British Cemetery with nearly 190 casualties of the Great War.

Corporal William John Weston   *3rd Bn Royal Marine Light Infantry*

Service No.	Ply/13437	Age:	32
Place of Birth:	Calne, Wiltshire	Home Country:	England
Date of Death:	11/08/1918	Cause of death:	Died
Memorial:	Calne		
War cemetery:	Portianos Military Cemetery		
Theatre of war:	Salonika		
Next of Kin:	William & Susan Weston		
Address:	24 Anchor Lane, Calne, Wiltshire		

William was a basket maker and seller, he enlisted in the Royal Marine Light Infantry on 20th October 1902, he served on many ships and would have seen much of the world.

In February 1915 William was part of the crew of H.M.S. Jupiter which sailed from Great Britain to Arkhangelsk, an ice bound Russian Port. The Jupiter was the first British ship to arrive at Arkhangelsk with a cargo of war items. She had broken through the ice field and suffered temperatures of minus 20 degrees. In recognition of this endeavor the Russian Emperor Nikolai II awarded the Crew of the Jupiter with Russian Medals and awards. William received the Russian Medal for zeal, and a life long pension, unfortunately the Russian revolution occurred and the pensions were not paid.

In March 1917 William was transferred to the 3rd Battalion Royal Marines and sent to Limnos. After the evacuation of Gallipoli, a garrison of the Royal Naval Brigade remained on the Greek island of Limnos. It is likely William died of disease while serving as part of

H.M.S. Jupiter, William Weston received the Russian Medal for Zeal while serving on her.

the Garrison. He is buried in the Portianos Military Cemetery with over 350 casualties of the Great War.

Captain Herbert Anthony Gale MC & Bar		*2nd Bn Wiltshire Regiment*	
Service No.	N/A	Age:	25
Place of Birth:	Calne, Wiltshire	Home Country:	England
Date of Death:	12/08/1918	Cause of death:	Died of wounds
Memorial:	Calne		
War cemetery	Aire Communal Cemetery		
Theatre of war:	France		
Next of Kin:	Honora G Gale (wife); - Alderman John Gale JP & Amelia Royal Gale		
Address:	The Sheiling Rookery Road Bournbrook, Birmingham; - Calne		

When the war broke out Herbert studying at Birmingham University, where he had entered into a years course as an analytical chemiste j Hoined the Officer Training Corps of the University and was later given a commission in the 6th Battalion Wiltshire Regiment, and was subsequently transferred to the 2nd Battalion Wiltshire Regiment. He first went to France in May 1916 and rose to the rank of Captain being awarded the Military cross in 1917. The official citation reads;

"This Officer has been a Platoon Commander since June 1916, and has been through all the offensives since that date on the Somme, the Ancre in 1916, at Whytschaete, and south east of Ypres in 1917. He has always shown exceptional zeal in the performance of his duties; his constant cheerfulness under very trying conditions and by his disregard of personal danger he has set a very fine example to his men."

Herbert wrote to his sister about his experiences in December 1916;

"We have been having rather an unusually wicked time in the trenches and lost a few good men, and now we are back in our billets behind. Our company mess has snaffeled about the least blown to pieces room in the village. Of course it has no windows, and the shutters do anything but shut as far as draught is concerned, but the ceiling is complete! Not only that, but in what is left of the fire place a bright fire burns. This was rather a good house, with

floor of beautiful tiles. We have actually been in the front line trenches where men have actually got stuck in thick clay mud right up to their waists in some cases. I worked nearly all night getting four men out, for they were in a bad way, and the place was very dangerous. The last one had been in nearly twelve hours when he was released. Of course when we got them out we dosed them with rum, and sent them to a dug out to have a rest in the warm. When I returned to company headquarters I had suddenly become quite a temporary hero, though nothing at all. I am perfectly certain, if I had not got on to the job personally the men would have remained there all the next day, or else died. The gratitude of the first chap was quite touching."

In October 1917 Herbert married Honora G Close who was the daughter of a member of Birmingham City Council, he then returned to the front.

Herbert went on to win a bar for the Military Cross for the action at Spanbroekmolen and Whytschaete on the 15th April 1918, the citation follows;

"For conspicuous gallantry and devotion to duty when commanding a company in the front line during an enemy attack. Under heavy shell fire throughout the greater part of the day, he beat off the enemy with rifle and Lewis-gun fire, kept the front line intact, and retained -touch with both flanks. This Officer who was the only officer in the Company, kept the front line intact and retained touch with both flanks. By his cheerfulness and personal gallantry he was largely indeed, responsible for the maintenance of the front line."

In August 1918 the news reached Calne that Herbert had died from wounds. The Wiltshires Chaplain wrote to Honora, Herbert's wife, expressing his deepest sympathy and gave the particulars of his death;

"He was bought down from the line badly wounded in the head by a shell. The doctor in the field ambulance said he was afraid he could not recover, but that there was just a chance. He was taken down to the casualty clearing station, where everything possible was done, but he died on Monday. He was buried in a cemetery just outside Aire. Personally I have not known your husband very long, but I liked him very much. His Military Cross and bar are a testimony to his bravery, and in his life he was true to his religion which he was not ashamed to profess. It was young Gladstone (who was killed in the war) who said "Life was not to be reckoned by it's length of days, but by the purpose which inspired it." The cause of liberty of the world and the deliverance of the oppressed is just that for which our Lord Himself laid down his life on the cross. Can you try to think of that."

The Wiltshires war diary for the day states:

"Captain H.A.GALE MC wounded badly in the head about 6am."

Herbert died at No. 54 Casualty Clearing station on Monday 12th August 1918 from wounds received on Friday 9th August 1918. Honora requested that his remains were returned to England to be interred in the family vault, but the army refused the request in accordance with official policy.

He is buried in Aire Communal Cemetery with nearly 900 casualties of the Great War.

Lieutenant Harry Bernard Wilson   *36th Trg Depot Royal Air Force*
Service No.   N/A   Age: 27
Place of Birth: Stratford on Avon   Home Country: England
Date of Death: 15/08/1918   Cause of death: Accident
Memorial: King Edward VI School, Stratford memorial
War cemetery: Stratford on Avon Cemetery
Theatre of war: Home
Next of Kin: Herbert & Ada Rosina Wilson
Address: Harpford, Stratford on Avon, Warwickshire.

Harry was educated at the King Edward VI School, Stratford on Avon. He volunteered for service and joined the 10th Battalion Royal Fusiliers and arrived in France on the 30th July 1915. He was then offered a Commission with the Royal Warwickshire Regiment and later transferred to the Royal Flying Corps and then onto the Royal Air Force.

On Thursday 15th August 1918 Harry was flying in the vicinity of Yatesbury aerodrome, his machine was to turn out of its course, do three turns then get into a spin and nose dive to earth. Bernard was killed instantly, the cause of death being a fractured scull.

Harry's body was returned to his parents and he was buried in Stratford on Avon Cemetery.

2nd Lieutenant Marcus Erald Rowe   *62nd Trg Depot Royal Air Force*
Service No.   N/A   Age: 24
Place of Birth: Springhill, Nova Scotia   Home Country: USA
Date of Death: 19/08/1918   Cause of death: Accident
Memorial: Winthorp Memorial
War cemetery: Yatesbury All Saints Churchyard
Theatre of war: Home
Next of Kin: Eli & Mary Ann Cranford Rowe
Address: 43 Wilsher Street, Winthorp, Massachusetts

Marcus was educated at Winthrop public school; his parents had moved to the town when he was four years old. In 1910 he started work with the Bay State Trust Company and in June 1917 he enlisted into the United States Naval Aviation Service, and in September was transferred to the British Imperial Flying Corps. He attended the University of Toronto, and soon graduated in aviation with honors and was then sent to Texas to finish his training. He then returned to Toronto and received his commission as Second Lieutenant. Marcus's words, characteristic of his whole life, as he tenderly kissed his mother good-bye and took the train for Halifax and sailed for England were:

" Everything will turn out all right, mother,"

On arrival Marcus was posted to Yatesbury aerodrome, here follows an extract from one of his letters;;

. *"Recently another fellow and myself went to church in a little town about a mile away from here. We were interested more than we would expect to be at home, on account of the simple but beautiful music in which all the people took a part. It was a quaint old church, built in the seventeenth century and nearly covered with English ivy. It was located in the center of a small cemetery.* (It is in this cemetery at Yatesbury that Marcus is buried.) *The choir consisted of eight little girls, about twelve years old, and a few men. They sang everything, including the Psalms, which they seemed to know by heart. They made one think of an*

Marcus Rowe and his grave in Yatesbury All Saints Churchyard.

English lark, they sang so softly and sweetly. The church was the same pattern as the Chapel of St. John in the Tower of London. We enjoyed ourselves, and as soon as we get the chance, we are surely going again."

Marcus had finished his training at Yatesbury and was posted to another aerodrome. On Monday 19th August Marcus was flying back to Yatesbury aerodrome to see some friends. When his machine was in the vicinity it was seen to get into a spinning-nose dive from which he failed to get out. The machine crashed to the ground and caught fire. Marcus was killed instantly.

Marcus's Mother received the following letter from Miss Mabel Huband, a British canteen worker;

"Dear Madam: Having known your son, the late Lieut. Marcus Rowe, so well, will you please accept my very deep and sincere sympathy. He was a great friend of mine from the first time he came to Yatesbury Camp. I had the greatest respect and admiration for him, as had every one who knew him. He was a perfect gentleman, and his loss is regretted by all. Last week I met his brother, Flight Commander Arthur W. Rowe, who came here and gave me your address, asking me to write you as I knew your son so well and had given him his last meal. He had left this camp a short time only, and had flown over to pay us a visit on the day he met his death, August 19. On August 23 he was laid to rest in the quiet little graveyard at Yatesbury. When the cross erected to his memory has been placed at his grave I will take a photograph and send to you. As long as it is possible to do so, fresh flowers shall be put there. His memory will ever be sacred in the heart of one who prays God to comfort his mother as only He can and will."

The second letter is from Mark's camp instructor Lieutenant George H. Heaton;

. *"My dear Mrs. Rove: It is with deep regret that I am writing to you about your dear son. I have been his instructor since he came to this station, and we became great friends in that short time. He was one of my keenest and ablest pupils and was very keen to get over to France to do his bit. But it was not to be so. Dear Mrs. Rowe, he died doing his duty as much as any fellow at the front. The Royal Air Force have lost in him one whom they can ill spare these days. I hope that you will accept my deepest sympathy in your great sorrow. And as his instructor, you can guess how I feel about him."*

The third is from the camp chaplain, it was dated Saturday 24th August 1918;

"My dear Mrs. Rowe: You will have heard ere this hour that your son was killed as the result of a flying accident at Yatesbury. I am writing to give you a few details of his crash and to offer you my sincere sympathy in the loss of such a gallant son.

On Monday last, August 19, he had flown over to Yatesbury, when he was seen to get into a spinning-nose dive from which he failed to get out. The machine crashed to the ground; and although help came up almost immediately, your son had passed beyond all human aid. He was killed instantly, so you will have the comfort of knowing he did not suffer at all. He had been on a course at Yatesbury a short time ago, and was, I believe, going to see some friends there, so it came as a shock to them to know that Lieutenant Rowe had crashed on their aerodrome and been killed. I, the Chaplain, with six other officers, went over to bury, him yesterday and the others acted as bearers at the funeral. His last resting-place is in the pretty-little cemetery of the village church, not far from the aerodrome, and his grave was covered with several wreaths sent by officers and friends, both at Yatesbury and here.

Words are useless things to express what one feels, but believe me, I sympathize with you deeply in your sorrow; your boy was a good lad, respected and liked by his fellow officers, and it will be some consolation to know that he died in the Great Cause of Freedom for which we are all fighting. may God be with you and comfort you in your trouble.
I am Yours very sincerely, A. Gordon Wright, C.of E. Chaplain."

Mrs Rowe also received a letter from the King & Queen expressing their sympathy. Marcus is buried in Yatesbury All Saints Churchyard.

Private Sydney Frank Blackford		*38th Coy Machine Gun Corps*	
Service No.	102839	Age:	20
Place of Birth:	Calne, Wiltshire	Home Country:	England
Date of Death:	20/08/1918	Cause of death:	Died
Memorial:	Calne		
War cemetery:	Bagneux British Cemetery Gezaincout		
Theatre of war:	France		
Next of Kin:	Mark & Emily Blackford		
Address:	1 Zion Lane, Calne, Wiltshire		

Sydney was the youngest son of Mark and Emily Blackford and by this stage in the war of their six sons three were now dead, one was a prisoner of war and two were still serving. Sydney originally joined the Wiltshire Regiment but transferred to the Machine Gun Corps.

He died in France where he was serving in the Machine Gun Corps and his mother, Emily Blackford, received the following letter from the Adjutant of his battalion;

"It is with very great regret I have to advise you of the death of your son, Sydney Blackford, on the 20th August at a casualty clearing station after an illness of about 18 days. He was admitted to hospital on the 9th August suffering from influenza, which developed into pneumonia. It was not thought at the time of his admission to hospital that his condition was at all critical, and notification of his death received today was a great shock to all his colleagues. He was a very willing young man, and the officers under whose command he came had great admiration for his courage and devotion to duty. My heart goes out to you in sympathy for your sad loss."

Emily received a further letter from the Adjutant while he was on leave in England dated September 8th and was free from censorship;

"I knew your boy well. In the taking of Pilkin Ridge, 31st July 1917, he was one of my runners. Early in the morning he was hit by a piece of stray shrapnel, but said nothing to any of us, who were unconscious of the fact. Through a long morning of difficulties he did his work with marvelous coolness and cheerfulness, and it was not until he fainted through pain of his wound that we realized he had been hit. Many brave deeds were done that day, and he was unfortunate not to receive a memento; but his acts were forgotten. On his return to the battalion we made him a runner, knowing full well he could be relied on under any circumstances to do what he could. Unfortunately illness cut short his life, though he has left us with a wonderful record of good heartedness and absolute devotion to duty. Personally, I feel I have lost a comrade, for he was always my right hand runner, whose place will be most difficult to fill. I feel sure he will get the best of all rewards in the hereafter. May God grant some consolation in the Great loss of your gallant son, and our loss of a staunch comrade and brave soldier. This note is rather personal, but I am sure the whole of headquarters and his comrades feel the sentiments I have tried to express."

Sydney's brothers Ernie and Lewis Blackford, were both to die in the war, Lewis was killed at the Somme in 1916 and Ernie had died nineteen days before on the 1st August 1918 while a Prisoner of war.

Sydney is buried in Bagneux British Cemetery, Gezaincout, with nearly 1400 casualties of the Great War.

21st AUGUST 1918 - THE SECOND BATTLE OF ALBERT

Private Arthur Culley   *16th Royal Warwickshire Regiment*

Service No.	35262	Age:	19
Place of Birth:	Calne, Wiltshire	Home Country:	England
Date of Death:	23/08/1918	Cause of death:	Killed in action
Memorial:	Calne		
War cemetery:	Adanac Military Cemetery Miraumont		
Theatre of war:	France		
Next of Kin:	Mr A & Emily Culley		
Address:	18 Mill Street, Calne, Wiltshire		

Nineteen year old Arthur was conscripted into the army and was sent to the 16th Service Battalion Royal Warwickshire Regiment. He was killed in action on Friday 23rd August during the British advances at The Battle of Albert. He is buried in Adanac Military Cemetery Miraumont which is north east of Albert. The cemetery contains nearly 1500 casualties of the Great War.

Private Percy Archibald Dolman		*14th Royal Warwickshire Regiment*	
Service No.	50623	Age:	18
Place of Birth:	Devizes, Wiltshire	Home Country:	England
Date of Death:	23/08/1918	Cause of death:	Killed in action
Memorial:	Calne		
War cemetery:	Adanac Military Cemetery Miraumont		
Theatre of war:	France		
Next of Kin:	Colour Sergeant A T & Annie Dolman		
Address:	Roundway Barracks, Devizes, Wiltshire		

Eighteen year old Percy was the son of Colour Sergeant Dolman of the Wiltshire Regiment who had retired when the war broke out but had re enlisted and after serving with the 6th Battalion Wiltshire Regiment in France he joined the 3rd Battalion Wiltshire Regiment in a training role. Percy too had originally joined the Wiltshire regiment but was sent to the 14th Battalion Warwickshire Regiment. He was officially the youngest soldier from Calne to be killed in the Great War.

He was killed in action on Friday 23rd August 1918 during the Battle of Albert and the British advance. He is buried in Adanac Military Cemetery Miraumont.

Eighteen year old Percy Dolman killed in action August 1918.

Private Frank Lawrence   *1st Bn Welsh Guards*

Service No.	4207	Age:	29
Place of Birth:	Calne, Wiltshire	Home Country:	England
Date of Death:	25/08/1918	Cause of death:	Killed in action
Memorial:	Not known		
War cemetery:	Mory Abbey Military Cenetery Mory		
Theatre of war:	France		
Next of Kin:	Bessie Grace Lawrence (wife); Frederick & Ellen Lawrence (parents)		
Address:	4 John Street, Burnham on Sea, Somerset; Axebridge, Somerset		

Frank was a masons labourer and it is likely he was conscripted into the Army and sent to the 1st Battalion Welsh Guards.

He was killed in action on Sunday 25th August 1918 during the British advance after the Battle of Albert. It is likely he was killed while recapturing the village of Mory where severe fighting took place. He is buried in Mory Abbey Military Cenetery, Mory with over 720 casualties of the Great War.

Private Frederick Harold Barton   *5th Bn Royal Berkshire Regiment*

Service No.	38934	Age:	26
Place of Birth:	Calne, Wiltshire	Home Country:	England
Date of Death:	26/08/1918	Cause of death:	Killed in action
Memorial:	Calne		
War cemetery:	Perrone Road Cemetery Maricourt		
Theatre of war:	France		
Next of Kin:	Charles & Sarah Jane Barton		
Address:	12 Anchor Road, Calne, Wiltshire		

Fred, a baker, volunteered for service joining the Royal Army Service Corps. In 1918 because of the lack of infantry soldiers many men in support corps were transferred to the infantry.

Fred was transferred to the 5th Battalion Royal Berkshire Regiment and at 2am on Monday 26th August 1918 they were at Bercodel, east of Albert. They had been ordered to attack German positions at Carnoy; they marched through the night on a compass bearing for three and a half miles and reached the forming up position at 4.45am. After a British barrage on the German positions the Royal Berks attacked. They were held up by German machine gun fire and suffered heavy casualties. The Germans then counter attacked and took a number of prisoners. Fred was killed during this action, most likely by German machine gun fire.

He is buried in Peronne Road Cemetery, Maricourt, with nearly 1000 casualties of the Great War.

Driver Jacob Francis Rawlings   *108th Bde Royal Field Artillery*

Service No.	94192	Age:	27
Place of Birth:	Pewsey, Wiltshire	Home Country:	England
Date of Death:	27/08/1918	Cause of death:	Died of wounds
Memorial:	Calne		
War cemetery:	Daours Communal Cemetery Extension		
Theatre of war:	France		
Next of Kin:	William Rawlings		
Address:	Quemerford Common, Calne, Wiltshire		

Jacob volunteered for service with the Royal Field Artillery and arrived in France on 31st August 1915. In September 1918 Jacob's father received news that his son had died of wounds.

The battery had been in action on August 27th when a shell exploded close by, wounding a number of men and horses. It was hoped at the time that Driver Rawlings wound was not fatal, but the letter announcing his death is dated September 4th. In offering Mr Rawlings the sympathy of the battery the writer said;

"Your son had been in the battery for about three years, and was very popular with all ranks. We all feel that we have not only lost a good soldier and a gallant comrade but also a friend."

Jacob is buried in Daours Communal Cemetery Extension with over 1200 casualties of the Great War

Private Ernest Edward Powell		*19th Bn Central Ontario Regiment*	
Service No.	814737	Age:	25
Place of Birth:	Calne, Wiltshire	Home Country:	Canada
Date of Death:	28/08/1918	Cause of death:	Killed in Action
Memorial:	Calne & Derry Hill		
War cemetery:	Vis En Artois British Cemetery, Haucourt		
Theatre of war:	France		
Next of Kin:	Ivy L Powell (wife); Edward & Elizabeth Powell (parents)		
Address:	109 Churchill Road, Wilesden Green, London; Studley, Wiltshire		

Ernest enlisted in the Canadian Army on Friday 11th November 1915 at Warkworth, Ontario. He had been a farmer in Canada prior to the war and on returning to England on leave he had married Ivy L Maidlow in the summer of 1917 at Wilesden.

On Wednesday 28th August 1918 the 19th Battalion were advancing on German positions east of Arras toward Cambrai but could not penetrate the German line due to terrific machine gun fire from German machine guns in concrete emplacements. It is likely that Ernest was killed during this attack. At the end of August 1918 the 19th Battalion had suffered the following casualties, killed 64, died of wounds 22, wounded 364, gassed 32, missing 24, making a total of 514. Ernest is buried in the Vis En Artois British Cemetery, Haucourt, on the road from Arras to Cambrai with nearly 900 casualties of the Great War.

Private Frederick John Bristow		*10th Royal Warwickshire Regiment*	
Service No.	43350	Age:	19
Place of Birth:	Calstone, Wiltshire	Home Country:	England
Date of Death:	04/09/1918	Cause of death:	Killed in action
Memorial:	Calne		
War cemetery:	Loos Memorial		
Theatre of war:	France		
Next of Kin:	John Francis Bristow		
Address:	5 Wood Street, Calne, Wiltshire		

Nineteen year old Frederick was the youngest son of John Bristow and they formerly lived at Calstone Mills before moving to Calne. Frederick was conscripted into the army and then sent to the Hampshire Regiment before being transferred to the 10th Service Battalion Wiltshire Regiment. He was killed in action during the British advance on Wednesday 4th September 1918 and is remembered on the Loos Memorial, with over 20,000 casualties of the Great War. He has no known grave.

Corporal Walter Reginald Powell   *8th Bn Gloucestershire Regiment*

Service No.	15041	Age:	26
Place of Birth:	Compton Bassett, Wiltshire	Home Country:	England
Date of Death:	06/09/1918	Cause of death:	Killed in action
Memorial:	Compton Bassett		
War cemetery:	Loos Memorial		
Theatre of war:	France		
Next of Kin:	George D & Mary J Powell		
Address:	Lower Lodge, Cherhill, Wiltshire		

Walter was the youngest son of George and Mary Powell. He had volunteered for service with the 8th Service Battalion Gloucester Regiment and arrived in France on 21st November 1915. Walter's mother received a letter from her son's platoon offcer dated September 12th in which he says that Corporal Powell was shot by a sniper while on patrol in France.

"*He was very popular with the men; he was a fine soldier and a man whom I greatly admired. He will be greatly missed by all the platoon, and as a non commissioned officer his place will be hard to fill. Our heartfelt sympathy goes out to you in your sad bereavement, and I trust you will find comfort in the thought that he died serving his country.*"

Walter is remembered on the Loos Memorial and has no known grave.

2nd Lieutenant Alexander Rose   *Royal Air Force*

Service No.	N/A	Age:	30
Place of Birth:	Glasgow, Lanarkshire	Home Country:	Scotland
Date of Death:	06/09/1918	Cause of death:	Accident
Memorial:	Not known		
War cemetery:	Glasgow Craighton Cemetery		
Theatre of war:	Home		
Next of Kin:	Alexander & Catherine Rose		
Address:	56 Clifford Street, Ibrox, Glasgow		

Alexander had originally joined the Highland Light Infantry and rose to the rank of lance sergeant. He received a commission in December 1916 and was then attached to the Royal Air Force.

During the evening of Friday 6th September 1918, Alexander was practicing flying his machine above Yatesbury aerodrome. At about 7.45 he made an attempt to land but took off again. Whilst turning he lost flying speed at about 100 feet from the ground with the result that the machine nose dived to earth and burst into flames. Alexander was killed instantly.

His body was returned to his parents and he is buried in Glasgow Craighton Cemetery.

Corporal Harold William Beazley   *8th Bn Somerset Light Infantry*

Service No.	31222	Age:	35
Place of Birth:	Calne, Wiltshire	Home Country:	England
Date of Death:	07/09/1918	Cause of death:	Died of wounds
Memorial:	Calne		
War cemetery:	Varennes Military Cemetery		
Theatre of war:	France		
Next of Kin:	Walter William & Elizabeth Beazley		
Address:	Genesta, Shelburne Road, Calne, Wiltshire		

Harold was the only son of Walter and Elizabeth Beazley, and was on the staff of C & T Harris. He was the local secretary of the Wiltshire Workingmen's Conservative Benefit Society and also secretary to the whist club.

He was conscripted into the army, originally joining the Devonshire Regiment and then transferring to the Somerset Light Infantry. He was shot in the chest on Saturday 7th September and died a few hours later at one of the casualty clearing stations based at Varennes.

He is buried in Varennes Military Cemetery with over 1200 casualties of the Great War.

Shoeing Smith Frederick George Edgar Bull   *112th Bde Royal Field Artillery*

Service No.	86568	Age:	30
Place of Birth:	East tytherton Wiltshire	Home Country:	England
Date of Death:	07/09/1918	Cause of death:	Killed in action
Memorial:	Chippenham – St. Andrews, Chippenham		
War cemetery:	Peronne Communal Cemetery Extension		
Theatre of war:	France		
Next of Kin:	Elsie Bull (wife); George & Ellen Bull (parents)		
Address:	19 Crickets Lane, Chippenham; Langley Burrell		

Frederick was a brewers labourer. At the end of 1912 he married Elsie E. Poole at Chippenham. He volunteered for service with the Royal Artillery and arrived in France on 27th September 1915.

He was originally a driver but was promoted to Shoeing Smith after the completion of a course and would have been responsible for ensuring horses of his battery were correctly shod.

He was killed in action on Saturday 7th September 1918 during the British advance. He is buried at Peronne Communal Cemetery Extension with over 1400 casualties of the Great War.

A casualty of the war.

Private John James Pontin   *6th Bn Wiltshire Regiment*

Service No.	3/86	Age:	20
Place of Birth:	Cherhill, Wiltshire	Home Country:	England
Date of Death:	22/09/1918	Cause of death:	Died
Memorial:	Cherhill		
War cemetery:	Grand Seraucourt British Cemetery		
Theatre of war:	France		
Next of Kin:	Simeon & Jane Pontin		
Address:	Cherhill, Wiltshire		

It is likely John was conscripted into the army and joined the 6th Battalion Wiltshire Regiment. His death was probably due to illness and he is buried in Grand Seraucourt British Cemetery.

Gunner Tom Ponting   *Bute Mountain Bty RGA*

Service No.	194969	Age:	39
Place of Birth:	Calne, Wiltshire	Home Country:	England
Date of Death:	25/09/1918	Cause of death:	Died
Memorial:	Bremhill - Foxham - East Tytherton Morovian Church		
War cemetery:	Karasouli Military Cemetery		
Theatre of war:	Salonika		
Next of Kin:	Lewis & Anne Maria Ponting		
Address:	41, Bremhill, Wiltshire		

Tom, a farm labourer, was a well known bell ringer in Bremhill. It is likely he was conscripted into the army being sent to the Royal Field Artillery and then transferred to the Highland Mountain Brigade of the Royal Garrison Artillery serving with the Balkan forces.

He died on Wednesday 25th September 1918 as the result of a fractured scull. He is buried in Karasouli Military Cemetery, Greece with nearly 1400 casualties of the Great War. His brother Arthur Ponting was killed in France in March 1918.

Private Herbert Harry Talbot   *7th Bn East Kent Regiment*

Service No.	G/17463	Age:	19
Place of Birth:	Hook, Wiltshire	Home Country:	England
Date of Death:	25/09/1918	Cause of death:	Died of wounds
Memorial:	Yatesbury		
War cemetery:	Doingt Communal Cemetery Extension		
Theatre of war:	France		
Next of Kin:	William J & Emily Talbot		
Address:	39, Yatesbury, Wiltshire		

Nineteen year old Herbert was conscripted into the army being sent to the 2nd Battalion London Regiment and then transferred to the 7th Service Battalion East Kent Regiment. It is likely he was wounded in actions around the Hindenburg Line at Epepy, France on 18th September 1918.

The Hindenburg line was a German fortification which stretched across France consisting of deep belts of barbed wire and concrete fortifications. It is also likely he died at a casualty clearing station at Doint, France, which is on the eastern outskirts of Peronne. He is buried in the Doingt Communal Cemetery Extension with over 400 casualties of the Great War.

Private Fredrick George Smart   *1st Bn Grenadier Guards*
Service No.   27894   Age: 30
Place of Birth: Calne, Wiltshire   Home Country: England
Date of Death: 27/09/1918   Cause of death: Killed in action
Memorial: Calne
War cemetery: Sanders Keep Military Cemetery Graincourt Les Havrincourt
Theatre of war: France
Next of Kin: John & Mary Smart
Address: Mill Street, Calne, Wiltshire

Fredrick was employed at Harris's as a sausage maker. He was conscripted into the 1st Battalion Grenadier Guards.

Sanders Keep was a German fortification 2 kilometres South-West of the village of Graincourt Havrincourt, which is ten kilometres south west of Cambrai. The fortification was stormed on Friday 27th September 1918 as part of the British advance during the Battle of the Canal Du Nord. It is likely Fredrick was killed in this action and he is buried in the Sanders Keep Military Cemetery with over 130 casualties of the Great War.

Gunner William Draper   *27th Siege Bty RGA*
Service No.   322899   Age: 38
Place of Birth: Hilmarton, Wiltshire Home Country: England
Date of Death: 27/09/1918   Cause of death: Killed in action
Memorial: Not known
War cemetery: Queant Communal Cemetery British Extension
Theatre of war: France
Next of Kin: David & Sarah A Draper
Address: The Daisy, Berwick St James, Wiltshire

William was a cowman. He was conscripted into the army and sent to the 27th Siege Battery Royal Garrison Artillery. He was killed in action on Friday 27th September 1918 during the British advance and was probably killed by German shell fire or ariel bombs. He is buried in Queant Communal Cemetery British Extension, which is south of Arras, France with over 270 casualties of the Great War.

Gunner Thomas Grubb   *44th Bde Royal Field Artillery*
Service No.   202474   Age: 25
Place of Birth: Ashton Keynes, Wiltshire Home Country: England
Date of Death: 28/09/1918   Cause of death: Killed in action
Memorial: Not known
War cemetery: Peronne Communal Cemetery Extension
Theatre of war: France
Next of Kin: Thomas & Sophia Grubb
Address: Cherhill, Wiltshire

Thomas was a carter on a farm. He was conscripted into the army and sent to the Royal Field Artillery probably because of his experience of working with horses. He was killed in action on Saturday 28th September 1918 in the vicinity of Peronne, most likely by German shell fire.

He is buried in Peronne Communal Cemetery Extension. His medals were never collected and in 1922 the Royal Artillery records office applied for their disposal.

Private Vernon Joseph Brewer   *1st Bn Dorsetshire Regiment*

Service No.	20990	Age:	19
Place of Birth:	Pickwick, Wiltshire	Home Country:	England
Date of Death:	29/09/1918	Cause of death:	Killed in action
Memorial:	Calne		
War cemetery:	Cerisy Gailly Military Cemetery		
Theatre of war:	France		
Next of Kin:	Joseph & Emily Jane Brewer		
Address:	Pickwick, Wiltshire		

Vernon was conscripted into the army and sent to the 1st Battalion Dorsetshire Regiment. On Sunday 29th September 1918 the Dorsets were taking part in the Battle of the St. Quentin Canal. At 11.45am the Dorsets moved forward to the Hindenburg outpost line on the St. Helene Ridge and one hour later they were ordered to move forward again. They crossed the canal by the bridge at Bellenglise, north of St. Quentin which was under fairly heavy shell fire and they incurred a few casualties. On the other side of the bridge machine guns and snipers were firing from the high ground on the right.

The Dorsets attacked La Fleche wood capturing three hundred and eighty prisoners, three 12 inch Howitzers, five 4.2 field guns and five machine guns. Two of the howitzers were taken back to England and were at the depot gates in Dorchester, which is now the Military Museum.

Vernon was killed during this action and is buried at Cerisy Gailly Military Cemetery. It is likely his remains were relocated to this cemetery at the end of the war.

Private Ernest Brown   *2nd Bn Worcestershire Regiment*

Service No.	241828	Age:	22
Place of Birth:	Heddington, Wiltshire	Home Country:	England
Date of Death:	02/10/1918	Cause of death:	Died of wounds
Memorial:	Bromham		
War cemetery:	Thilloy Road Cemetery, Beaulencourt		
Theatre of war:	France		
Next of Kin:	Henry & Mary Brown		
Address:	Beacon Hill, Bromham, Wiltshire		

Ernest was a farm labourer and it is likely he was conscripted into the army. On 29th September 1918 the 2nd Worcesters were taking part in the Battle of St. Quentin Canal and it is probable Ernest was wounded during this battle.

He died of his wounds at one of the casualty clearing station based at Beaulencourt, France.

Lance Corporal Frank Walter Frankling   *26th Bn Royal Welsh Fusiliers*

Service No.	48857	Age:	36
Place of Birth:	Westbury, Wiltshire	Home Country:	England
Date of Death:	04/10/1918	Cause of death:	Killed in action
Memorial:	Calne & Hale, Cheshire		
War cemetery:	Ploegsteert Memorial		
Theatre of war:	Belgium		
Next of Kin:	Ellen Frankling (wife); Frank & Annie Frankling (parents)		
Address:	Slater Ing Hall, Hebden Bridge, Yorkshire; 31 New Road, Calne		

Frank, known as Walter, was a cycle repairer and married Ellen Cobden in the summer of

1908 at Hale, Cheshire.

He was conscripted into the army and sent to the 26th Service Battalion Royal Welsh Fusiliers. Walter was killed in action on Friday 4th October 1918 when the Royal Welsh were operating in the area of the River Lys northern France. He is remembered on the Ploegsteert Memorial and has no known grave. The war memorial in Calne states W. Franklin.

Private Edward John Drew   *2nd Bn Royal Dublin Fusiliers*

Service No.	14899	Age:	26
Place of Birth:	Calne, Wiltshire	Home Country:	England
Date of Death:	07/10/1918	Cause of death:	Killed in action
Memorial:	Calne		
War cemetery:	Prospect Hill Cemetery Gouy		
Theatre of war:	France		
Next of Kin:	Joseph & Harriet Drew		
Address:	13 Castle Street, Calne, Wiltshire		

Edward, known as Ted, volunteered for service with the Wiltshire Regiment at the beginning of the war, however because some of the Irish regiments were short of recruits a number of men from Wiltshire were transferred to these regiments. Ted was sent to the 2nd Battalion Royal Dublin Fusiliers and while landing at Gallipoli on the 9th August 1915 he was shot in the arm. He then saw service at Salonika where he was again wounded and after a period of leave in England he returned to France.

He was killed during the final advances of the war. Official records state he was killed in action but a memoriam of the time states he died of wounds. He is now buried in Prospect Hill Cemetery, Gouy, France and if he had died of wounds it would have probably been at the 18th Field Ambulance station which was based at Gouy. Teds brother, Fred Drew, was killed in action in France in 1917, and the following memoriam appeared in a local paper in November 1918:

> " We know not what they suffered
> We did not see them die
> O could we but have seen them
> If just to say goodbye"

It would appear that Ted's medals were not collected and in 1922 the records office requested permission for their disposal.

Private George Lucas   *7th Bn Wiltshire Regiment*

Service No.	12385	Age:	37
Place of Birth:	Yatesbury, Wiltshire	Home Country:	England
Date of Death:	07/10/1918	Cause of death:	Killed in action
Memorial:	Yatesbury		
War cemetery:	Prospect Hill Cemetery Gouy		
Theatre of war:	France		
Next of Kin:	Thomas & Jane Lucas		
Address:	20, Yatesbury, Wiltshire		

George was a carter on a farm. He volunteered for service and joined the 7th Battalion Wiltshire Regiment. He arrived in France on 21st September 1915 and the 7th Battalion then served in Salonika, Grecce and then returned to France in July 1918. On Sunday 6th October

1918 the Wiltshires were at Prospect Hill near Gouy and at 11.30am they attacked the Germans north of Guisencourt Farm. They were held up by barbed wire and machine guns. They suffered heavily with over two hundred casualties between 4th and 6th October 1917 and it is likely George was one of them. He is buried in Prospect Hill Cemetery Gouy.

Private Rowland William Roberts   *7th Bn Wiltshire Regiment*

Service No.	22999	Age:	29
Place of Birth:	Cherhill, Wiltshire	Home Country:	England
Date of Death:	07/10/1918	Cause of death:	Died of wounds
Memorial:	Cherhill		
War cemetery:	Tincourt New British Cemetery		
Theatre of war:	France		
Next of Kin:	John & Emily Roberts		
Address:	Cherhill, Wiltshire		

Rowland was a farm labourer. He was conscripted into the army and sent to the 7th Battalion Wiltshire Regiment. It is likely he was wounded during the action between 4th and 6th October 1918, when the Wiltshires suffered over two hundred casualties. He subsequently died of wounds on Monday 7th October 1918 probably at a casualty clearing station nearby.
He is buried in Tincourt New British Cemetery with nearly 1900 casualties of the Great War.

Private Herbert Edward Martin   *13th Bn Welsh Regiment*

Service No.	54684	Age:	28
Place of Birth:	Calne, Wiltshire	Home Country:	England
Date of Death:	08/10/1918	Cause of death:	Killed in action
Memorial:	Purton		
War cemetery:	Prospect Hill Cemetery Gouy		
Theatre of war:	France		
Next of Kin:	Edward J & Annie Martin		
Address:	Windham Cottage, Purton, Wiltshire		

It is likely Herbert was conscripted into the army being initially sent to the Worcestor Regiment, then the Hertfordshire Regiment and finally to the 13th Service Battalion Welsh Regiment.
He was killed on Tuesday 8th October during the British advance on the German lines east of Gouy, France and is buried in Prospect Hill Cemetery, Gouy.

Gunner Walter Rivers   *Howitzer Bde Royal Marine Artillery*

Service No.	RMA/13877	Age:	24
Place of Birth:	Goatacre, Wiltshire	Home Country:	England
Date of Death:	11/10/1918	Cause of death:	Killed in action
Memorial:	Lyneham		
War cemetery:	Vadencourt British Cemetery Maissemy		
Theatre of war:	France		
Next of Kin:	John and Fanny Rivers		
Address:	Freegrove Cottage, Goatacre, Wiltshire.		

Left: Walter Rivers.

Below: No.2 Howitzer Royal Marine Artillery.

Walter was the eldest son on John and Fanny Rivers and before the war was a farm labourer. He enlisted at Bristol on 13th January 1914 and was on active service from the outbreak of the war. He arrived in France on 3rd October 1917 and was posted to No. 2 Howitzer on 10th October 1917 who were operating in Belgium. The 1st Siege Battery Royal Marine Artillery was serving with the British 4th Army in 1918 and was used to support the British advance. The Royal Marine Artillery was equipped with huge 15 inch Howitzers which had maximum range of 10,795 yards, firing a 1,400 pound shell and each gun had a crew of 60 men. Walter was killed in action near St.Quentin, on Friday 11th October 1918 one month before the Armistice was to take effect. He is buried in the Vadencourt British Cemetery, Maissemy, with nearly 550 casualties of the Great War.

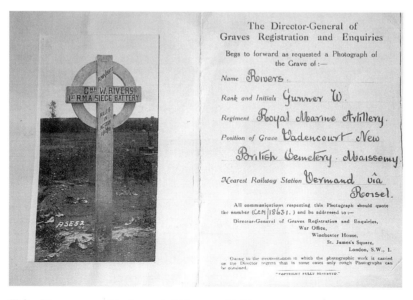

Walter Rivers grave registration card which was sent to his parents.

Private Francis James Henly   *2nd Bn Worcestershire Regiment*

Service No.   57682   Age: 19
Place of Birth: East Tytherton, Wiltshire   Home Country: England
Date of Death: 14/10/1918   Cause of death: Died of wounds
Memorial: Bremhill - Foxham - East Tytherton Morovian Church
War cemetery: Beaulencourt British Cemetery Ligny Thilloy
Theatre of war: France
Next of Kin: William J & Ruth Henly
Address: 57 Wick Hill, Bremhill, Wiltshire

Nineteen year old Francis was conscripted into the army and sent to the 2nd Battalion Worcestershire Regiment.

It is likely he was wounded during the pursuit of German Forceato the Selle. He probably died in one of the casualty clearing stations near Beaulencourt British Cemetery, Ligny Thilloy, where he is buried.

The Bremhill memorial gives the name Frederick James Henly.

Private Reginald Tom Raisley Cook   *1st Bn Royal Inniskilling Fusiliers*

Service No.   45033   Age: 18
Place of Birth: Manningford Abbas, Wiltshire   Home Country: England
Date of Death: 15/10/1918   Cause of death: Killed in action
Memorial: Compton Bassett
War cemetery: Tyne Cot Memorial
Theatre of war: Belgium
Next of Kin: William & Mary Jane Cook
Address: 59 Compton Bassett, Compton Bassett, Wiltshire

Reginald, known as Tom, was likely to have been conscripted into the army and sent to the 1st Battalion Royal Inniskilling Fusiliers.

He had just had his eighteenth birthday when he was killed in action during the Battle of Courtrai when the Britsh forces advanced through Belgium. He is remembered on the Tyne Cot Memorial and has no known grave. His brother William Cook had died of wounds in Iraq in 1917 and his twenty four year old sister Winifred was to die of illness four days later on the 19th October 1918.

Corporal Sidney Walter Cowdry   *HMS Argus Royal Air Force*

Service No.   208500   Age: 21
Place of Birth: Allington, Wiltshire   Home Country: England
Date of Death: 22/10/1918   Cause of death: Died
Memorial: Cherhill
War cemetery: Dunfermline Cemetery
Theatre of war: Home
Next of Kin: Frank & Fanny Cowdry
Address: 17, Cherhill, Wiltshire

H.M.S. Argus was the world first aircraft carrier with a flush deck which enabled wheeled aircraft to be used. Walter was a member of the repair and service crew for the aircraft. He died of pneumonia on Tuesday 22nd October 1918 on the hospital ship Garth Castle. He is buried in Dunfermline Cemetery, Scotland.

Rifleman Albert Edward Sayers   *2/17th Bn Rifle Brigade*
Service No.   P/1455   Age: 35
Place of Birth: Charlesworth, Berkshire   Home Country: England
Date of Death: 22/10/1918   Cause of death: Died
Memorial: Not known
War cemetery: La Kreule Military Cemetery Hazebrouck
Theatre of war: France
Next of Kin: Frederick & Maria Sayers
Address: Lodge, Bowood, Wiltshire.

Albert, a gardener, was the son of Frederick Sayers who was the lodge keeper at Bowood. It is likely he was conscripted into the army and sent to the 2/17th Rifle Brigade. He died most probably of disease or illness at one of the casualty clearing stations based at La Kreule, near Hazebrouck, France. He is buried in the cemetery there with nearly 600 casualties of the Great War.

Corporal Herbert John Ford MM   *2nd Bn Royal Dublin Fusiliers*
Service No.   15841   Age: 26
Place of Birth: Ilfracombe, Devon   Home Country: England
Date of Death: 26/10/1918   Cause of death: Died of wounds
Memorial: Chippenham - Calne - St Paul's Church Chippenham
War cemetery: Abbeville Communal Cemetery Extension
Theatre of war: France
Next of Kin: Frederick John & Fanny Ellen Ford
Address: Chippenham, Wiltshire.

Herbert, known as Bert, had been adopted by his uncle and aunt, Mr and Mrs Jones of 3 York Place, Calne. He had been employed at C & T Harris Bacon Factory for a number of years and afterwards worked in the stores department at Saxby and Farmers Ltd of Chippenham. He volunteered for service in September 1914 joining the 5th Wiltshire Regiment but was later transferred to the Royal Dublin Fusiliers and went to the Dardanelles with them arriving on 9th August 1915. He saw active service in Salonika, Palestine and France. He was seriously wounded in Salonika in September 1916 and was sent to Malta for treatment. On his return to duty he was sent to France and he had been home on leave from there in July 1918.

Bert died of wounds on Saturday 26th October 1918 most likely received at the battle of the Selle during the final advance through Picardy. In June 1919 it was announced he would posthumously receive the Military Medal.

His fiancé Kate Bailey was heart broken using the following words to express her grief;

"In loving memory of my dear Bert
Who died from wounds received in France,
If only round the bedside
I could but just have stayed
Or seen that lonely spot
Where my dear boy is laid
But the hardest part is yet to come
When the heroes all come home
I shall miss among those cheering lads
The face of my darling boy
From his sorrowing Kit (Kate Bailey)"

Air Mechanic 3rd Class Sidney Ernest Hall   *Royal Air Force*

Service No.	288146
Place of Birth:	Blunsdon, Wiltshire
Date of Death:	28/10/1918
Memorial:	Calne
War cemetery:	Calne Holy Trinity Churchyard
Theatre of war:	Home
Next of Kin:	Ellen Sarah K Hall (wife); Thomas & Emily Hall (parents)
Address:	1 The Close, Oxford Road, Calne; Blunsdon

Age: 44
Home Country: England
Cause of death: Died

Sidney was a coal merchant and had married Ellen Sarah K. Smith in Calne in 1896. He was most likely conscripted into the forces being sent to the Royal Air Force. He died most likely of illness or disease at Grantham, Lincolnshire, and his body was returned to Calne where he is buried in Holy Trinity Churchyard.

Gunner Percy Zebedee   *10th Mountain Bty RGA*

Service No.	301282
Place of Birth:	Calne, Wiltshire
Date of Death:	28/10/1918
Memorial:	Calne
War cemetery:	Haifa War Cemetery
Theatre of war:	Palestine
Next of Kin:	James & Louisa Zebedee
Address:	The Marsh, Calne, Wiltshire

Age: 26
Home Country: England
Cause of death: Died

Percy was a baker. It is likely he was conscripted into the army being sent to the Royal Garrison Artillery. He died at the 33rd Combined Clearing Hospital at Haifa, Israel, on Monday 28th October 1918 of malarial fever. He is buried in the Haifa War Cemetery with over 300 casualties of the Great War.

Right: The grave of Sidney Hall in Calne Holy Trinity Churchyard.

Below: Members of a mountain Battery going into action.

Corporal William Emanuel Beames MM   *2nd Bn Leinster Regiment*

Service No.	5372	Age:	34
Place of Birth:	Devizes, Wiltshire	Home Country:	England
Date of Death:	01/11/1918	Cause of death:	Died of wounds
Memorial:	Devizes		
War cemetery:	Terlincthun British Cemetery Wimille		
Theatre of war:	France		
Next of Kin:	Gertrude Beames (wife); Francis & Jesse Beames (parents)		
Address:	Sunnyside, The Marsh, Calne; Broadlease Lodge, Hatmoor, Devizes		

William was a market gardener. He married Gertrude Heath at Devizes in 1915 and it is likely he was conscripted into the army being sent to the Dorsetshire Regiment where he won a Military Medal. He was then transferred to the 2nd Battalion Leinster Regiment and was wounded in action during fighting in the final days of the war. He succumbed to his wounds at one of the base hospitals in the area. He is buried in Terlincthun British Cemetery Wimille with over 3000 casualties of the Great War. His wife inserted the following memoriam in a local paper;

"My dear husband gave his life for his Country "Thy will be Done"

From his loving wife Gerty"

Private Fred Heath   *H.M.S. Brittania RMLI*

Service No.	PO/17762	Age:	25
Place of Birth:	West Tytherton, Wiltshire	Home Country:	England
Date of Death:	09/11/1918	Cause of death:	Died
Memorial:	East Tytherton Morovian Church		
War cemetery:	Portsmouth Naval Memorial		
Theatre of war:	At Sea		
Next of Kin:	Sidney & Kate Heath		
Address:	West Tytherton, Wiltshire		

H.M.S. Britannia after the explosion she took two hours to sink.

Fred, a farm labourer, volunteered for service with his brother on 9th September 1914 and joined the Royal Marine Light Infantry. After he completed his training he was posted to H.M.S. Britannia, a pre-dreadnought battleship which had been launched in 1904.

He was killed on 9th November 1918. The Britannia was on her way to Gibraltar when she was torpedoed by the German submarine UB 50. After the first explosion caused by the torpedo the Britannia listed to port and there were two further explosions, the last being in her cordite magazine. Fred was killed by one of these explosions. The ship sank after two and a half hours with the loss of 50 of her crew. Fred is remembered on the Portsmouth Naval Memorial, his brother Maurice was killed in action in October 1917 at the battle of Passchendaele.

Private Albert Edward Large   *Royal Marine Light Infantry*

Service No.	PLY/14313	Age:	29
Place of Birth:	Burton Hill, Wiltshire	Home Country:	England
Date of Death:	09/11/1918	Cause of death:	Died
Memorial:	Calne		
War cemetery:	Calne Holy Trinity Churchyard		
Theatre of war:	Home		
Next of Kin:	John & Elizabeth Large		
Address:	Moredon Villa Moredon, Swindon, Wiltshire		

Albert was a farm labourer and enlisted in the Royal Marines on 11th December 1907. Before the war he served on many ships traveling around the world as far as Hong Kong. He served all through the war and died of disease just two days prior to the armistice. His body was returned to Calne.

Right: The grave of Albert Large in Calne Holy Trinity Churchyard.

Below: Stretcher Bearers on their way to an aid post.

11

ARMISTICE DAY - MONDAY 11 NOVEMBER 1918

The War is over but the deaths continue:

Private Reginald Deane Pinnell   *2nd Bn Wiltshire Regiment*

Service No.	28272	Age:	17
Place of Birth:	Chippenham, Wiltshire	Home Country:	England
Date of Death:	13/11/1918	Cause of death:	Died
Memorial:	Not known		
War cemetery:	Mont Huon Military Cemetery Le Treport		
Theatre of war:	France		
Next of Kin:	John Dudley & Maria Pinnell		
Address:	Sunnyside, The Marsh, Calne		

It is likely Reginald lied about his age because he should have been eighteen and a half to serve on the continent at this time. He originally joined the Royal Wiltshire Yeomanry but was transferred to the 2nd Battalion Wiltshire Regiment.

   He died of pneumonia at one of the hospitals based at Le Treport on Wednesday 13th November 1918, two days after the armistice. He is buried in Mont Huon Military Cemetery, Le Treport, with over 2000 casualties of the Great War.

2nd Lieutenant Leo Edwin Aldrich   *37th Trg Depot Royal Air Force*

Service No.	N/A	Age:	21
Place of Birth:	Elyria, Ohio	Home Country:	USA
Date of Death:	14/11/1918	Cause of death:	Accident
Memorial:	Ridgelawn Cemetery Ohio		
War cemetery:	Bath Locksbrook Cemetery		
Theatre of war:	Home		
Next of Kin:	Helen Seymour Aldrich (wife); Edwin and Agnes Aldrich (parents)		
Address:	169 North Canyon Boulevard, Monrovia, California, USA		

Leo was an American who enlisted in the Canadian Air Force before coming to England. He had been stationed at Yatesbury for three months for his final training. On Thursday 14th November 1918 he and a colleague, 2nd Lieutenant McDougall, were ordered to go to Filton near Bristol to pick up an aircraft and return to Yatesbury.

   At about noon, as the machine made it's way back to Yatesbury, it was observed by Mr Glass a farmer of of Newleaze farm near Chippenham. He watched the aeroplane for sometime, because there seemed to be something wrong with the engine, he could hear it misfiring and starting to stall. Suddenly, while at a considerable height, the machine turned down its nose and dropped like a stone. Mr Glass and another went to the field where the machine had dropped and helped to get the officers out of the machine. The aircraft was badly smashed and the engine was imbedded in the ground, both men were still in their seats but the pilot, Leo, was unconscious and trapped behind the engine and it took half an hour to free him. Leo was suffering from a fracture at the base of the scull, a crushed chest, a fracture to the right leg and a dislocated right ankle. 2nd Lieutenant McDougall was not badly injured but was suffering from shock. Leo was taken to the war hospital in Bath, but died later that evening. He was buried in Bath Locksbrook Cemetery with full military honours.

Bombardier Victor Edward Bernard Bye   *Royal Field Artillery*

Service No.	76258	Age:	22
Place of Birth:	Grittenham, Wiltshire	Home Country:	England
Date of Death:	27/11/1918	Cause of death:	Died
Memorial:	Calne		
War cemetery:	Calne Holy Trinity Churchyard		
Theatre of war:	Home		
Next of Kin:	Henry & Ellen Bye		
Address:	13 North Street, Calne		

Victor was the son of Henry Bye who had fought the Zulus at Rorke's Drift. After leaving school Victor was employed by C & T Harris and Co. in Calne but early in 1914 he enlisted in the army joining the Royal Field Artillery. At the outbreak of hostilities he crossed to France with the original Expeditionary Force arriving on 5th October 1914, and was in the retreat from Mons. He was wounded in the head and following his recovery took part in numerous engagements, from which he emerged unscathed until December 1917, when he was severely wounded in the right leg. He was evacuated to England and sent to a Red Cross Hospital in High Wycombe. He was given leave in October 1918 and returned home to Calne

The grave of Victor Bye in Calne Holy Trinity Churchyard.

Below: Messines Road looking toward Messines Ridge after the war.

and spent time with his mother. On his return to High Wycombe he was transferred to the Military Camp at Caterham, near Richmond, Yorkshire. Soon after his arrival he contracted influenza, pneumonia supervened, his condition became critical and on 22nd November his mother was telegraphed and asked to come. She journeyed the next day to Caterham and initially her presence seemed to rally him. He made such good progress that when she left on Tuesday 26th November he felt well enough to get up and he looked forward to returning home at Christmas; but the day after his mother's departure he passed away. His body was brought to Calne and he was interred at Holy Trinity Churchyard with full military honours.

Corporal John William Onslow   *1/4th Bn TF Wiltshire Regiment*

Service No.	200367	Age:	22
Place of Birth:	Hillfarrance, Somerset	Home Country:	England
Date of Death:	12/12/1918	Cause of death:	Died
Memorial:	Calne		
War cemetery:	Kantara War Memorial Cemetery		
Theatre of war:	Egypt		
Next of Kin:	Richard & Mary Onslow		
Address:	51 Curzon Street, Calne		

John was a territorial soldier with the Wiltshire Regiment and most likely traveled to India with the 1/4th Battalion Wiltshire Regiment in 1914 for garrison duties. In September 1917 the 1/4th Wiltshires were transferred to Egypt where they began a campaign against Turkish forces fighting through Palestine.
   John died of disease at one of the Hospitals in Kantara, Egypt.

Private Algernon Green   *1/4th Bn TF Wiltshire Regiment*

Service No.	200563	Age:	25
Place of Birth:	Calne, Wiltshire	Home Country:	England
Date of Death:	15/12/1918	Cause of death:	Died
Memorial:	Calne - Calstone & Blacklands		
War cemetery:	Kantara War Memorial Cemetery		
Theatre of war:	Egypt		
Next of Kin:	Peter W & E J Green		
Address:	26 Theobalds Green, Calne, Wiltshire		

Algernon, a carter and farm labourer before the war, was a territorial soldier. Like John Onslow he also died of disease at one of the Hospitals in Kantara, Egypt. He is buried with John Onslow in Kantara War Memorial Cemetery.

Private Robert Guppy   *180th Coy Labour Corps*

Service No.	568190	Age:	36
Place of Birth:	Portland, Dorset	Home Country:	England
Date of Death:	17/12/1918	Cause of death:	Died
Memorial:	Yatesbury		
War cemetery:	Tournai Communal Cemetery Allied Extension		
Theatre of war:	France		
Next of Kin:	Daisey M. Guppy (wife); Robert & Susan Guppy (parents)		
Address:	28, Yatesbury, Wiltshire		

Robert, a baker, enlisted in the Hussars on 15th January 1901 at Dorchester and served in India from 1903 to 1908. In 1909 he returned to England and left the army being placed on reserve. He was called up on 5th August 1914 when the reserves were mobilized at the commencement of hostilities, arriving in France on 16th August 1914. On 31st August 1915, Robert married Daisy Maud Lillian Kempton, and on 17th October 1917 their son Cyril Robert was born. On 17th August 1918 he was compulsorily transferred to the Labour corps. He died suddenly on the night of Tuesday 17th December 1918 of heart failure following a bout of chronic bronchitis and asthma.

   His personal property was returned to his wife and consisted of; letters, photos, disc, note book, wallet, religious medallion, badge, pouch, 2 pipes and 2 pairs of spurs. Robert is buried in Tournai Communal Cemetery Allied Extension with nearly 700 casualties of the Great War.

Rifleman Frederick Ralph   *3/6th Bn London Regiment*
Service No.   R/40858   Age: 18
Place of Birth: Calne, Wiltshire   Home Country: England
Date of Death: 24/12/1918   Cause of death: Died
Memorial: Calne
War cemetery: Calne Holy Trinity Churchyard
Theatre of war: Home
Next of Kin: William & Elizabeth Jane Ralph
Address: 7 London Road, Calne

It is likely eighteen year old Frederick was conscripted into the army and was originally sent to the Royal Army Service Corps. He was transferred to the 3/6th London Regiment who were serving in England. He died on Christmas Eve 1918 of disease. It is unlikely that he would have received any Medals due to his length of service, and the fact that it was all in England. His body was returned to Calne and he was buried in Holy Trinity Churchyard.

The grave of Frederick Ralph in Calne Holy Trinity Churchyard.

Below: a destroyed British tank at the end of the war.

Private George Amos Oxx   *2nd Bn Wiltshire Regiment*
Service No.   25801   Age: 36
Place of Birth: Woodbridge, Suffolk   Home Country: England
Date of Death: 28/12/1918   Cause of death: Died
Memorial: Calne
War cemetery: Terlincthun British Cemetery Wimille
Theatre of war: France
Next of Kin: Edith M Oxx
Address: 2 Castle Street, Calne

George was a hardware shop assistant and had come to Calne in 1904 as an assistant to Mr E. W. Brown in the High Street. He established himself as a favorite in the town, being of a genial disposition and courteous manner. He was a member of the Castle Street Baptist Church, and was a strong supporter of the Brotherhood movement, being a popular speaker at meetings, both in Calne and the wider district. In the summer of 1913 he married Edith M. Angell, who was the sister of Councilor A G Angell of Calne. He joined up in June 1916 at the same time as Rev. Guyton Thomas, then minister of Castle Street. He joined the 2nd Battalion Wiltshire Regiment and proceeded to France. George was made a signaler and during the German advances in May 1918 he was reported missing and for a time no news was heard of him, later it was known he was prisoner of the Germans. He should have been sent to Germany, but it was believed he was kept behind the German lines, where he was subjected to harsh treatment and exposure and contracted tuberculosis. When the armistice was signed he was turned adrift by the Germans and was on the way home in France when he was taken ill. His friends heard nothing of him from 20th October 1918 until news of his death arrived in early January 1919. He had been taken to a Canadian Hospital in Boulogne after the armistice where he died on Saturday 28th December 1918.

Aircraftsman 1st Class Walter Woodward   *35th Sqdn Royal Air Force*
Service No.   61214   Age: 26
Place of Birth: Highway, Wiltshire   Home Country: England
Date of Death: 26/02/1919   Cause of death: Died
Memorial: Calne Methodist Church
War cemetery: Calne Curzon Street Churchyard
Theatre of war: Home
Next of Kin: William & Julia Lugg
Address: Butlers Buildings, Calne

Walter was a labourer and died most likely of disease in Calne on Wednesday 26th February 1919. He is buried in the nonconformist Curzon Street Churchyard.

Private Albert James Harding   *2nd Bn Wiltshire Regiment*
Service No.   18211   Age: 40
Place of Birth: Yetminster, Dorset   Home Country: England
Date of Death: 26/02/1919   Cause of death: Died
Memorial: East Tytherton Morovian Church - Foxham
War cemetery: Foxham St John the Baptist Churchyard
Theatre of war: Home
Next of Kin: Ada Maude L Harding
Address: Foxham, Wiltshire.

Above left: The grave of Walter Woodward in Calne Curzon Street Churchyard.

Above right: The grave of Albert Harding in Foxham St .John the Baptist Churchyard.

Albert was a farm labourer, and married his wife at Foxham at the beginning of the year in 1902. They had met when they had both been employed as servants for different households in Yatton Keynell. He volunteered for service with the 2nd Battalion Wiltshire Regiment and arrived in France on the 1st June 1915. He died at Southampton, most likely of illness, on Wednesday 26th February 1919. His body was returned to Foxham and he was buried in St. John the Baptist Churchyard.

Private Godfrey Freegard		*1st Bn Somerset Light Infantry*	
Service No.	38002	Age:	20
Place of Birth:	Studley, Wiltshire	Home Country:	England
Date of Death:	28/02/1919	Cause of death:	Died
Memorial:	Calne & Derry Hill		
War cemetery:	La Louviere Town Cemetery		
Theatre of war:	Belgium		
Next of Kin:	William & Martha Freegard		
Address:	114 Norley Lane, Studley, Wiltshire		

It is likely twenty year old was conscripted into the army joining the 1st Battalion Somerset Light Infantry. He died, most likely of disease, at No 30 Casualty Clearing Station based a La Louviere, Belgium; the town is sixteen kilometetres from Mons where the British army was engaged in it's first action with the Germans in 1914.

Private Charles Walter Pottow   *Machine Gun Corps*

Service No.	Not known	Age:	24
Place of Birth:	Cherhill, Wiltshire	Home Country:	England
Date of Death:	02/04/1919	Cause of death:	Died
Memorial:	Not known		
War cemetery:	Calne Holy Trinity Churchyard		
Theatre of war:	Home		
Next of Kin:	Albert & Fanny Pottow		
Address:	Calne, Wiltshire.		

Walter was discharged from the machine gun corps at the end of the war and took a job as a machine operator with CT Harris of Calne. He died of influenza followed by pneumonia on Wednesday 2nd April. His mother Fanny died on the same day of influenza. His brother Edwin had died of wounds in may 1917.

Shoeing Smith Edward Reeves   *1st Bn Wiltshire Regiment*

Service No.	7201	Age:	36
Place of Birth:	Lyneham, Wiltshire	Home Country:	England
Date of Death:	19/05/1919	Cause of death:	Died
Memorial:	Hilmarton		
War cemetery:	Hilmarton St Laurence Churchyard		
Theatre of war:	Home		
Next of Kin:	Ellen Kate Reeves (wife); James & Clara Reeves (parents)		
Address:	Goatacre, Wiltshire.		

Edward, a labourer, was the youngest son of James & Clara Reeves, and joined the Wiltshire Regiment on 1st October 1900. He was first posted to St.Helena and then served in India. He left the army and traveled to Canada and Australia. At the Outbreak of war he returned from Australia and joined his old unit the 1st Battalion Wiltshire Regiment. He was wounded in the neck and left shoulder in November 1916 and after his recuperation returned to the front. On 2nd March 1918 he was admitted to 77th Field Ambulance with measles, sent to a base hospital and after a short spell in hospital he was given a months leave. In July 1918 he passed a Shoeing Smith Course, which was a qualification that enabled him to shoe the Battalions horses. In December 1918 he was admitted to hospital in France and then sent to Brighton, where it was found he was suffering from valvular disease of the heart. He was transferred to the military Hospital in Colchester where he died on Monday 19th May 1919. He was buried with full military honours at Hilmarton St Laurence Churchyard. Edward's nephews Walter Rivers and William Rivers had been killed during the war. The inscription on his grave stone reads;

"Only those who have Loved and Lost
Can realise what the War has Cost"

Driver Frederick John Burchell   *Royal Army Service Corps*

Service No.	T/370861	Age:	31
Place of Birth:	Calne, Wiltshire	Home Country:	England
Date of Death:	05/07/1919	Cause of death:	Died
Memorial:	Not known		
War cemetery:	Calne Holy Trinity Churchyard		
Theatre of war:	Home		

Above left: The grave of Edward Reeves in Hilmarton St. Laurence Churchyard.

Above right: The grave of Frederick Bruchell in Calne Holy Trinity Churchyard.

Next of Kin: Ellen Burchell (wife); Fred & Martha Burchell (parents)
Address: 25 Cressings Road, Witham, Essex; 3 Oxford Terrace, The Marsh, Calne

Frederick, known as John, was a butcher and the oldest son of Fred & Martha Burchell. At the end of the year in 1916 he married Ellen Crow at Dunmow, Essex. It is likely he was conscripted into the army joining the Royal Army Service Corps. He died most likely of disease on Saturday 5th July 1919 at Eastbourne and his body was returned to Calne for burial in Calne Holy Trinity Churchyard.

Lance Corporal Percy George Chivers   *Royal Defense Corps*
Service No.   47827   Age: 26
Place of Birth: Calne, Wiltshire   Home Country: England
Date of Death: 08/07/1919   Cause of death: Died
Memorial: Calne
War cemetery: Calne Holy Trinity Church
Theatre of war: Home
Next of Kin: Thomas & Alice Alberta Weston
Address: 26 Church Street, Calne, Wiltshire

Percy was a shop assistant, his father had died and his mother Alice, had married Thomas Weston. He volunteered for service with the Somerset Light Infantry arriving in France on 29th December 1915. It is likely he was wounded and unfit for front line service and returned to England. He joined the Royal Defence Corps, which was a military force set up to guard

The Grave of Percy Chivers in Calne Holy Trinity Churchyard.

Below: The Iron harvest shells are still found today.

important installations in Great Britain. He died at Salisbury on the 8th July 1919 probably due to illness. He is buried in Holy Trinity Churchyard.

Private Percival James Coleman   *2nd Bn Wiltshire Regiment*
Service No.   8340   Age: 28
Place of Birth: Yatesbury, Wiltshire   Home Country: England
Date of Death: 20/05/1920   Cause of death: Died
Memorial: Not known
War cemetery: Cherhill St James the Great Churchyard
Theatre of war: Home
Next of Kin: Henry James & Ellen Coleman
Address: Cherhill, Wiltshire

Percy was a regular soldier and at the outbreak of war he was based at Gibraltar with the 2nd Battalion Wiltshire Regiment. The Wiltshires returned to England and on 14th October 1914 Percy and the Wiltshires landed at Zeebrugge, Belgium. He fought all through the war and it is likely he died of disease at Bath on Thursday 20th May 1920. He is buried in Cherhill St James the Great Churchyard.

Gunner William Arthur Strange   *Royal Garrison Artillery*
Service No.   326865   Age: 28
Place of Birth: Tytherton, Wiltshire   Home Country: England
Date of Death: 04/06/1924   Cause of death: Died of wounds
Memorial: Not known
War cemetery: Not known
Theatre of war: Home

Next of Kin   Henry & Mary Strange
Address: Tytherton Lucas, Wiltshire

In the small church of Tytherton Lucas there is a memorial on the wall in memory of William, a farm Labourer who died in 1924. I believe the words engraved on it are an epitaph to all those who were casualties of the conflict it simply states;

"AFTER MUCH SUFFERING

THE RESULT OF

SERVICE IN THE GREAT WAR"

Above: The memorial to

William Strange in St.Nicholas, Tytherton Luccs.

Right: Peace day celebrations 19th July 1919 British artillery near the Rhine in Germany.

12
REMEMBRANCE

The news of the signing of the armistice reached Calne about mid-day on Monday 11 November 1918, and occasioned the greatest delight and satisfaction. Work in nearly every trade and profession was suspended for the remainder of the day, and large crowds perambulated the streets. In the afternoon there was a united open air thanksgiving service held at the Strand, where a large number assembled.

In 1920 plans were made to build a permanent War Memorial, which cost £1200 and by Armistice day 1921 it was in place. At 11 o'clock the two minutes silence was observed, and in the morning the Mayor deposited a laurel wreath on the War Memorial. It bore the inscription .
"In grateful remembrance."

On Thursday 11 November 1920 Lady Lansdowne unveiled the War Memorial at Bremhill St. Martin Churchyard and a service of dedication followed which was attended by a large number of parishioners.

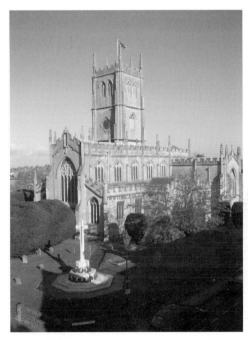 

Left: Calne St. Mary's Church and War Memorial. *Right: Bremhill St. Martin Church and War Memorial.*

Left: East Tytherton Morovian Church Memorial.   -   Right: Foxham St. John the Baptist Church Memorial
Both have listed many of the same names as Bremhill.

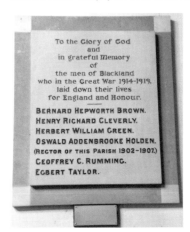

Left: Blacklands St. Peter's Church Memorial which is identical to Calstone St. Mary the Virgin Church Memorial

Centre: Hilmarton St. Laurence Church Memorial Window depicting St. George and Gordon of Khartoum.

Above right: Heddington St. Andrew Church Memorial.

Right: Cherhill St James the Great Church
Memorial.

Above left: Compton Bassett War Memorial.   Above right: Compton Bassett St. Swithin Church Memorial.

Above left: Yatesbury All Saints Church War Memorial.   Above right: Derry Hill War Memorial.

Derry Hill War Memorial was unveiled by Lady Lansdowne in May 1920. In her brief speech Lady Lansdowne recounted that two months before the Great War was declared she was talking with her late son Lord Mercer Nairne about death, and he said to her;

"Shall I tell you, mother, the death above all others that I should prefer to die?

I should like to die in action, fighting for my Country."

MAPS

The Western Front

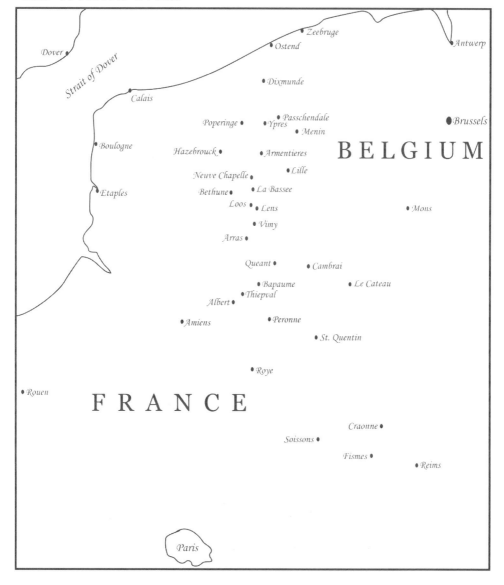

Dover •   Strait of Dover   Calais •   Ostend •   • Zeebruge   • Antwerp

• Dixmunde

• Boulogne   Poperinge •   Ypres •   • Passchendale   • Brussels

Hazebrouck •   • Armentieres   • Menin   **BELGIUM**

• Etaples   Neuve Chapelle •   • Lille

Bethune •   • La Bassee

Loos • • Lens   • Mons

• Vimy

Arras •

Queant •   • Cambrai

• Bapaume   • Le Cateau

Albert • • Thiepval

• Amiens   • Peronne

• St. Quentin

• Roye

• Rouen   **FRANCE**

Craonne •

Soissons •

Fismes •   • Reims

Paris

Gallipoli 1915 to 1916

Mesopotamia 1914 to 1918

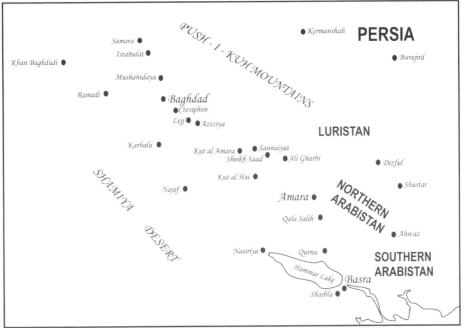

Balkans 1914 to 1918

Palestine 1914 to 1918

A-Z OF MEMORIALS

Abbeville Communal
Cemetery Extension
Herbert John Ford
Adanac Military
Cemetery Miraumont
Arthur Culley
Percy Archibald Dolman
Aire Communal Cemetery
Herbert Anthony Gale
Albert Communal Cemetery
Percy Gordon Bridges
Alexandria Hadra War
Memorial Cemetery
Albert George Daniels
Amara War Cemetery
Arthur Edward Angell
George Brewer
Frederick George Wheeler
Arras Memorial
Alfred James Angell
Walter George Cole
Clement James Eatwell
Herbert William Hillier
Carol James Pocock
Frederick Slade
Herbert John Sutton
Frederick Willis
Artillery Wood Cemetery
Harry Lucas Hillier Perrett
Authuile Military Cemetery
Edward Slade
Bagneux British Cemetery
Gezaincout
Sydney Frank Blackford
Bailleul Communal Cemetery
Extension Nord
Egbert Taylor
Barlin Communal Cemetery
Francis William Gingell
Basra Memorial
Walter Angell
William John Cook
Ernest George Dean
George Gingell
Frederick Goddard
Frederic George Greenstreet
Sidney Selman

Bath Locksbrook Cemetery
Leo Edwin Aldrich
Lewis Scott White
Beaulencourt British
Cemetery Ligny Thilloy
Francis James Henly
Beaumetz Les Cambrai
Military Cemetery No 1
George Stone
Bedford House Cemetery
Herbert John Butler
Herbert Henry Rumming
Beersheba War Cemetery
Frederick Henley
Belgian Battery Corner
Cemetery
Frederick George Clifford
Bethune Town Cemetery
Sidney Herbert Matthews
Albert Thomas Taylor
Bradford Bowling Cemetery
Edward McEvoy
Bramshott St Mary
Churchyard
William Howard Simpkins
Brandhoek New Military
 Cemetery
Francis Sidney Williams
Thomas William Lawrence
Flangham
Bremhill St Martin
Churchyard
George Charles Chubb
Brighton Bear Road
Cemetery
Borough Cemetery
Henry Newman Cole
Brookwood Military
Cemetery
Stanley Howard Pilkington
Buffs Road Cemetery
William John Fussell
Bully-Grenay Communal
 Cemetery French Extension
Thomas Victor Cross
Cabaret Rouge British
Cemetery

Caix British Cemetery
Gerald Henry Perrett
Calne Curzon Street Cemetery
Geoffrey Charlton Paine
Rumming
Walter Woodward
Calne Holy Trinity Churchyard
Reginald Thomas Bull
Frederick John Burchell
Victor Edward B Bye
Percy George Chivers
Ernest Hall
Albert Edward Large
Edwin George Pottow
Charles Walter Pottow
Frederick Ralph
William Sinclair
William Henry Watkins
Cambrin Churchyard Ext.
Joseph Richard Brazier
Cambrin Military Cemetery
William Ebden Wilkinson
Canada Farm Cemetery
Francis Victor Sage
Carnoy Military Cemetery
Lewin Blackford
Cement House Cemetery
Frederick Charles Smith
Cerisy Gailly Military
 Cemetery
Vernon Joseph Brewer
Chatham Naval Memorial
Robert Wait
Cherhill St. James The Great
Churchyard
Percival James Coleman
City of London Cemetery and
Crematorium Manor Park
Albert Davies
Cologne Southern Cemetery
Ernie George Blackford
Thomas Baker
Coxyde Military Cemetery
Arthur Charles Smith
Croydon Mitcham Road
Cemetery
Stanley Arthur Burree

Dalziel Airbles Cemetery
Charles Findlay
Daours Communal Cemetery
Extension
Jacob Francis Rawlings
Dartmoor Cemetery Becordel
Becourt
William Pyt Bennett
Arthur Edward Strange
Deir El Belah War Cemetery
Edwin Minty
Dive Copse British Cemetery
Sailly Le Sec
Rowland Charles Lane
Doingt Communal Cemetery
Herbert Harry Talbot
Doiran Memorial
Arthur John Sumbler
George Weston
Doiran Military Cemetery
William Henry Hyde
Doullens Communal Cemetery
Extension No 1
Arthur Francis Ponting
Duisans British Cemetery
Etrun
Colin Garnett Fell
Thomas Balfour Gornall
Dunfermline Cemetery
Sidney Walter Cowdry
East Mudros Military
Cemetery
Charles Ponting
East Tytherton Moravian
Burial Ground
Alfred Pocock Long
Ecoivres Military Cemetery
Mont St Eloi
Herbert Ernest Archard
Erith Brook Street Cemetery
Albert Higgs Vinson
Estaires Communal Cemetery
Ernest John Angell
Etaples Military Cemetery
Harold Butcher
Stephen Gilbert Haines
Gilbert Allen Ponting
Etretat Churchyard Extension
Reginald Herbert George Jones

Euston St Genevieve
Churchyard
William Henry Alfred Fitzroy
Ferme-Olivier Cemetery
Henry Short
Feuchy Chapel British
Cemetery Wancourt
Ernest Edward Carpenter
Fifteen Ravine British
Cemetery Villiers Plouich
Oswald Addenbrooke Holden
Ford Park Cemetery
(Plymouth Old Cemetery)
Pennyco
Edward Drew
Foxham St John the Baptist
Churchyard
Albert James Harding
Givenchy En Gohelle
Canadian Cemetery Souchez
Tom Weston
Glasgow Craighton Cemetery
Alexander Rose
Godewaersvelde British
Cemetery
William Henry Fry Vines
Gordon Dump Cemetery
Ovillers La Boisselle
George Bruce Fletcher Hunt
Grand Seraucourt British
Cemetery
John James Pontin
Haifa War Cemetery
Percy Zebedee
Hammersmith Old Cemetery
Percival Francis Crommelin
D'Erf Wheeler
Heene St Botolph Chruchyard
Extension
John Leslie Colbourne
Helles Memorial
Geoffrey Peter Guillebaud
Frederick Elms
Harry Thomas
Heninel Croisilles Cemetery
Bernard Hepworth Brown
Hill 10 Cemetery
Herbert John Gunning
Hillington St Mary
Churchyard
Edgar Kinsey Reynolds

Hilmarton St Laurence
Churchyard
Edward Reeves
Francis William Haddrell
Hooge Crater Cemetery
Percival John Hacker
Hove Old Cemetery
Frank Bernard Brown
Jerusalem War Cemetery
John Alfred Gingell
Kantara War Memorial
Cemetery
Algernon Green
John William Onslow
Karasouli Military
Cemetery
Tom Ponting
Kemmel Chateau Military
Cenetery
Walter Henry Rivers
Kirkee 1914-1918 Memorial
Edward Chandler
William G. L. Marshman
John Taylor
Ernest Frederick Wild
La Ferte Sous Jouarre
Memorial
Charles William Hillier
Harry Stanley Toppin
La Kreule Military
Cemetery Hazebrouck
Albert Edward Sayers
La Laiterie Military
Cemetery
George Peak-Garland
La Louviere Town
Cemetery
Godfrey Freegard
Lancashire Cottage
Cemetery
Reginald Alfred Freegard
Larch Wood Railway
Cutting Cemetery
Lionel Frank Henly

Le Touret Memorial
Alec Chapman Atlay
William John Bennett
Alfred Cleverly
Ernest Arthur Elsip
Albert Fry
William Henry Gee
William Golding
Albert W Henly
Oliver Arthur Henly
William John Keevil
Harold John King
Frederick Knight
Albert Selby
Frank Stapleford
Frederick James Wheeler
Francis James Wilkins
William Wiltshire
Leeds Beeston Cemetery
George Stanley Howard
Leicester Gilroes Cemetery
John Herbert Whiston
Level Crossing Cemetery
Fampoux
Fred Cleverley Robbins
Lijssenthoek Military
Cemetery
Frederick Doble Smale
Frederick Herbert Summers
Sidney Miles Toppin
Llanyre St Llyr Churchyard
Thomas Thompson
Pritchard
Locre Hospice Cemetery
Walter Alfred Soley
London Cemetery and
Extension Longueval
Herbert William Green
Lonsdale Cemetery Authuile
Charles John James
Loos Memorial
Frederick Albert Angell
Frederick John Bristow
Edward John Dash
Harry Parsons
John Henry Pearce
Walter Reginald Powell
Luton General Cemetery
Stanley Burnet

Lytham St Cuthbert
Churchyard
Henry William Adam
Maroilles Communal
Cemetery
Walter Brindle
Merville Communal
Cemetery
John Newman
Mikra Memorial
Henry Richard Cleverly
Mont Huon Military
Cemetery Le Treport
Reginald Deane Pinnell
Mordington Burial Ground
Edward Leadbetter Gray
Mory Abbey Military
Cenetery Mory
Ernest Charles Hunt
Frank Lawrence
Mylor St Mylor Churchyard
John Boyd Chamberlin
New Southgate Cemetery
Ruby Harold Morton
Nieppe Bois (Rue Du Bois)
British Cemetery Vieux
Berquin
Maurice Gough
Nouex Les Mines
Communal Cemetery
Herbert George Ealey
Oosttaverne Wood
Cemetery
Francis William Hornblow
Passchendaele New
Cemetery
Walter John Cook Brittain
Peronne Communal
Cemetery Extension
Frederick George E Bull
Thomas Grubb
Peronne Road Cemetery
Maricourt
Frederick Harold Barton
Arthur Weston
Ploegsteert Memorial
Reginald James Vclifford
Frank Walter Frankling
Ploegsteert Wood Military
Cemetery
Walter Alfred Hillier

Pont Du Hem Military
Cemetery La Gorgue
John Slade
Portianos Military Cemetery
Samuel Beer
Wiliam John Weston
Portsmouth Naval Memorial
Fred Heath
William George Robinson
James Henry Summers
Alfred Tuck
Pozieres Memorial
Frederick Watson Carpenter
Albert Edward T Gunning
Percy James Matthews
Walter John Morley
Frederick Joseph Park
Prospect Hill Cemetery Gouy
Edward John Drew
George Lucas
Herbert Edward Martin
Puchevillers British Cemetery
Charles Fortune
Queant Communal Cemetery
British Extension
William Draper
Querrieu British Cemetery
Maurice Herbert Lawrence
Railway Dugouts Burial
Ground
Ephriam John Baker
Ramleh War Cemetery
Godfrey Lawes Godfrey
Ramsgate and St Lawrence
Cemetery
Charles Leonard Price
Reninghelst New Military
Cemetery
Henry George Panting
Rue Du Bois Military
Cemetery Fleurbaix
John Keith Atlay
Arthur Besant
Salonika Lembet Road
Military Cemetery
Arthur George James Freegard
Sanctuary Wood Cemetery
Stewart Cecil Hawkins

Sanders Keep Military Cemetery Graincourt Les Havrincourt
Fredrick George Smart
Sarigol Military Cemetery Kriston
Frederick William Cleverly
Serre Road Cemetery No 2
Jesse Edward Lewis
Shellingford St Faith Churchyard
Adam Goddard
Sissonne British Cemetery
Reginald Watson Lewis
Soissons Memorial
Herbert Thomas J Fortune
Reginald George Coombs
Somer Farm Cemetery
Joseph Topp
St Sever Cemetery Extension Rouen
Edward Andrews
Alfred James Davis
Ernest William Hillier
Arthur Raymond Marshall
Strabane Cemetery
William Kerr Magill Britton
Stratford on Avon Cemetery
Harry Bernard Wilson
Templux Le Guerard British Cemetery
Arthur Sidney Dunne
Terlincthun British Cemetery Wimille
William Emanuel Beames
George Amos Oxx
The Huts Cemetery
Albert Charles Dewey Drewett
Thiennes British Cemetery
Jacob Andrews
Thiepval Memorial
Frederick Edward G Angell
Frank Atwood
Albert Diccox
Ernest William Hacker
William Ernest Rose
Henry Herbert Strange
Arthur Robert Summers
Percy George Weaver

Thilloy Road Cemetery Beaulencourt
Ernest Brown
Tincourt New British Cemetery
Rowland William Roberts
Torreken Farm Cemetery No 1
Clement John Strange
Tournai Communal Cemetery Allied Extension
Robert Guppy
Townstall St Clement Churchyard
Ernest Osborne Tracey
Trowbridge Cemetery
Ernest Bennett
George Victor Jim Elmes
Tyne Cot Cemetery
Maurice Heath
Tyne Cot Memorial
Victor Arthur Bull
Reginald Tom Raisley Cook
William Edward Corderoy
Roland George Manners
George Herbert Moody
Henry James Reeves
Vadencourt British Cemetery Maissemy
Walter Rivers
Varennes Military Cemetery
Harold William Beazley
Villers Faucon Communal Cemetery
Charles Thomas Stanley Cox
Vis En Artois British Cemetery Haucourt
Ernest Edward Powell
Wancourt British Cemetery
Frederick George Drew
Warwick Cemetery
Gilbert Thomas R Pettigrew
Wimereux Communal Cemetery
Henry Herbert Slade
Leopold Arthur Walker
Wytschaete Military Cemetery
Frederick Evans

Yatesbury All Saints Churchyard
Walter Earl Carter
Wilfred Arthur D Carter
Arthur Measures Chatterton
Reuben John Davidson
James Horace Farnham
John Thomas Gibson
Harold Edwin Goodwin
Robert Emmett Gorman
Thomas Herald
Frederick Cyril Hoey
Alfred Stanley Hunt
Marcus Erald Rowe
Walter Sondheim
William Edward Tate
Eric Charles Terry
Marcus Erald Rowe
Charles Gerald V Smith
Alexander Vinogradoff
Ypres Menim Gate
Percy Henry Angell
Montague R Bridgeman
Frederick Bull
William Frederick Godwin
Alford Edward Heavens
Daniel Hillier
Leslie Edward J Lawrence
Arthur Edward Bruce O'Neill
William Rivers
Maynard Summers
John James Taylor
Ypres Reservoir Cemetery
Charles William Gingell
Ypres Town Cemetery
Charles George Francis Mercer-Nairne